GHOST MAGNET

BY

JONI MAYHAN

Cover design by Joni Mayhan

Any resemblances to actual places, people (living or dead), or incidents that happened that are not listed are purely coincidental. Prior approval has been obtained from all parties who are mentioned in this book.

Also by Joni Mayhan

True Paranormal Non-fiction

Signs of Spirits – When Loved Ones Visit

Ruin of Souls

Dark and Scary Things – A Sensitive's Guide to the Paranormal World

Ghost Voices

Bones in the Basement – Surviving the S.K. Haunted Victorian Mansion

The Soul Collector

Devil's Toy Box

Ghostly Defenses – A Sensitive's Guide for Protection

Paranormal Fiction

Lightning Strikes (Angels of Ember Dystopian Trilogy– Book 1)

Ember Rain (Angels of Ember Dystopian Trilogy – Book 2)

Angel Storm (Angels of Ember Dystopian Trilogy – Book 3)

The Spirit Board (Winter Woods – Book 1)

The Labyrinth (Winter Woods – Book 2)

The Corvus (Winter Woods – Book 3)

ACKNOWLEDGEMENTS

How do you really thank someone for saving your life?

That might sound somewhat melodramatic, considering we're talking about ghosts and not avalanches, but that doesn't make it any less important. The people who played roles in this book saved me in more ways than one.

Thank you, first and foremost, Sandy MacLeod for always being there beside me, no matter how dark the situation became. Having someone who was on the same evolutionary path was essential. I'm fairly certain I wouldn't have survived without you.

My mentors throughout this voyage helped me by giving me tools to work with and by saving me countless times. Thank you Barbara Williams for your support and sound advice; to Kaden Mattison for teaching me about energy; to Chris George for showing me the golden egg method of protection; to Jose Prada for your knowledge and protection; and lastly, to Michael Robishaw for literally saving my life.

Much appreciation is due to fellow author Gare Allen for tirelessly editing my book, chapter by chapter, and for providing much needed author support.

My beta readers were given a very tight deadline and they pulled through like champs. Thank you Tami Stevens, Jill Anne and Eileen Landry.

Finally, to all those who allowed me to share our experiences together, you have my deepest gratitude: Barbara Kirk Niles, Pamela Howell, Mary Lou Moriarty, Crystal Pina, Ken Murray, Raymond Richard, Gina Bengtson and Jeff Legere.

Contents

For Sandy Macleod – Thank you for always being my light in the darkness

PRELUDE

June 2016

I chased the miles, driving as fast as I could manage, my eyes constantly seeking the rear view mirror, terrified at what I might find in my backseat.

In my heart loomed a horror I couldn't wrap my mind around. Had this really happened to me again?

Did another demon latch onto me?

Why was this happening?

Was I marked in some way, creating a beacon they could easily follow?

I could hear the entity's words inside my head. They rattled around like a loose screw in a frantically racing machine.

When it gets dark, I will show myself to you and cause you to have an accident.

I saw his scenario unfold in my mind, playing with such perfect detail that it felt more like a memory than a vision. I would watch dusk settled on the horizon as I crossed the border into Kentucky, still hours away from home. I would feel his presence before I actually saw him, catching movement out of the corner of my eye as a passing car illuminated the interior of my car.

I'd turn with a gasp and he would be there in all his immortal glory, grinning at me with teeth that were crusted with cemetery dirt. His face was as black as the inside of a crypt, making the whites of his eyes seem brighter, almost as though they were illuminated by an internal fire, reminding me of something from a Halloween display. His white shirt was neatly pressed beneath his slim black jacket, but I only saw this detail for a moment. My eyes were too fixated on his horrible sneer. It made me want to crawl inside of myself and find a place to hide where he couldn't find me.

He wanted to tear my flesh from my bones with those horrible teeth, one painful bite after another, and then spit me out, claiming my soul as his own until he had pulled every ounce of light from it.

"God, help me," I whispered.

I wanted a cigarette, even though I hadn't smoked for more than two years. The need was so strong, I nearly pulled over at the next exit to purchase a pack, before I realized that cigarettes weren't going to help me with this.

What I needed was someone to sweep in and save me. I needed a miracle because this thing was in my backseat, patiently waiting for darkness to fall.

That was all I could think about.

Darkness and what it would bring.

CHAPTER 1

IN THE BEGINNING

At first glance, there is nothing remarkable about me.

I'm average height and weight, with dark blonde hair and green eyes.

At heart, I'm a true introvert. I like quiet activities, often indulging in long thought-purging walks with my dog or camping out at home, reading or binging on Netflix.

Sometimes, when the creative urge strikes me, I paint pictures that I usually give away to friends and family. I like to wear clothes that are comfortable, typically something along the lines of jeans and a t-shirt. If you saw me at the grocery store, you'd probably identify me as a suburban mom, someone with grown kids and a normal everyday life. Nothing could be further from the truth.

In reality, there is something quite startling about me.

Despite my outward appearance, there is a hidden element inside of me that has made my life a living hell. I've alluded to it in several of my other books, but I haven't divulged the full extent of the nightmare that I live with every single day.

I am a ghost magnet.

I'm not sure how it started, but it's been with me since childhood. My earliest memories come from the age of four years-old.

Bedtime was a true horrorfest for me. As soon as my mother tucked me in, I begged for her to turn on a nightlight before she left the room. If she tried to close my bedroom door, essentially cutting me off from the rest of the family and the blessed light that filtered through my doorway, I'd nearly go into hysterics.

"No! Please, leave it open!" I wailed.

She stared at me for a moment, probably wondering if she should follow the advice from the child rearing books that were piled on her nightstand and just force me to get used to it. In the end, she sighed and ended up leaving the door open a crack.

(Above) The log cabin where I first encountered ghosts

Even with the meager light, it wasn't much better. The dead would still find me. If I thought that the light was a means of keeping them at bay, I was sorely mistaken. The light only served to allow me to see them better. They liked the fact that I was isolated and frightened. They would wait until my mother's footsteps receded down the hallway before they would emerge from the shadows.

My first indication that they were there came with a noise. It was a buzzing in my ear that mimicked the way the television sounded when the station went off the air. I heard it drift across the room, getting louder as it got closer. I tucked my head under my covers and hugged my stuffed animal close, trying to remember my prayers. If I cried out for my parents, my pleas were often met with frustration.

"Joni, go back to bed. There's nothing to be afraid of. There's no such thing as ghosts," they would tell me, and that would be the end of it.

When I finally managed to fall asleep, my night was filled with terrifying nightmares. This continued throughout my childhood. By the time I was seven years-old, I began having night terrors. I would race around the house, fleeing from something my parents couldn't see, tears streaming down my face. No matter what they did, they couldn't wake me up. They had to just wait it out.

Eventually, I would come out of the nightmare, bits and pieces of the dream world still clinging to my mind. I often had the same dream over and over again. A tall skinny man with an evil smile and a black hat pursued me, chasing me through the woods to the site of an old chair lift. Once I got onto it, thinking I was escaping him as I was carried high into the dark night, I began hearing his voice in my ear.

Come with us or we will take your family, one by one.

We'll start with your little sister. She will be most delicious.

And then we'll take your mother, and then your father, while we make you watch.

I would wake up, feeling disoriented and confused as I stared up at my parents who looked as though they'd just seen a ghost themselves.

Not long after that, I began experiencing excruciating migraine headaches, something that would follow me into adulthood. They came on just after lunch and would completely drain me of energy and a will to live. Within an hour, I would be vomiting up anything I ate that morning, the pain in my head so severe, I couldn't function. I would hole myself up into a dark room and pray that sleep would take me away from the pain.

My mother whisked me off to every doctor and specialist she could think of. My head was examined inside and out thoroughly, but they couldn't find anything wrong.

Typically, migraine headaches start when a child enters puberty, but it started far earlier for me, which made no sense to the specialists. They put me on medications that caused me to fall asleep at school, but didn't prevent the onslaught of pain. After a while, they threw their hands up and sent me home to deal with it.

"Maybe she'll outgrow them," they said.

Perhaps they should have looked at what they couldn't see instead. What they didn't realize was that I was born with abilities that would mark me forever.

I began retreating inwardly, avoiding other kids and adults as much as possible. I discovered a love for books, something that kept my mind off of everything else going on in my life. I learned to ignore the strange feelings that came over me when my ears would begin to buzz with the sound of static.

During this time, my parents began fighting which led to a pretty nasty divorce. The doctors began blaming my migraines on the divorce, but I wasn't sure that was the reason. Something was wrong inside my head, something nobody could fix.

As an adult, I can look back and see the progression of events as though they were schematics on a blueprint. Children with metaphysical abilities often go through physical changes as well. Attempting to adapt to something so terrifying changed the way my brain functioned. I'm also pretty sure all those x-rays and magnetic probings didn't help much either.

All this would continue throughout my childhood and into my adulthood without explanation. I wouldn't understand why I sometimes just "knew things" and hated crowds until I was in my mid-forties.

The truth was: I might have looked like an ordinary child, but there was something fairly extraordinary about me from the very start. Unfortunately, it would take several decades of suffering before I truly understood what was going on.

CHAPTER 2

THE MAN AT THE ROCK WALL

Life has a tendency of getting in the way. That's what happened to me.

In 1984, I met a man who would later become my husband. We moved in together and then got married in 1986. Since his family lived in Massachusetts, it wasn't long before he began talking about us moving there too.

I hated the idea of being so far away from my own family, but the temptation of a new location was alluring. Soon after we got married, we packed up our two dogs and our meager possessions and hauled them a thousand miles east, where we set up our new home.

Jobs were far more plentiful in Massachusetts, so it wasn't long before we were both working full time positions. We scrimped and saved and bought our first home in 1988. A year later our daughter Laura was born.

For many years, I had shut down my abilities. If my ears began ringing at odd times, I blamed it on tinnitus. If I felt as though I was being watched, I brushed it off. Unfortunately, this wasn't easy to do considering the house we moved into was haunted.

I documented this story in my 2015 book *Devil's Toy Box.*

The haunting at our new house was unimaginable. The entity that lived there had mastered the ability to move objects and knew how to frighten me. He turned my happily-ever-after into a nightmare that I was forced to endure for eleven long years.

We eventually escaped the house, leaving the haunting behind us. We built a house in Oakham, Massachusetts, which I thought would eliminate the possibility of another haunting. In some ways, I was right, but in other ways I was very wrong.

The property where we built the house had once been part of a large family farm. After purchasing a book about the history of our new town, I learned that family that once owned the land had been an integral part of Oakham since the early 1800's.

(Above) The Oakham house the first winter we moved in, before I built the rock wall.

We walked the property, trying to find the perfect spot to put a house and ended up settling on a hill in the middle. I imagined it planted at the apex of the land, looking down over the valley of pines and undergrowth like a castle on a hill.

Once the foundation was laid, we were distraught to learn that the front yard would drop off several feet from the front door. The contractor planned on just leaving it that way, not wanting to invest the time and resources on actually making it look pretty.

I walked back and forth in front of the wall, trying to figure out what to do about it while my two children, Laura and Trevor, played in the yard. Laura was ten and her younger brother was four, which put them at prime ages for sibling arguments. Trevor wanted to follow Laura everywhere she went, but Laura was having none of that.

We had only been in the house a few months, surviving our first winter there. It was now March and the snow was rapidly melting and the yard was full of robins, which was a good sign that spring was approaching.

Since moving there, I had enjoyed the luxury of staying home with the kids, but it was something I knew wouldn't last. I wanted to take full advantage of my time off. Getting the yard in shape was at the top of my list.

Laura scooped up a handful of melting snow and lobbed it at her brother, who protested loudly.

"Be quiet for a minute!" I scolded them, trying to figure out what to do with the front yard to make it look better. If we left it like it was, the entire concept of having our dream home would be ruined for me. It just wouldn't look right.

Inspiration found me as I tripped over a large rock that had been uprooted during the excavation of the basement. As I glanced around, I realized there were hundreds, if not thousands of rocks. I would build a wall.

It was an ambitious project. I started it the next morning and finished nine months later as the first snow of the season began to fall. It was a grueling job that made my arm muscles as hard as the stones themselves, but it was satisfying all the same. Ironically, it also gave me a deeper look into the history of the land from a perspective I wouldn't have imagined beforehand.

Since the wall was nearly seventy feet long and four feet tall, I needed a lot of stones. While I found a great deal of them scattered in the yard, it wasn't enough to finish the job. Behind the house, near the old cart path, I found an old stone wall that had eroded back into the ground and began cannibalizing it for my new wall.

Back in the 1800's New England farmers often built walls surrounding their properties. It gave them a definite border between their property and their neighbor's land, but it also served an even greater purpose. It gave them somewhere to put the rocks.

New England soil is saturated with rocks. Sometimes they even pop up from the ground on their own. This is something you learn fairly quickly. All you have to do is dig a hole in your yard and you'll hit so many rocks, you'll soon find yourself swearing at the ground.

As I began pulling rocks from the old wall, I heard a high pitched hum. It reminded me of the sound I heard when I was near a ghost. This one was a bit different though. Unlike the buzzing I heard at our last house, this one felt more passive.

I found myself tuning into it, reaching deeper into the sound for more information. Soon, images began flooding my mind. I saw an older man with fly-away white hair that was several months past its last haircut and a beard that brushed his chest. He was wearing a faded blue plaid shirt that was halfway unbuttoned, displaying a stained white undershirt beneath it. Old fashioned overalls hung off him by one shoulder, the denim soft and worn.

(Left: a photo of the man I saw at the rock wall)

I saw him leaning against a shovel, sweat pouring off him in buckets as he rested for a moment. "Damn rocks," he muttered to himself before picking the shovel back up to continue his job.

As the image faded from my mind, I found myself again seeing the landscape in front of me as it was now. When I saw the man, the land surrounding him was open and treeless, but now there was a forest.

I shook my head, trying to determine if the image I saw was real or just my imagination. All my life I was told that I had an active imagination, something I often utilized in my writing and in my craft projects, but this was something altogether different. The image was so clear, it was almost as though I saw a snapshot in my head.

I wasn't sure what to do with the information. After living in a haunted house for eleven years, the last thing I wanted to do was tell my husband. While he eventually believed me after experiencing some of the activity himself, he probably wouldn't have faith in me this time, so I just kept this knowledge to myself. Our marriage had become tedious enough on its own. I didn't need to tempt fate with more paranoia about something that might not even be valid.

I just tucked it away somewhere inside my mind and mused about it when I plucked rocks from the old wall. If he was truly there, he didn't seem to mind me tearing apart his old wall. Years later, I would happen upon a picture of Oakham from the 1800's. In it was a man who looked eerily similar to the one I saw in my mind. He was identified in the picture as the man who once owned the farm.

The man continued to visit with me while I completed my wall, but he never made any advances towards me. He just watched me work, becoming my invisible companion as I nearly broke my back hauling rocks from one wall to another. It was an interesting realization for me though. It was the first time I encountered a ghost that didn't scare me.

Unlike the scary man who haunted our last home, this man just wanted to share the moment with me. He didn't want anything from me and had no interest in scaring me. He was just there, watching.

It made me realize that ghosts weren't the scary things I thought they were. Granted, some of them were horribly frightening, but some of them weren't. They were just people who no longer had bodies.

We only ended up living in the Oakham house for five years before our marriage fell apart. The house then went onto the real estate market and my husband and I parted ways.

He found another house in Oakham that was priced to sell because it needed extensive work, and I found a house in nearby Barre.

My new house was an old colonial that sat right on the main road going into town. It was much smaller than my dream home, but had promise. I began mentally decorating the rooms and adding much needed landscaping along the bare foundation.

Two weeks before my moving truck was due to arrive, I was hit with devastating news. The sellers backed out. They took the house off the market and refused to sell.

This put me in a horrible position. Not having any family in the area, I had nowhere to go. I ended up putting my belongings into temporary storage and moved into an efficiency motel a half hour away.

My realtor worked feverishly to find me a new house, knowing my situation wasn't good. Not only was I separated from my kids due to their school schedule, but I was also separated from my pets.

My ex-husband agreed to keep my pets for me, but they were forced to spend their days in a utility closet in the basement due to his allergies. When I visited them, they gave me the saddest expressions, as if telling me to do something.

"I'm trying," I whispered to them as I left with tears in my eyes.

When a house came onto the market, I was elated. Once I went to see it, the feeling fell apart like a sandcastle on a windy day. It wasn't what I wanted and I didn't like the way it felt inside.

There was a very good chance it was haunted, but I didn't have any other choices. I could either stay in the motel and continue looking or I could take a chance.

I should have kept on looking.

CHAPTER 3

THE BARRE HOUSE

The house in Barre certainly wasn't my happily ever after house. It wasn't even close. It was the kind of house that new families start out in while saving for something nicer. It wasn't the kind of house that a forty-something year-old divorced woman with a head full of dreams bought.

It was less than 900 square feet, which was nearly a third of the size of the house I just left. Squat and square, it boasted a hip roof, and was surrounded by asphalt, something that I found less than desirable.

I walked around it, taking in the faded beige siding and the old windows.

(Above) The Barre house after a typical New England snowstorm

"What's up with all the asphalt?" I asked the realtor as I eyed the ring of pavement that surrounded the house. Even the sidewalks and back patio, if you could call it that, consisted of the same black pavement. It was ugly and utilitarian, built for purpose but not for appearance.

"I'm not sure," she said, clearly not in the mood to humor me any further. It was apparent she was tired of showing me house after house. She just wanted to sell me something and move onto the next client.

The inside of the house was a pleasant change from the outside. It had polished hardwood flooring in the living room and fresh carpeting in all the bedrooms. The kitchen had been recently renovated and had brand new cabinets and flooring. Even though the house was small, the abundance of windows gave it a sunny persona.

I quickly learned that it was a flipped house. A realtor bought it from the bank after it went into foreclosure and did a quick down-and-dirty renovation before putting it back on the market for nearly $80,000 more than they bought it for.

I spoke to the realtor who had flipped it and learned a little more about the family who lived there before me.

"The kitchen walls were crusted with food," he told me. "It was so bad, we had to remove all the sheet rock and replace it."

It made me wonder about those people. I knew they lost the house to foreclosure, but I knew very little about them otherwise. Looking around, it seemed strange to think that other people once lived their lives within these four walls. I tried to envision it, but couldn't get past the mental imagery of the food stained walls.

Thanksgiving had come and gone, finding me attempting to cook a turkey in a tiny oven for two children who would have rather been with their father at his enormous house. If they spent the night with me, they either had to crowd into my bed with me or sleep on the sofa in the living room. There wasn't a massive television and a family room set up for their use. There was one room that served as the kitchen and the living room and another one that was just large enough for a bed and dresser.

The motel was located in a less than savory area. When I came home from work, I often saw working girls leaving their rooms several doors down. As the street lamps came on at dusk, I watched cars pull up in the parking lot and make exchanges through the windows. It was a far cry from my three acre lot in Oakham.

I mourned the loss like a death. Not only had I lost my marriage, I also lost my family. My children spent more time with their father and his new girlfriend than they did with me and holidays became a blank spot on the calendar.

As Christmas rapidly approached, I felt a twinge settle in my soul.

I couldn't imagine setting up a tree in the tiny living space and trying to pretend that everything was alright when it really wasn't. Before I could catch it, my mind would flash to the previous season, to the grand white fir set up in front of the double windows, glistening with white lights.

My work days at the pet store had nearly drained me entirely. As part of an annual fundraiser, I had set up a Christmas tree lot in the parking area near my store, hoping to sell enough trees to make a profit for my chosen charity.

Not only was I attempting to manage a multi-million dollar store, I was also managing a second business of selling those trees. I had invested several thousand dollars of my own money for the initial purchase, but was still in the red. If I sold every tree I had purchased, I would make over $2000 for my charity. If I didn't, I'd have to eat the shortcomings.

I didn't have a lot of time for deep thinking. All I could consider was Christmas finding me in the efficiency unit, celebrating two doors down from prostitutes and drug dealers. I called the realtor and told her my decision.

"I'm going to buy the Barre house," I told her, the tone in my voice speaking volumes of my lack of enthusiasm. I'd treat it like a stepping stone, moving on to a better house as soon as possible.

Three days before Christmas 2005, two things happened simultaneously. I sold the last tree at work and I moved into my new house.

As I unpacked the mountain of boxes, trying to find a spot for everything, I heard a knock at my door. I opened it to find my realtor standing on the sidewalk with a Balsam fir in her hands.

"I wanted to bring you a house warming gift and figured you wouldn't have time to get a tree!" she said, her face lit up with enthusiasm.

I nearly groaned in her face.

***

The house had three small bedrooms. Two were located at the front of the house, with another one in the back. Even though the front bedrooms were larger, I felt drawn to the back bedroom.

It was positioned on the dark side of the house. When the sun rose in the east and set in the west, it would barely be touched by sunlight, providing me with a perfect place to sleep.

I painted the walls the color of a terra cotta flowerpot, with dusty smudges of white painstakingly dabbed on with a sea sponge. I wanted something different, something my now ex-husband couldn't deny me. He often frowned at my odd color choices, preferring white walls instead. Now, I could do whatever I wanted. I could paint them Princess Pink if I wanted to.

I filled the room with cherished treasures I had spent years collecting. A metal framed bed went below one of the windows and was flanked on either side with matching iron lamps with lavender lamp shades. I hung gold framed photos on the wall, giving the room a definite feminine touch. A painting that my grandmother gave me hung beside the door, next to a collection of colorful scarves and old pocketbooks. It wasn't a room that would ever be featured in a magazine spread, but it had my personality stamped all over it.

I imagined it becoming my sanctuary, a place where I could retreat to when the world got to be too much for me. I filled my nightstands with paperbacks and bought a TV to put on my bureau. I added plump pillows and a fluffy afghan for my cats to cuddle on.

I quickly went to work on the other rooms as well, painting the kitchen a cheery lemon yellow and the living room a calm sage green. Since most of my possessions didn't fit in the tiny house, I hauled them down to the basement, which was my least favorite place in the house.

Something about it gave me the creeps. I don't know if it was the musty smell of mold or the low ceilings. Even the lighting contributed to the creepy demeanor, with single light bulbs hanging in the center of each room.

One section of the basement appeared to have been somewhat renovated. I say "somewhat" because it was a half-hearted effort. A sheetrock ceiling and walls had been constructed, but were crumbling and moldy from the constant moisture that seeped in through the foundation. If I planned to use the room, I'd have to invest in a dehumidifier, something I couldn't afford at the moment.

I roamed the basement rooms with a flashlight, dodging the cobwebs that hung like garland from the open rafters, my sense of intrigue turning to anxiety in a matter of moments.

In one of the basement rooms, I found an old-fashioned medicine cabinet hanging on the wall. I stood and stared at it for a long moment, trying to make sense of it. Why hang a medicine cabinet in the darkest corner of a basement? The thought gave me a chill as I imagined someone actually living down there.

There wasn't any plumbing in the basement, so a medicine cabinet didn't make any sense. If someone attempted to use it for anything other than storage, he'd have to bring a flashlight just to see his reflection in the mirror.

As I walked back into the large room, where the oil tank and boiler were housed, my eyes caught a startling sight.

The wall had once been painted white, but had aged to the color of cemetery stones. Sporadically scattered along the wall were dark smudges with drips running down from them.

I stopped dead and stared at it, feeling a sense of unease come over me. For all the world, it looked as though someone had lined up a group of people and shot them in their heads. I shuddered at the thought, willing the images in my mind to disintegrate.

Surely, if a murder happened here, I would have known about it. I think the realtor would have been forced to tell me. It still left me feeling disconcerted.

As I stared at those dark splotches, it was as if the energy was rising from the wall, implanted with the horrid memories that created them. Cold chills rose on both of my arms and I felt my stomach clinch with anxiety.

What else could it be?

Either someone created an elaborate hoax or something very bad had happened in my basement. Before the images of death and horror could get a firm grip on my mind, I turned away. It wasn't something I was prepared to deal with.

I hastily retreated back up the decrepit stairs, finding my way back to my bright sunny kitchen. My two cats blinked at me from the couch in the adjacent living room where they soaked in the sunshine from the picture window.

"Hey babies," I cooed at them.

They purred as they looked at me.

Besides my two fat tabby housecats, Gatorbug and Skeeter, I also had a black Border Collie mix I rescued from a shelter the

(Above) Gatorbug and Skeeter

(Above): Ripley

previous year named Ripley. The three of them were like family to me.

As I settled into the Barre house, I again became aware of the energy that lingered there. I felt it the first time I walked through the house, but it wasn't something I could put my finger on. It was simply there. But as time progressed, it separated itself from the shadows and began letting itself be known.

After a few months, it became clear to me. I had moved into another haunted house.

Chapter 4

The Haunted Pet Store

My first year in the Barre house was busy. Besides trying to make my new house a home, I had a high volume pet store to run.

I didn't happen upon my job by accident. Before I got pregnant with my daughter Laura, I managed a small pet store in the town of Sudbury. The company went belly-up while I was on maternity leave, so I took time off to focus on raising my daughter. It was a nice break and I enjoyed every moment of it, but money was tight. By the time Laura started Kindergarten, I was back at work, trying to earn a much needed income.

I started working as a cashier at a local pet store chain and was promoted to an assistant manager position within the year. I was a hard worker, full of ideas to help grow the business and soon found myself accepting a general manager position within the company.

For several years, I moved from location to location, fixing up neglected stores and then turning them over to a new manager. After giving birth to my second child, I learned that the company had been sold to a national chain. I decided to take the time off to raise Trevor like I had with his sister.

Soon after I finished the stone wall at the Oakham house, I was pressured to find another job. Living on one income was difficult and more money was needed.

I applied for a general manager position at the large pet store chain that bought out my old company, but didn't get the job. Instead, they offered me an assistant manager position, one I took gratefully. After a year of proving myself to them, I was offered a general manager position at another location.

The Shrewsbury store was located in a run-down shopping plaza near the edge of the Worcester border. It attracted a wide range of shoppers. Not only did we get the needy customers, who insisted on employing me as their personal shopper while they painstakingly perused the store, but we also got the shoplifters from the bad parts of town. Trying to maintain some sort of balance between the two could have been a full time job in itself.

Shortly after I took over the store, the employees began telling me about Fred. Apparently, they felt the building was haunted.

"How do you know his name is Fred?" I asked.

One of my team leads stepped forward. She was a pretty young blonde with an open smile. She had been with the company for many years and knew the ins and outs of the store better than anyone.

"Follow me and I'll show you," she said.

I followed Carrie to the back of the store, praying for a pause between shoppers to satisfy my curiosity.

The store was long and narrow, reminiscent of a bowling alley. It had low drop-ceilings that were adorned with brown water stains and old rusty shelving that had been repainted red so many times, the paint had bubbled.

She brought me to an employee bathroom that was painted dark green. It made the already small room feel like an algae coated closet.

Someone had tacked up glittery stickers along all the walls, depicting cartoonish sea life. It took me a moment to realize they were hoping to make the bathroom feel like the inside of an aquarium. With their unfortunate color choice, it felt more like being trapped inside of a decaying septic tank instead.

"Right after we painted it, this appeared," she said, pointing to a jagged line of words.

Fred was here.

I stared at it, trying to understand what she was telling me. It was obvious that someone had scratched the words into the paint. How was that paranormal?

"Didn't someone just scratch that into the wall?" I asked, stating the obvious.

She smiled. "That's what we thought when we first saw it, but we painted over it again and it reappeared each time."

I must have given her an incredulous look. I've been told that my emotions play out clearly on my face, no matter how hard I try to hide them. This time was no different.

"Well, that's what we think anyway. I guess it could have just leaked through the new paint," she said, attempting to discard her earlier enthusiasm.

I felt as though I'd just taken a lollipop away from a starving child. Her expression went from elated to disappointed in two seconds. Besides my inability to hide my emotions, I also have a tendency to speak my mind without thinking about the consequences. This is something I still continue to work on.

At that moment, someone paged me to the cash register, so I didn't have time to pursue the conversation any further. I wouldn't have to wait long for another example though. Several days later, something else happened.

We often worked over-night shifts. With a store as busy as ours, it was impossible to get all our tasks done when the store was filled with shoppers.

Armed with extra-large coffees, we started at ten o'clock in the evening as the last of the shoppers exited through the automatic double doors. Twenty pallets full of product had arrived earlier in the day and we were eager to get it onto the shelves.

My head receiver pulled the pallets out onto the floor near the area where the product was located and a group of people would begin tearing it apart, placing the items on the corresponding shelves.

After several hours of this, we stopped to take a well-needed break. I took a sip of my now cool coffee and plopped down on the edge of a pallet full of wild bird seed, praying I didn't split the bag open in the process.

Without warning, a thumping noise went across the store intercom.

It sounded exactly like a heartbeat.

Everyone in the group paused, looking up at the ceiling as though expecting to see some mammoth beast lurking there.

"What the hell was that?" I asked.

Carrie laughed, amusement lighting up her face. "That was Fred."

"No way," I said, jumping off the bird seed pallet. I made my way into my office to inspect the intercom system. During the day, it was hooked up to an MP3 system that broadcasted music and promotional blurbs throughout the store. At night, it was thankfully disconnected, giving us a break from the canned music none of us had ever heard of before.

Typical of that type of system, the music was muted when someone used the intercom to page a message. "Manager to the register" was the most frequent phrase used.

Nothing was amiss. Everything was working like it normally did. By the time I returned to the sales floor, the sounds of a beating heart had stopped.

"Do you hear that often?" I asked, feeling the first sensation of trepidation.

"Just during overnights usually," one of the employees told me.

The logical side of me dismissed it as faulty equipment. The store was old, which meant that the electrical components were also aging, but a heartbeat? That was a little surreal to me. It was difficult to explain.

I quickly forgot about it until the next event transpired.

One day, I was merchandising some new product into the current plan-o-gram, while internally cursing at the person who designed the product layout. Instead of making sure the items would all fit on the same shelf, the corporate merchandiser had simply shrunk the image on the page. It meant that I'd have to rework the entire design to fit everything in the already tight spot.

As I knelt in front of the shelving unit, the automatic front doors opened. I glanced up, thinking that a customer had walked through. It was our customary policy to greet them as they came into the store and offer assistance. When I looked up, nobody was there.

Even though I had been sitting there for over fifteen minutes, I wondered if I had somehow triggered the invisible eye that detected movement. I waved my hands over my head, but the door fell closed again and remained that way.

"That's weird," I mumbled to myself and then returned to my project. A few minutes later, it happened again.

An employee walked past and took notice of the situation. She smiled at me.

"That must be Fred," she said breezily.

Since coming to the store, the employees were hell-bent on convincing me that the store was haunted. Even though I had lived through a haunting of my own, I had a difficult time accepting their theory at face value.

People often get spooked and will lump together several experiences, hoping to make a noteworthy story out of them. I wasn't necessarily buying it, although I was getting closer.

The following day, I came back to my display and began tweaking it to make it look better and the door didn't budge. I stared at it, almost willing it to move, but it refused.

Several days later, as I was covering the register for a cashier who was on break, it began happening again. This time, I was far enough away from the doors to know that I wasn't causing it to open. It was almost as though it was doing it on purpose to capture my attention. I put a call into the company who serviced the doors for us.

The man came out the following day and tore apart the mechanism. He worked for nearly an hour before he put it all back together again.

"Nothing is wrong with it," he told me matter-of-factly.

"What do you mean? It sometimes opens on its own. Something must be wrong," I told him.

He shrugged. "I don't know what to tell you. Nothing is wrong with it."

If I wasn't convinced that the building was haunted, the next event would make me a believer.

Carrie and I often got to the store several hours before it opened. While she cleaned the small animal compartments, I finished up paperwork and did small projects that I couldn't do when the store was opened.

I was in the middle of tearing apart a display, when Carrie approached me, her face blanched of color.

"Oh my God! You won't believe what just happened to me," she said.

I started to ask her to elaborate, but she motioned with fluttering hands for me to follow her. "I have to show you," she said.

She led me back to the rear of the store and pointed at the double doors.

The doors were solid with small windows at the tops that led to the receiving area where we kept the excess product that wouldn't fit on the shelves. When I tried to push them open, they refused to budge.

"You know my routine. I go back into the back and get the portable vacuum in the mornings and then push it through these doors to get to the front of the store. After I was finished with them, I went to put it back and the doors wouldn't open," she said and then pried the door open with her fingers to show me what was on the other side.

Two heavy boxes were in front of the doors, preventing them from being pushed open. This was strange to me because we didn't keep boxes of product near the door. They were either lined up on a shelf on the other side of the room or they were left on the pallet until we could put them away.

As I inspected the shelf where the boxes are kept, my heart nearly froze. There were two open spaces that were identical in size to the boxes she found in front of the doors. It looked as though someone had picked up the boxes and carried them to the doors. I didn't know what to say.

The following weeks found me anxious about going into the back storage room by myself. If I could have avoided it altogether, I probably would have, but some of the supplies I needed were kept there.

It wasn't long before I began hearing the same static sound that I've always associated with ghosts. I stopped dead in my tracks the first time I heard it, my heart hammering inside my chest.

Was there really a ghost here?

I would flip the lights on in the morning and practically race to the back of the store. The backroom was dimly lit. No amount of lighting could have eased my fears though. If this was a ghost, he was nothing like the man at my rock wall. This was more like the creepy guy who haunted my former house. I got cold chills just thinking about it.

"I'm just going to go back and get a few peg hooks and then I'll be gone," I would say aloud, hoping none of my employees would hear me. Then I'd race to the far back corner of the room where the shadows were the darkest and grab what I needed before bolting out of the room.

It felt weird talking to thin air, but I hoped that by explaining my intentions, he would leave me alone.

On one of these occasions, I nearly barreled over Carrie as she came through the double doors. She laughed at the expression on my face.

"Now do you believe me?" she asked.

I did, but there wasn't much I could do about it. I didn't want to admit it for fear that the employees would be too frightened to come to work. Finding good associates was difficult enough. Losing them over a haunting would have been devastating.

Several months later, the final piece of the puzzle dropped neatly into place.

I came into the store two hours prior to opening time, my mind filled with thoughts of our upcoming inventory. Once a year we were required to count every piece of product in the store, to insure our inventory counts were accurate. It was a time consuming process that I dreaded every year. Not only would it eat up all my work time, it would also force me to work longer hours.

That morning, I wanted to go through some of the back-stock in the back room and put away everything that could fit on the shelves. As I was walking down the long aisle towards the rear of the store, I saw a man standing at the end of one of the aisles, inspecting one of my displays.

He was dressed as though he belonged in the 1940's with a long trench coat and a newsboy cap. He was close to my height, judging by the shelves he was standing in front of, which was fairly short for a man. The fact that he was in the store at all was astounding. Even more surprising was his coloring. He was made entirely of shades of grey.

From his jacket to his shoes, he was grey and white, looking exactly like an old newspaper photo. I only saw him for two or three seconds before I walked past an aisle display. By the time I got around it, the man was gone.

I knew for a fact that the front doors were locked. The only people in the store were me and Carrie.

"Carrie!" I called out, while racing to the spot where I saw the man. While I was pretty sure he wasn't a physical person, judging by the grey tones, I couldn't simply dismiss it as paranormal without searching the store first. If someone had somehow snuck into the store, I needed to know about it.

Carrie came running and we searched the store together, not finding any trace of the man. Both the front and back doors were securely locked, as well.

Once we finished, we retreated outside for a cigarette. After I took my first deep drag, my hands were still shaking.

"I guess I finally met Fred," I told her.

"I guess you did," she said with a sense of accomplishment.

I did a bit of research on the property and learned that it had been a gas station in the 1940's and 50's. Later, after the gas pumps were removed and the building was demolished, it became a graveyard for old semi-truck trailers. I was told that homeless people would camp out in them until the police chased them away again. The man I saw pretty much fit the description of what I thought a man from the forties would look like. Was he a former gas station owner who was still hanging around his property?

The questions piled up on top of one another with no logical explanation. I had been under the assumption that someone had to die at the location before it could become haunted, but after researching the topic I learned this wasn't true. Ghosts sometimes hung out at places where they spent a lot of time while they were alive. If the man worked at the gas station, or even owned it, it stood to reason that he might hang around there after death.

It made me wonder what he was doing. It was obvious that he wasn't seeing a vision from the past by the way he was inspecting the flea and tick endcap so carefully. Was he trying to make sense of the new-fangled products? I didn't know, but I was insanely curious about him and wanted to learn more.

Years later, while I was at a national meeting, I met a man who had once managed my store. He had since been promoted to a district manager position in Arizona, which gave him a sense of clout. I knew he would be hesitant to talk about ghosts given his job title, but I couldn't let the opportunity pass without at least trying. I asked him about Fred as soon as I tracked him down.

He gave me a steady look, his expression border-lining between intrigue and apprehension.

"I saw him one morning. I need to know what you saw," I told him. The expression on my face must have been the deciding factor because he pulled me aside to a place where no one else could hear us talk.

He then told me about the heart beat on the intercom and about the front doors that sometimes opened on their own. Then he told me a story I hadn't heard before.

"One night as we were locking up, we stood at the front of the store near the doors and saw a man race across the store and disappear into the fish department. We searched the store from top to bottom and never found anyone," he told me. That was confirmation enough.

As much as I didn't want to admit it, not only was I living in a haunted house, I was also managing a haunted store.

Chapter 5

Motel Ghosts

After one of my supervisors at work saw my Christmas tree lot, I was soon offered a regional promotion.

"Anyone who thinks outside the box like that is someone I want on my team," he told me. Most of the other stores had done far less for the charity drive, setting me apart from the crowd.

I went from managing a retail store to becoming a regional manager, covering five states. I was gone all day, from dawn to dusk, driving to the stores in my area to evaluate and coach them on their pet grooming and training programs. Twice a month, I was required to travel to New Jersey and New York, where I spent several days visiting the stores in the vicinity.

I loved my new job, but really despised all the traveling involved, especially the overnight trips. It often brought me nose to nose with the paranormal world.

I found this out quickly during a trip to Long Island, New York. I was traveling with a group of regional associates who were doing a tour of the area to prepare the stores for an upcoming visit from a high-level company Vice President. This happened several times a year and I was always expected to participate.

While I loved the freedom of my promotion, I never looked forward to the group outings. Egos were always evident as my peers attempted to outshine each other in hopes of garnering attention from our superiors. I've never been good at playing that game. I do what I do without a need to gloat over it. Even when I tried, I came off flat and false. It reminded me of being back in high school, trying to be something I wasn't and failing miserably at it.

Our group toured several stores during the day, met for dinner at a nice restaurant that evening and then retired to our rooms where we would catch up on our unread emails.

I was exhausted when I finally got to my room. Holding a forced smile all day left me with a dull throbbing headache. All I wanted to do was to fall into bed and sleep, but after my experiences in the Paterson hotel, I needed to make sure I was secure first.

The room was long and narrow, much larger than most rooms I had stayed at in the area. When real estate prices were extraordinarily high, the hotel rooms often reflected this. I once stayed in a room in Times Square that was barely big enough for a bed and a dresser. This room was at least ten times that size.

The wall on the right side of the room was home to two queen-sized beds, with a small sofa, desk and entertainment cabinet consuming the opposite wall. The bathroom was located at the far end. Besides the size, it looked like any other hotel room I'd ever stayed at, with one exception. This room had drop ceilings.

I was familiar with drop ceilings after living in a house that had them in the living room. If you lifted one of the panels, you could see all the way up to the ceiling. If the walls between the rooms didn't extend to the ceiling, it would be conceivable for someone to slip over the wall, gaining instant access to my room.

It was a ridiculous concept. Why would anyone want to get into my room? It wasn't like I was traveling with a queen's ransom that someone would want to steal. Besides, nobody was in the hallway when I unlocked the door, so they would have no idea who was next door. Still though, I couldn't get the thought out of my mind.

I found my way to the bathroom and took a quick shower, washing away the residue of the long day and easing my aching muscles. As soon as I was finished, I pulled on a pair of sleep shorts and a t-shirt and headed back into the room.

The minute I walked in, I knew I wasn't alone. One quick glance around the room dispelled this idea, but I couldn't shake the feeling. I felt as though I was being watched.

I grabbed my laptop and hopped into bed, hoping for a distraction to take my mind off my fears. I would answer a few work emails, which would hopefully help me fall asleep. As soon as I opened my computer and turned it on, my ears began ringing with a static sound.

I froze.

It seemed to be coming from the other end of the room, near the bathroom. I found my eyes drawn to the ceiling near the wall, half expecting to see the ceiling panel move.

I snapped my laptop shut and scrambled out of the bed. Every cell in my body urged me to bolt from the room, but where would I go?

If I raced down to the lobby in my night clothes, I'd be met with inquisitive stares. I couldn't even imagine contacting one of my work associates regarding my fears. I worked far too hard for my promotion just to throw it away on an irrational fear. After all, there was clearly no one in my room.

I studied the air around me, my heart pounding frantically.

What could I do?

I couldn't imagine the teasing I'd get from my coworkers later. "Did you see another ghost, Joni?" My superiors wouldn't find it nearly as amusing, possibly reassessing my ability to perform my job.

I eased back onto the bed and put my back against the headboard. While I could still hear the buzzing sound, nothing moved in the room. It wasn't exactly comforting, but it was all I had at the moment.

After a few minutes, I relaxed a bit. It had been a long day. Maybe I was just imagining things. I slid my laptop back onto my lap and began responding to emails sent to me by the stores I covered. It didn't take me long to lose myself in my work and temporarily forget about my situation.

Some of the emails were easy to answer, but others required extensive research, which took me the better part of an hour. As I finished my last message, I was getting ready to close my laptop and think about going to sleep when the bathroom light snapped on.

I stared across the room, feeling the same sense of unease wash over me. I might have imagined the buzzing sound, but this was something I couldn't dismiss so easily.

Would someone or something come walking out of the bathroom?

I watched the rectangle of light for what felt like an eternity before easing up from my bed. I glanced around the room, looking for something to defend myself with, but didn't see anything that even remotely resembled a weapon. The closest thing was the table lamp, but I didn't want to take the time to unplug it and remove the lampshade. Instead, I crept across the room and approached the bathroom.

The bathroom fan whirred loudly, blocking out all other sounds in the room. If the buzzing tone was happening, I couldn't hear it. I slipped into the bathroom and whipped open the shower curtain.

Nothing was there.

I took a deep breath and let it out with a sigh. Even though I knew I was alone, I still had a situation to consider. How did the light come on by itself?

I turned my attention to the wall switch. It was a standard mechanism. I turned it off, causing the light and fan to cut out, plunging me into near total darkness.

"Shit!" I swore and flipped it back on again before something could reach out and grab me. The light and fan came back on again, returning the bathroom to normal.

"What the hell?" I whispered.

I made another sweep of the room, taking care to inspect the spaces beneath the two beds and the interior of the closet. No one was there.

Thoughts of the ghost at my home and the one at my old store returned to me. Every time I felt something was nearby, I heard the same buzzing tone in my ears. Was I hearing ghosts?

It seemed illogical to me that every place I went to was haunted. Was the world so full of ghosts that they were crowded shoulder to shoulder together, or was I drawing them to me?

I didn't have any easy answers, so I headed back to my bed. We were starting early the next day, visiting another handful of stores. I needed to be at the top of my game, not bleary-eyed and groggy from a lost night of sleep. I turned on a lamp near the small sofa and jumped back into bed, making a massive leap so nothing could grab my ankles from under the bed.

Part of me fear was hinged firmly on my lack of knowledge. What could a ghost do to me? Could it slip into my body while I was asleep and take me over? Would the Joni who appeared at the corporate breakfast table the next morning be someone altogether different than the Joni who checked into her hotel room the night before?

Could they hurt me?

I had watched enough horror movies to fill my mind with possibilities. I imagined hands closing around my throat as soon as I closed my eyes. If I managed to turn on the lamp, I would find the room empty.

As those scenarios raced through my mind, I realized that none of them were the ones that scared me the most. My greatest fear was to wake up and find one standing beside my bed.

When my daughter was small, she often walked in her sleep. Sometimes she would walk to the side of my bed and just stand there until I woke with a gasp. It always took my mind several seconds to comprehend what I was seeing. For those terrifying three seconds, I always thought she was something else.

Sleep found me after an eternity of lying there, listening to the sounds of the hotel. People shuffled down the hallways at odd hours of the night, talking too loudly. The air conditioner turned itself on with a roar that nearly sent me skyward several times, while someone in the next room randomly thumped against the wall. I soon found myself falling into a dark pit of nightmares where someone was chasing me. I woke with a start hours later.

I sat up in bed, trying to figure out where I was. The room was pitch black. I couldn't see a single thing in the darkness. As the dregs of sleep fell away, I remembered where I was. With a sense of panic, I pawed the nightstand beside my bed, trying to find the lamp.

It came on with a click, illuminating the room with a soft glow. Nothing was out of place except for one thing. I had left a lamp on, but now it was turned off.

I crept out of bed, approaching the lamp as though it was a snake coiled in the grass. I turned it back on to make sure the bulb hadn't simply burned out, but it came on with a flourish. I turned it off and back on again, thinking that maybe it just had a faulty switch, but it worked perfectly.

I spent the rest of the night propped up in my bed, waiting for daylight to find me. Nothing else happened, but that didn't alleviate my fears. Something was in the room with me that night and I knew it.

I met my coworkers and supervisors early the next morning. The circles under my eyes were evident and several people inquired about them.

"Couldn't sleep?" one of them asked.

"No. I have a hard time sleeping in hotel rooms," I told him, not wanting to divulge the truth. What would I say? There was a ghost in my room?

It would be the first of many times that I would live through a horrific event that I couldn't talk about. If I did, people would think I was crazy and I'd lose all chances of hanging onto the job I so desperately needed.

Experiences like that continued to happen to me in various hotels. Lights came on by themselves and strange noises sounded in the other parts of the rooms. Several times, I felt the distinct pressure of someone sitting on the bed with me and was actually touched on the cheek once. It didn't matter how fancy the room was. If there was a ghost in the general vicinity, it found me.

I eventually discovered a hotel in West Orange, New Jersey that had a good feel to it. The room was located in the older section of the building and had the added bonus of being at ground level with a small porch. I could sit out there and smoke when the urge struck me, while I watched the traffic pass by on the road out front.

Nothing happened to me in that room, so I continued to request it for my return trips to the area. On my fifth or sixth visit, I heard the distinct buzzing sound enter my room, but it didn't have the same aggressive emotions attached to it. It felt more like the man at the stone wall, which made me more comfortable.

As I drove home from my trip, I had to smile. Had I become so at ease with the concept of ghosts that I was now placing them into categories? Scary or safe? I wasn't sure, but it would forever change the way I felt about staying at hotels.

Unfortunately for me, back home was no different than I left it. In fact, the ghosts seemed to be angry that I left for so long.

Chapter 6

My Paranormal Side-Kick

It was evident that something strange was happening to me. Everywhere I went, I began picking up the sound that alerted me to the presence of ghosts.

It didn't matter if I was at the grocery store or driving past a cemetery, it became far more prevalent. It came at me, unwanted and without reservation. I couldn't turn it off or even block the sound. In some ways, it was similar to having an indicator button that couldn't be disabled. Perhaps the worst part was having to keep all that to myself.

I really didn't have many friends. For most of my life I had worked as a manager and resisted the urge to become friends with my associates. If I hung out with them socially, it would have completely decimated the employee/manager boundary, making it impossible to do my job.

The few friends I did have weren't interested in the paranormal. I wasn't certain if they even believed in ghosts. It wasn't a topic we discussed. The only thing I had was my pets and they ended up teaching me more than I bargained for.

My house was quickly becoming a ghost hotel. Not only was I hearing the tone that I had always associated with ghosts, I began to realize that there was more than one of them. Some of the tones were high and crystal clear, while others were low and filled with static. As I tuned into them, I counted at least five different ghosts in my house.

None of them had the same menacing feeling to them that I felt with the one in the hotel room, but it wasn't exactly a comforting thought either. Even though I had been hearing the sounds since childhood, a part of me simply disregarded them as being real. Somehow, I had been able to deny the legitimacy of them. In some ways, it was probably self-preservation. I wasn't mentally ready to deal with this on the grand scale it would become, so I wouldn't allow myself to fully believe in it. It was much easier to pretend it wasn't happening than to except the truth of the matter. Now that I had broken down that wall, there was no going back. I was in it for the long haul.

It wasn't long before I began to notice that my cats were tuned into the same thing I was sensing.

The bond I shared with my pets went deeper than a normal pet/owner relationship. I could feel them and often interpret their moods. When one of them was ill, I knew it even if they were hiding their symptoms. I don't know if I was simply reading their body language or if I was deciphering their energy, but I was always aware of what they were feeling.

At this point in my development, I was insanely curious about everything that was happening to me. I began reading books and articles on paranormal websites, hungry for answers. What I found out about my connection with pets made perfect sense to me. Not only was I gifted with the ability to sense ghosts, I was also an Empath.

Empaths are people who are tuned into the energy surrounding them. They can tap into the energy and pull information from it. This was especially true with people and animals they were close to.

As I read more, I also learned that Empaths often struggle with all this excess energy. They absorbed it like human sponges. When the energy overflowed in their bodies, it would often cause them to react in a physical way. Some people develop signs of depression and anxiety, while others get blinding headaches.

Some empaths are even able to tap into the energy of the dead as well as the living. Was this how I was interpreting whether a ghost was safe or scary? Was I tuning into their energy? I wasn't sure, but I wanted to know more.

The articles recommended a process called "grounding" to help purge off the extra energy that an Empath absorbs. There were various methods suggested, but the one that resonated with me was to imagine my feet planted twenty feet into the ground like the roots of a tree. I would then imagine a white light beaming overhead. As I took a breath, I pulled the white light into the crown of my head. As I exhaled, I would push the extra energy down my body and into my feet where it could be absorbed into the ground.

Once I did that, I went onto the second part of the exercise, which involved shielding myself from pulling in more energy. For this, I had to imagine pulling the white light from above my head downward to my body, creating a protective bubble that surrounded me.

I found the bubble shielding to be helpful in everyday life. I used it when I was forced to endure large crowds of people and even used it on airplanes during some of my longer work trips.

Another symptom of being Empathic involved animals. Not only were Empaths more connected to animals, they often drew them in. It made me think about my childhood and how animals would naturally gravitate to me.

My own pets were no exception. They felt like souls who shared my space, not just "things" that people collected. I recognized the fact that they had emotions and thoughts, just like I did. They were also picking up on the paranormal activity in my house, just like I was.

My two brown tabby cats would sit and watch something move around the room. The first time I noticed it, I naturally thought they were watching a bug.

"Whatcha looking at, Gatorbug?" I asked the older of my two cats. Gatorbug was a sweet cat with beautiful thick black stripes. Of the two cats, he was the most affectionate, always preferring to be by my side.

I looked around the room to see what he was watching when I realized I was hearing a tone. As I turned my head, I was amazed to realize that I could actually pinpoint the location it was coming from. To my utter surprise, Gatorbug began watching the exact same spot where the sound was coming from. If it moved, he followed it to the next place I heard it. Soon, my other cat Skeeter was watching it too.

(Above Skeeter and Gatorbug sharing the futon)

Were my cats picking up on ghosts too?

This was unreal to me. I was curious about this, so I did some more research and learned that a cat's eyesight is far different than ours is. They can see a larger extent of the ultraviolet range, which made perfect sense to me. From my research I knew that paranormal investigators were experimenting with cameras that captured more of the light spectrum and were coming back with some very chilling images.

Once I realized what was going on with my cats, I used it to my advantage. They truly helped me validate what I was hearing, but I still wished I had someone to talk to about everything I was experiencing. The thoughts and concepts were bubbling up inside of me and I had no one to discuss it with. Furthermore, I was lonely.

While I've always been something of an introvert, I still crave human companionship just like everyone else. Sometimes weekends passed by without a single human encounter.

I began the arduous search for other human beings. Not certain where to start, I created a profile and began online dating. I probably don't need to go into this in depth because the consequences were predictable. I was meeting nothing but men hoping for a quick hookup, which definitely wasn't what I was looking for.

In my frustration, I reached out to an old friend from Indiana who was also experimenting with online dating and asked his opinion.

He suggested that I should focus on finding friends instead of boyfriends and told me to check out Meetup.com to see if there were any paranormal groups listed there. He used the site frequently to find kayaking friends and found it to be helpful.

I took his suggestion and found a meetup group nearby. After a bad experience with one group, I was eventually introduced to another meetup leader, a woman by the name of Sandy MacLeod.

I went to one of her events and we hit it off right away.

At first glance, Sandy's appearance was a contradiction to the person she really was. She had an air of quiet confidence about her. With her dark red hair and glasses, she looked like someone who taught English 101 at the local community college. She was soft spoken and articulate, someone who chose her words carefully before releasing them out to the world.

During the course of the night, I found myself drawn to her, asking her questions about her past investigations. She had been to many that were featured on the various paranormal television shows I watched, but there was more than that. I was envious and intrigued.

(Above) Joni and Sandy in Salem in 2012

I believe that sometimes people's souls recognize one another. I've had this happen before. When I meet someone, I get an immediate impression. Sometimes, I either really connect with them or I don't. I tend to listen to this little voice in the back of my head and will often follow it to see where it leads. In Sandy's case, it led to a friendship that is immeasurable.

I didn't tell her about my gift that night, preferring to absorb as much wisdom and knowledge as I could from her instead. She had a bag full of paranormal gear and she went through it and demonstrated how it all worked, even going as far as allowing us to use it ourselves. She showed us how to use an EMF meter that detects electromagnetic energy, which is often a sign that a ghost was present.

I found that concept extremely alluring. If I had a piece of equipment that could verify what I was feeling, I would have the validation I needed. The only equipment I had at that time was a digital voice recorder, but I had no idea how to use it. Through the process of the night, she showed us how to conduct EVP (electronic voice phenomena) sessions, where we used our recorders to attempt to record ghost voices. By the end of the night, I was hooked. There was no going back for me. I would become a ghost hunter regardless of any obstacles thrown my way.

I've always believed in watching for strange synchronicities. Sometimes life shoots us signs and directions that we're supposed to follow. They often appear out of nowhere, but are always profound enough to garner our attention. If we follow them, they often act like dominos, tipping over one into the other. All we have to do is pay attention and follow them.

When we look back at our past, we can see these dominos and understand how one situation led us to another and another until we reached the place where we are supposed to end up.

(Left) Joni at Waverly Hills

Another synchronicity occurred during this same time frame. My sister who lived in Indiana set up an investigation at Waverly Hill Sanatorium, a famously haunted tuberculosis hospital located in nearby Louisville, Kentucky. Even though my sister had never investigated the paranormal before, she knew from our conversations that it was something I was interested in. When I told Sandy that we were going, she asked if she could join us. I was elated. Having a real ghost hunter with her years of experience, not to mention all of her fancy gear, was astounding.

Since I was already planning on being in the Midwest to visit my family in Indiana, Sandy met me at Waverly Hills. We spent the night walking the haunted hallways, experimenting with her equipment and basically learning how to investigate the paranormal.

When I listen back to the audio I recorded, I have to laugh at all my errors. At that time, I knew nothing about the delicacy of recording ghost voices and made so many mistakes. We walked around while recording and captured our footsteps on the audio, covering up any possible ghost voices. We didn't mark the audio verbally when someone coughed, yawned or had a stomach growl, but we had an enjoyable time, all the same.

One thing I learned during that investigation still remains with me. I learned how to feel the energy of a location, further tapping into my Empathic abilities.

"It feels so sad here," Sandy said.

I stopped in my tracks and looked at her, realizing that I felt it too without really acknowledging it. It was something that just lingered in the air, almost like an invisible fragrance.

The more I focused on it, the stronger it got. I would have dismissed it as imagination, but the tears that rolled down my cheeks wouldn't let me. This feeling was real and I was connecting with it.

We explored every inch of the building that night that we were allowed to investigate, not leaving the property until nearly four o'clock in the morning. As soon as I returned back home from my trip, Sandy and I made plans to get together again soon.

CHAPTER 7

THE CEMETERY GHOST

Meeting Sandy and having someone to share my experiences with truly catapulted me into the paranormal realm. Instead of being frightened by my ability to sense the dead, I began embracing it instead.

Sandy's theories about the paranormal world soon became my own. I especially coveted her sense of compassion.

Instead of seeing ghosts as dark, scary things that wanted to steal my soul, I began seeing them as people without bodies. Although this concept really took root for me when I met the ghost man at my stone wall, her impact served to make it more insightful.

She began to teach me how their personalities often remained with them after death. Just like in life, there were good people and bad people. Their situation seldom changed in death. A negative, grumpy man who hated all of humanity would probably end up being a nasty ghost, while a gentle, honest man would probably stay somewhat the same.

Unfortunately for me, I couldn't always tell them apart. Sometimes nasty ghosts pretended to be nice souls in order to gain my trust. It made me distrustful of all of them, despite how they felt to me.

Since New England is filled with old cemeteries, Sandy suggested that we start there. They were easily accessible and offered a plethora of souls to connect with.

The first cemetery we decided to explore was located not far from her house in Hubbardston, Massachusetts. Located on several acres of flat land, it was close to the busy road, offering us a measure of protection from the living.

Cemeteries can be dangerous places for more than one reason. They are often secluded, providing a perfect lurking spot for people with unethical purposes.

While Hubbardston wasn't known for having high crime, or any crime for that matter, it still paid to be vigilant. Enough women and children have disappeared over the years in other quaint Massachusetts communities to make it a possibility.

Thick dark woods bordered the cemetery on three sides, with the main road lining the fourth. We parked on the thin grassy strip that separated the cemetery from the road and got out of the car.

It was a mild September afternoon. The sky was a perfect powder blue, a beautiful backdrop for the orange and yellow foliage on the autumn trees. I wanted to meet Sandy earlier, but I had to finish a report for work. By the time we got there, the sun rode low in the sky, only giving us an hour or two of daylight.

I stopped at the entrance and looked around. Streaks of bright sunlight pierced through the trees, sending fingers of light into the graveyard, giving it an angelic appearance. I wished I could have latched onto the imagery, but it didn't feel like it looked. Something about it was dark and foreboding.

"I'm not sure I like the way it feels," I commented.

Sandy looked around, squinting at the dark line of trees along the left side of the cemetery.

"Me neither," she said. She continued to stare into the woods, so I followed the line of her gaze and was able to make out the glint of metal through the branches.

"Is that a house?" I said, shielding the bright sun from my eyes with a cupped hand. As I stared, I could see a part in the trees that suggested a long driveway.

"I think so," she said noncommittedly. Not much got to Sandy. She just trudged through things that would cause me to pause and reconsider. Even though she was often cautious and would dig her heels in if she felt something wasn't in her best interest, she was also the bravest person I knew.

"I can't imagine living so close to a cemetery," I said, feeling an edge of apprehension come over me.

"Oh, I don't know. I've always found cemeteries to be somewhat serene," she said. "During the Victorian era, people would often use them for family get-togethers. They'd have picnics there."

The thought was astounding. I couldn't imagine picnicking at the feet of the dead. I felt my stomach curdle just thinking about it. Somehow dead bodies and fried chicken just didn't go together.

I took one more glance at the glint of metal through the trees before we started off into the cemetery.

Many of the stones were fairly new, but there were several at the back edge of the cemetery that dated back to the 1800's. I found myself drawn to a unique stone with two overgrown bushes flanking it.

When the bushes were planted, the placement must have made sense, but they now nearly buried the stone in greenery. It gave the grave an abandoned, creepy feeling to it, something that made me shudder and turn away.

I thought Sandy was still beside me. I started to comment about the overgrown bushes, but caught sight of her walking across the cemetery towards the far other corner.

(Left) The grave with the overgrown bushes

As I started off towards her, my ears began picking up a buzzing sound. I stopped mid-step and looked around, as though I expected to see something materialize in thin air.

There was a ghost nearby.

I turned to look at the grave that was nestled in the bushes. Was the noise coming from there? Had my curiosity woken the dead?

The sensation it gave me was like grasping onto barbed wire. The energy wasn't gentle and inquisitive. It felt almost menacing, like something that would take pleasure in ripping me apart, limb by limb. I hastened my steps and caught up with Sandy.

The sound triggered a memory. As I approached the grave that Sandy was studying, I was surprised I hadn't thought of it sooner.

"You know, sometimes when I drive past here, I hear that buzzing tone," I told her.

She turned and studied me. "The ghost sound?"

"Yeah and I'm hearing it now too. I think it's coming from that grave in the corner that's surrounded by bushes."

"Let's check it out and see if they will talk to us," she said, taking off in that direction.

A part of me was happy that I had moved away from the grave. The last thing I wanted to do was to return to it, but I pushed back against my apprehension. This was why we were here, right? If I started running away every time I heard a ghost, I'd never make contact with the dead.

I swallowed my fear and trudged on.

By the time I made it to the stone, Sandy already had her digital recorder out. I pulled mine out of my pocket and began fumbling with the switches, trying to remember how to turn it on.

Sandy waited until I found the switch and began recording. She spoke directly into her recorder, providing the name of the cemetery, the date and time, as well as the fact that I was with her so she would know these details later when she listened back to the audio she recorded.

"I'm Sandy and this is my friend Joni. We come in peace. We just want to know if there is anyone here who would like to speak with us," she said, leaving a gap of space after her sentence before she continued.

I knew from past experience why she did this. The dead often have a difficult time communicating. Sometimes it takes them fifteen to thirty seconds to respond to our questions. If we shoot rapid-fire questions at them, we might accidentally talk over a response.

"Is there someone here with us?" she asked.

The ringing tone in my ears grew louder.

I began to see a picture of an old man in my mind. He was grey in color, almost like a living corpse, with long arms and a sneering smile. His sparse white hair was plastered to his head and his clothing was nothing more than rags.

I wanted to run, but I held my ground, not wanting to show fear. I knew from my research that fear often feeds the dead. They used the heightened emotional energy as fuel to grow stronger and scarier.

"Are you the man from that grave?" I said, looking at the decrepit gravestone. The man had died more than fifty years ago at an age that was appropriate for the image in my mind's eye.

Sandy asked a few more questions before we moved along to another section of the cemetery. The entire time I followed along behind her, I couldn't get that image out of my mind. After a while, I couldn't take it any longer. The sound was getting stronger as though he was tagging along behind us.

I told her about the image in my mind.

"Then we should probably leave," she said. "We don't want him to get too curious about us."

When we got to the car, Sandy pulled a sage stick out of her equipment back and began digging through her pockets to find a lighter.

"Let's do a quick smudging to make sure nothing follows us as a precaution," she suggested. I heartedly agreed, knowing that the smell of burning sage often changed the vibration of the air, causing negative energy to dissipate. If something nasty was hanging around us, it would act as a deterrent.

She finally got the sage stick lit and instructed me to stand in front of her with my arms stretched out to the sides. She then went all around me, insuring that the smoke had touched all parts of my body, including the souls of my feet, which she had me raise one at a time.

After she finished, I did the same to her. We quickly stubbed out the stick and then got into the car, not wanting to give anything a chance to break through the temporary boundary.

As we drove away, I caught myself staring into the woods at the glimmer of light that came through the trees and thought I saw something move. I couldn't be sure, but I would wonder about it in the days to come.

As it turns out, he would be one of the first ghosts to follow me home.

CHAPTER 8

A GHOST IN MY HOUSE

I didn't notice the ghost for several days. I was so caught up with my busy work schedule, it took some time for the reality to sink in, but the truth was undeniable. Something had followed me home from the cemetery.

Several days after our cemetery excursion, I came home from visiting stores in Rhode Island, my mind filled with work issues. One store didn't have enough pet groomers and was using a cashier to bathe all the groomer's dogs, which was a company violation. Another store wasn't offering dog training classes, something I was getting beat up by my supervisors about. It was as though I was expected to wave a magic wand around and make all the issues disappear. All I wanted to do at that point was to change into my sweat pants and t-shirt and plop down on the couch for several hours of thought-free TV and allow my mind to unwind.

My dog Ripley met me at the door with other ideas. She was a mix of so many breeds, it was difficult to determine her parentage, but she looked and acted much like a border collie. With her high energy level and adept motivating skills, she had me well trained. Part of our evening ritual involved a long walk after dinner and she wasn't letting me get out of it. I held her at bay until I could scarf down a quick bowl of cereal and then grabbed her leash.

Our normal walk took us down a two-lane blacktop road near my house. Traffic was fairly steady, so I kept her on a leash for the duration. She always stuck close to my side, only veering off track when something especially smelly caught her attention and she needed a minute or two to investigate it.

By the time we got home, I had worked up a good sweat and had purged away most of my work stress. I loved the therapeutic benefits of walking. It gave me time to process my thoughts. I didn't necessarily solve all my problems, but I usually found a way to deal with them by the end of the walk.

As I came through the door, ghosts were the last thing on my mind, but I heard the tone immediately. It was almost as though he was waiting at the threshold for me. I let Ripley off her leash and closed the door behind me, feeling a sense of discomfort wash over me like a cold bucket of water.

For once, I was thankful I didn't have my 14 year-old son that night. He stayed with me four days out of the week and spent the remainder of the week with his father. Given the circumstances, I was glad he wasn't there.

How would I explain these things to him?

He wasn't the kind of kid who was even remotely interested in the paranormal world. If he came into the room while I was watching a creepy show, he would pivot on his heels and walk back out again unless I changed the channel. I wasn't sure if it scared him or if he just wasn't interested, but I wasn't going to let it interfere with our time together.

My daughter probably would have handled it better, but she was seldom around. Since she chose to live with her father full-time after the divorce, I only saw her on random weekends.

I took a deep breath to steady myself. I needed to handle this now.

"If someone is here, you are not welcome. You need to leave immediately and go back to where you came from!" I said in a strong voice, knowing it sometimes worked for other people.

The tone didn't falter. If nothing else, it grew louder. I could almost feel him laughing at me. Unlike the other ghosts that were in my house, this one was strong. If I was able to ignore the others and pretend they weren't there, he wouldn't give me that option. I could all but see him.

As I walked down the long hallway to my bedroom, I could hear him right on my heels. I paused when I got to my bedroom, uncertain what to do. Normally, I would shower and then put on comfortable night clothes, but this didn't seem like a smart decision. Having an invisible intruder beside me in my own home, a place where I should feel safe, made me feel violated.

Could I really just undress and shower knowing that someone was watching me?

"Don't show any fear," I reminded myself, not wanting to give this monster any more ammunition to use against me.

I took a deep breath and tried to slough off the anxiety.

I turned on the shower, fully aware that the hitchhiker was still following me. If he had been a living person, I could have called the police to have him arrested, but they couldn't do anything about a ghost. I'd have to try something different.

I read somewhere that if you ignored them, they sometimes grew bored and went away. Even though he completely creeped me out, I decided to give it a shot. I undressed quickly and took the fastest shower known to man and then put on my night clothes.

I plopped down on the couch and turned on the television. I found that if I cranked the volume up to a high setting, I couldn't hear his tone. Despite the overwhelming sensation of being watched, I was able to get through the evening. Bedtime was another matter though.

After nearly twenty years of marriage with a partner who preferred to sleep in total darkness, I had grown out of my need for a nightlight. I kept the room as dark as the inside of a tomb, even going as far as hanging light-blocking curtains and blinds over the windows so I didn't wake with the first blush of dawn. Things were different now though.

As soon as I turned off the light, I could feel him closing in on me. He drifted beside my bed and hovered close to my body. I could see him in my mind's eye, grinning with rotten teeth, savoring the impact he was having on me.

I could sense his energy beside me as though he was made of skin and bones. He took a deep breath and let it out directly in my face, making my hair move with the current. The smell of rotting flesh filled my nose.

I couldn't prevent the terror that spiked through me.

"Oh God!'

I reached out and snapped on the nightstand lamp, fully expecting to see him standing there.

Nothing.

The room was empty.

I let my arm fall back to my side. Why was this happening to me? Hadn't I been through enough over the course of the past few years with the divorce and the move?

There was no way I could just close my eyes and fall asleep. That would be like sleeping beside a knife-wielding serial killer. What was he capable of? Could he kill me in my sleep?

I retreated to the living room where my two cats were stretched out on the sofa. They gave me slow, sleepy blinks as I turned on the lamp.

"Why are you guys hanging out here?" I asked them, as if expecting a response. I actually already knew the answer. If I was aware of the dead guy in my bedroom, they probably were too. They were just smarter than me and didn't even try going into the room.

I turned on the television and was a bit horrified to find it already tuned into a paranormal show. I gasped and hurriedly switched it to something a bit less frightening.

As I mindlessly watched an old sitcom, I thought about all the paranormal shows I had watched over the years. Being sensitive to the energy of the dead often left me yearning for more information. Unlike true psychic mediums, I didn't get the full picture. I only got bits and parts.

I read as many books as I could find and watched the shows as though hoping for a road map. Unfortunately, the information I was getting was only serving to make me more apprehensive. I began to wonder if I was making things worse for myself.

Was it possible that I was igniting some sort of internal beacon when I watched paranormal shows? I had to wonder. I often sensed them drift into the room while I was watching something spooky. There was so much I needed to know.

Somehow, I managed to fall asleep on the couch and woke up several hours later, feeling as though I had slept on bare concrete. Every joint in my body was stiff and sore.

"This is ridiculous."

I pulled myself off my couch and marched back to my bedroom. I wasn't going to let some invisible dead guy ruin my day tomorrow because I was too groggy and sore to function.

I climbed into bed and yanked the covers up to my neck, trying desperately to ignore the buzzing sound. Instead of turning the room into its normal dark cave, I left the nightstand lamp on and rolled over onto my side.

Sleep must have found me because the next thing I remember was a thump at my bedroom door. I opened my eyes in time to see a dark shadow person dart across my room and disappear into my closet.

With a shriek, I sprang out of bed and ran into the hallway. I slammed the bedroom door behind me, ready to race out of the house in my night clothes. My heart pounded in my chest as my mind filled with pure panic.

I paused in the hallway and looked back at my bedroom door, expecting to watch it open.

"Oh my God," I whispered to myself.

What would I do?

Who would I call?

I wanted to jump in my car and drive as far as I could, but where would I go? I didn't have any friends or family nearby and couldn't afford a hotel.

My mind raced as I stood there, not knowing what to do.

Was it a ghost, a real intruder or just a dream?

If I called the police and they didn't find anything, I'd be embarrassed. With my heartbeat thumping in my temples, I edged back to the bedroom door.

If someone was in my bedroom, they had nowhere to go. There wasn't another doorway and the only windows were blocked by furniture.

I pressed my ear to the door to listen.

It was quiet.

As I was pulling away, something scratched on the inside of the door. I nearly came unglued and let out another shriek, only to hear the scratching followed by my dog's woeful whine.

"Oh, Ripley…" I had forgotten that she was in the bedroom with me. If someone was in there, she would have been barking and growling. That left two other possibilities. It was either a dream or a ghost.

Ripley whined again, pulling me out of my indecisiveness. Either way, I couldn't leave her in there alone.

I dug deep and gathered every ounce of courage. I had to be brave. I yanked the door open and flipped on the overhead light.

The room was empty.

My body trembling, I looked in the closet and under the bed, finding nothing. I wasn't sure what to do, but one thing was certain. I wasn't sleeping in that room.

I spent the rest of the night on the couch, not even daring to close my eyes for a second. I watched one cheesy sitcom after another until it was time to get ready for work.

I left the house by 9am and visited some of my local Massachusetts stores, not having the energy to venture very far away. By the time I made it back home, my head was spinning with work related issues. As I put my key in the keyhole, I was greeted by the buzzing sound.

I should have been terrified, but anger took the lead instead.

This was the last thing I wanted to deal with after having a day from hell. It was intrusive and disruptive, almost like having a homeless person move in and take over my house.

I'd like to say that I am brave, and maybe I am to some extent, but this was a case where I was pushed to become braver than I felt.

Without even changing out of my work clothes, I stomped into my bedroom and dug through my dresser until I found a stick of sage. I wasn't sure if it was going to be any more effective than the smudging that Sandy and I did at the cemetery, but I wasn't putting up with this any longer.

I lit the sage and proceeded to walk around all the rooms in my house, filling it with light and love.

"I fill this space with light and love. I ask for my angels and spirit guides to remove any negative energy that lingers here. This is my house and I take it back!" I said in each of the rooms. By the time I finished, the house felt a bit better.

The ringing sound had faded to a point where I wasn't certain who was still there. The tone was similar to what I had been hearing before the new ghost made his arrival, so I took some measure of comfort in that.

That night, my cats joined me in the bedroom again, which made me feel immensely better. I did make one change to my nighttime routine though. Instead of sleeping in pitch darkness, I dug out an old nightlight from a box in the closet and plugged it into the wall.

If I was going to live with the possibility of having ghosts in my house, I wasn't going to do it in the dark.

CHAPTER 9

CAPTAIN SIBLEY'S GHOST

When Sandy suggested going to yet another cemetery, I should have been smart and declined, but I was intrigued by the cemetery she proposed.

I've always been a curious person. I can't handle an unsolved mystery. Avoiding something tantalizing just wasn't in my nature. They say that curiosity killed the cat and it would probably be my eventual demise as well, but I was helpless to resist.

Riverside Cemetery wasn't just a picturesque cemetery hidden down a rutted gravel road. It was also the location of the Naramore monument.

In 1901, Elizabeth Naramore murdered her six children for fear they were going to be taken away from her. Poverty stricken and living with an abusive husband, Elizabeth Naramore went to the town for help. When officials visited the residence, they determined that the children would need to be put into foster homes. Before they could do that, Elizabeth killed them, from oldest to youngest, and then attempted unsuccessfully to commit suicide.

While the Naramore deaths were tragic, the children wouldn't die in vain. After the dust settled, lawmakers created new laws to protect children in similar situations. In the 1990's a monument was erected in remembrance of the lost children.

The stone sat off to the side of the cemetery beneath a wicked looking old tree with branches that could easily transform into talons. Over the years, people have left toys on the monument. Most of them are moss-covered and faded, giving them a distinctively eerie appearance.

We spent a bit of time at the monument, but didn't feel any spirit energy lingering there.

"It's just a monument. I think the bodies are buried somewhere else," Sandy commented.

With that, we moved along to the actual cemetery.

I had researched the cemetery's history years prior to our first visit, which was most of the reason why I decided to chance going there. After my experience with the last cemetery, I knew I was pushing my luck, but I refused to miss out on an opportunity due to fear. In my world, fear is a demon unto itself. If you pamper it like a spoiled child, you allow it to grow stronger. I chose to devote my time and attention to courage instead.

I knew I needed to do something different though. Merely smudging ourselves at the last cemetery hadn't been effective. I decided to add God to the mix.

Before we entered into the cemetery, I said a prayer, asking God and my guardian angels to watch over me and keep me protected. I hoped it would be enough.

The cemetery was serene and quiet, dabbled with a mixture of old and new stones. Birds sang in the surrounding treetops and a soft breeze blew across the meadow-like space.

There were so many layers to the cemetery. Not only was it the location of the Naramore monument, it was also a reminder of the history of the area. It sat at the edge of a community once known as Coldbrook Springs.

Coldbrook Springs was a bustling town back in the 1800's with two hotels, a bowling alley, a blacksmith shop, post office, billiard hall, a box mill, school, and nearly 35 houses. It was removed in the 1930's as part of the Quabbin Reservoir project. Now, it is nothing but a memory.

In the 1930's, the state of Massachusetts bought all of the buildings and then demolished them. The reservoir they were building would provide Boston and all its suburbs with drinking water. Five other towns were also destroyed, many of them becoming flooded and submerged beneath the still waters.

Even though Coldbrook Springs wasn't in the immediate area, it was located directly on the Ware River, which was one of the primary water resources for the reservoir. The officials were afraid that run-off from the town's industry would contaminate the water that flowed into the reservoir, so the town was demolished. Residents were relocated to nearby towns of Oakham, Barre, and Hubbardston, and the town simply ceased to exist.

Besides a few foundations, the cemetery is virtually all that remains of the old town. We walked the grounds, taking in the mixture of old and new headstones. Even though the cemetery was virtually hidden down a maze of gravel roads, people were still using it to bury their dead. Several of the graves were even adorned with fresh flowers.

We stopped at a few graves and attempted to do EVP sessions to see if we could capture any responses, but weren't getting any results. I wasn't hearing any of the ghost tones, which I took as a sign that no one was present.

I really wanted to test my abilities. If I heard the ghost tone and we were able to record an EVP, it gave me far more validation. I desperately needed the confirmation. More than anything, I needed to know that I wasn't just imagining what I was experiencing.

As we walked back towards the entrance, I was drawn to a group of tombstones. As I got closer, I began hearing a faint buzzing sound.

The stones were old and faded, the words difficult to make out on the worn slate stone. The first stone listed the name of a Catherine Sibley, who lived from 1805 to 1874. Beside her grave was the grave of her husband, Captain Charles Sibley, who lived from 1808 to 1849. And sadly, beside his was the grave of their four children. This was what caused me to pause.

They were listed, one after another, telling a heartbreaking story. Three out of their four children died within days of one another.

We just stood there, taking it all in, trying to wrap our minds around the tragedy of losing four children. My heart went out to their parents.

I am always very respectful of the dead, and with this comes a sense of compassion. From my research, I knew that some souls didn't automatically go to Heaven like they're supposed to. When faced with a tragic death, some lose their way and become earthbound. We wanted to make sure this wasn't the case. We pulled out our digital recorders and conducted a short EVP session.

"Captain Sibley, are you still here?" Sandy asked.

The response was heart wrenching. "Yes, Heaven won't take me."

To listen to the EVP, type the following information into your computer's browser:
https://soundcloud.com/jonimayhan/captain-sibley-yes-take-me

The EVP is faint and must be listened to with headphones on high volume. For reasons I can't explain, the audio has faded over the years, perhaps from being transferred too many times, or possibly for other reasons. Maybe I was the only one meant to hear it.

After listening to it, I couldn't stop thinking about this poor family and the possibility that the father was still lingering around his grave over 160 years later.

I went back to Captain Sibley's grave the following week.

In the quiet of the cemetery, I sat beside his headstone and just talked to him. Even though my ears picked up the faint buzzing of a lost soul, I didn't know if he was listening or not, but I wanted to help him if I could. I told him about the natural process of what happens to us after death.

"When we die, we're supposed to cross over into the white light, moving to the place where we're supposed to go. Some people call it Heaven," I said. I looked around at the quiet bank of trees, wondering if he was there, or if I was simply talking to myself. I had to continue though.

I knew that some people were capable of helping souls cross over into the white light, but I wasn't sure of the process. I just trusted my instincts and began talking to him.

My voice sounded like a prayer as I began speaking. "Look for the white light. It's right above you. All your family is waiting for you. Call out to them to help you cross through." I took a deep breath and then added something I hoped would help. "God loves you and welcomes you with open arms. Go find the peace and serenity you deserve." And then I cried.

I went back several weeks later to see if Captain Sibley was still there. The cemetery was quiet and my ears didn't pick up any of the tones I usually associate with ghosts.

I turned on my digital voice recorder and asked again. "Captain Sibley, are you still here?" Later when I listened to the recording, all I heard was birds chirping in the background. I wouldn't be certain until years later when I returned to the cemetery with a psychic medium who confirmed his crossing, but I had a feeling that he had listened to my words. After enduring the agonizing loneliness of a cemetery for more than a century, he was finally at peace.

It was perhaps the first time that I felt like my abilities were more of a blessing than a curse. If I could help this one lost soul, then maybe eventually I could help others.

CHAPTER 10

THE PARANORMAL TEAM

Thanks in part to Sandy's paranormal meet-up group, I had the opportunity to experience many haunted venues. During this time, Sandy began to realize that she had metaphysical gifts as well.

When my ears began ringing, she often felt a strange sensation on her head. It was as if her scalp was crawling. We began researching it and learned that she was probably clairsentient.

People who are clairsentient often feel the presence of ghosts physically. It seems to be different for everyone. Some people feel it as cold chills, while others feel a tightening in their guts. I was thrilled that she was experiencing something too because we were able to use each other for validation.

If Sandy felt the head tingling at the same time I heard the ghost tone, we felt as though we were on the right path. We began using other paranormal equipment too for further validation.

If we felt as though a ghost was near, we would turn on an EMF detector to see if it confirmed our feelings.

Initially, it seemed strange to me that we would both be gifted. What were the odds of that? Were we drawn together by some sense of fate, knowing that we would eventually need each other? Or was I somehow contagious?

That possibility sounded ridiculous to me, but I wasn't discounting anything at that point. The rollercoaster I was riding was precarious and terrifying, full of loops and dips that I couldn't see coming until I was in the middle of them. If I wanted off, I couldn't see the exit. I was apparently bolted to my seat for the duration of the ride.

At some point during this time, I also began to realize that I was able to determine the location of the ghost. The sound I was hearing wasn't constant. It seemed to fade or grow stronger as I moved around the room. I began turning my head during investigations to help pinpoint the location of the ghost. This helped us know where to place our paranormal equipment in hopes of capturing evidence.

It wasn't enough for us though. Sometimes devices like EMF detectors can be set off by non-paranormal situations. We often found electrical panels and malfunctioning electric devices that caused the meter to fluctuate. Electronic devices such as cell phones and walkie-talkies could make other meters light up as well. What we needed was a mentor, but we weren't having much luck finding one.

While investigating the haunted Houghton Mansion, a place where Sandy once saw the apparition of a little girl in the basement, we met someone who would change the course of our spiritual paths.

***

The Houghton Mansion is a somber place with a sad story.

In the spring of 1914, A.C. Houghton took several friends and family members for a pleasure drive in their new Pierce-Arrow Touring Car. When the car hit a soft shoulder of the road, it tumbled down the steep embankment, rolling over three times, killing Houghton's daughter Mary and her childhood friend, Sybil Hutton. Feeling immense guilt over the accident, the driver of the car, John Widders, a longtime friend and servant of the Houghton's, put a gun to his head three days later and ended his life. Mr. Houghton died ten days later, possibly from undiscovered injuries incurred during the accident. Most of them never left the mansion.

(Above) The Houghton Mansion

In 1920, Houghton's surviving daughter sold the mansion to the Masons, who built a tremendous Temple behind the house. The mansion has been under the care of the Lafayette-Greylock Lodge ever since, adding another layer to the haunting.

Like most of Sandy's meet-up's, there was a mixture of people at the event. One of these people was a man I'll call Adam for the sake of preserving his privacy.

Adam was like a bull in a paranormal china shop. It was obvious that most of his training came from watching paranormal television shows, especially the ones that used provocation to elicit responses from the dead. He spent most of the night yelling at the unseen entities, demanding that they show themselves.

Sandy and I rolled our eyes a few times before she finally called him out on his behavior.

"Adam, please don't do that. You don't know who you're talking to," she reminded him. "You might think you're talking to a negative spirit, but you could actually be talking to a child."

She was right and I was thankful she finally said something. When one member of a group uses such aggressive tactics, it makes it dangerous for everyone else involved. What if it was an angry ghost and it decided to retaliate? We'd all be put in danger. Plus that, it just irritated me. He was aggressive and rude, not the kind of person I wanted to spend an evening with.

During the course of the evening, I overheard him talking to several other people in our group, telling them about this great paranormal group he was a member of. He was actively attempting to recruit new members and wanted to know if they were interested.

My first reaction to this was predictable. I got angry.

"Who in their right mind would join a group that condoned such behavior?" I told Sandy. As it turned out, several people did. Lured by the possibility of investigating on a regular basis, he ended up recruiting four people that night.

Several days later, Sandy called me to deliver some unexpected news.

"I'm thinking about joining that group," she told me.

I was speechless. "You're kidding me, right?"

"No, really. I looked into them and they are a legitimate paranormal group. I don't think Adam is a good example of what they have to offer." She went on to suggest that we might even be a good example for Adam to follow. "If he sees the way we investigate, maybe he will change his tune."

Sandy was the first to join. I held off, mostly due to my stubborn nature. I had dealt with too many people like him in my past, bullies who didn't care who they pushed to get what they wanted. I didn't cave in until Sandy told me about the leader of the group.

"She's a psychic medium and I think she might be able to help us," she told me.

Having a bonafide psychic medium to work with was like striking gold for us. We had been working with each other to develop our abilities, but there was still so much we didn't know.

Over time, we both learned to determine the gender of the ghost. For me, it was all about the pitch of the tone. A high pitch signified a female ghost, while a lower sounding tone meant it was male. Sandy felt the genders in different parts of her head. A female often caused the front part of her head to tingle, with males affecting the back of her head.

We were also beginning to develop another ability, as well. If we tuned into the triggers that we both got, we could pull more information. This often came in images.

I had already experienced this with the man at the rock wall and the first cemetery ghost. Once I listened to the tone, I immediately got a picture in my mind's eye of what I thought they looked like. My mind images were often single images, almost appearing like snapshots, while Sandy saw a moving picture which was more like a video recording.

Was it possible that our abilities were evolving?

This made me both elated and terrified at the same time. It was exhilarating to imagine having open communication with the dead. I imagined getting to ask an unlimited amount of questions and getting answers in return. In turn, I would learn more about my own mortality.

The flip side of this was the lack of control. If one ghost followed me home from a cemetery, would this just open the floodgates for more to follow?

I needed answers and an opportunity was being presented to me. I'd be a fool not to take advantage of it.

I agreed to join the group with Sandy and made plans to meet the psychic medium. For the sake of anonymity, and to avoid a potential lawsuit somewhere down the road, I'll call her Leesa.

She was one of those people who had a presence about her. I couldn't understand what it was, but I felt drawn to her. It was apparent she had that effect on everyone. Wherever she went, she seemed to be accompanied by an entourage, as though she was a high profile celebrity.

She claimed to have worked with the state police to help them solve several missing persons cases and had a long line of people willing to back up her claims. That was enough for me, at least in the beginning.

Our first investigation was held at an old motel in Maine. It belonged to a friend of hers who allowed us to investigate, providing we kept the location a secret. The last thing she wanted was for people to shy away from staying there because it was haunted.

(Above) Outside the motel

Teams were established as soon as we got there and I was dismayed to discover that I wouldn't be accompanying Leesa. Sandy and I were put together with two other newbies, which almost turned the investigation into another meet-up event.

This was more troublesome for Sandy than it was for me. She was growing weary of her role as a teacher and wanted to be a student instead, but we made the most of the event.

We walked into the rooms and conducted EVP sessions, hoping to capture voices of the dead on our digital recorders. The energy in some of the rooms felt heavier than others, so we focused our attention on those rooms.

Because we were both so new at mediumship, we decided to eliminate possible cross-contamination.

"Let's write down our impressions instead of blurting them out," Sandy suggested. "Then, we can compare notes afterward and see how accurate we are with one another."

It seemed like a great idea. During one of her events, a budding medium in the group had been quite vocal in her impressions, announcing every ghost she felt nearby. It made it difficult for the rest of us to get valid findings. If she told us there was a man in the corner wearing a stovepipe hat, that was all we could think about, whether she was accurate or not.

We tried this new method in a room where we felt the energy the heaviest. Both Sandy and I picked up on a sad woman with long dark hair. Sandy felt that she was an older woman who was in anguish over losing a child and I thought she was a younger woman who had committed suicide. One person also picked up on a female, but saw her with blond hair and thought she was angry. The fourth person in our group thought it was a lost child.

We weren't sure what to do with this information. While it was interesting that Sandy and I were close in our findings, the other two budding mediums had felt something altogether different.

"That wasn't very helpful," Sandy said as we left the room.

I wasn't certain if it was helpful or not, but it might be a starting place. An idea came to me.

"Let's go find Leesa and see what she thinks," I suggested.

Sandy thought that was a good idea, so we hunted down the group's psychic medium and brought her back to the room. We didn't tell her what we thought. We just asked her what she felt instead.

She walked around the small room, staring into the air. I watched her closely, as if hoping to glean some tidbit of information.

The tone in the room was definitely female. I knew this clearly. In some way, I think I was also evaluating our new psychic medium friend. If she said it was a male, I probably wouldn't have trusted another word she said. I'm not one of those people who buys everything at face value. You have to prove it to me first.

After a few minutes, she walked out of the room and sat down on one of the metal lawn chairs that was parked outside the door.

"There's a female there. I see her in her mid-thirties with long dark hair. I think she killed herself and is sad that she left a child behind," she said.

Sandy and I were stunned. As my eyes met Sandy's a thousand questions bounced between us. In some sense, I think this scared us more than we expected. Being a medium wasn't an easy path. It meant we would both probably have a lifetime of dead people to contend with. How could we possibly navigate through something like that?

The flip side of the coin was that we had just received the validation we were looking for. We were both right, but had picked up different aspects of the haunting. If we combined our efforts, we would be stronger, providing we survived.

I had read about mediums who were so bombarded with dead people, they eventually lost their minds. Some of them became recluses and cut themselves off from the world because it was too difficult to navigate. I certainly didn't want that happening to either of us. It wasn't something I was prepared to handle, so I decided to press on with the psychic medium instead.

"Sandy sees her as being in her fifties and I see her as being in her twenties. Why would we see her at different ages?" I asked.

"That just might be how she's presenting herself to you. Sandy is older, so she might be showing herself as older to Sandy so she'll accept her more readily," she said.

While I was absorbing this information, she said something that would shake me to the core of my being.

"I don't know if you realize this or not, Joni, but you have several ghosts attached to you. They've been following you around all night."

I don't know if this information surprised me or not, but it wasn't good. I was still collecting dead people.

Chapter 11

My First Mentor

I was overjoyed to finally have a psychic medium willing to work with me. I had so many questions they piled up inside of me like an unruly game of Tetris.

Finding gaps in Leesa's schedule was another matter.

She juggled a family and a career, which made her life busy to begin with. Fitting in investigations, as well as time to mentor both me and Sandy was difficult at best.

Soon after we joined her group, Adam went along the wayside. As it turns out, his behavior was difficult for everyone to handle. He began picking fights with other team members and was eventually ejected from the group.

Since he was the director for the Massachusetts portion of the group, Leesa asked me if I would take over for him.

I was astounded and more than a little frightened by the prospects. Even though I had a full year of experience under my belt, I wasn't where I thought I should be. Leading a paranormal group wasn't a small task.

Besides setting up frequent investigations and overseeing them, I also had to review all of the evidence they collected during each investigation before selecting the best pieces to present to the client. The one thing I did have on my side was management abilities.

Because of my training with the pet stores, I was organized and knew how to handle people. Sandy would have been the obvious choice, but her time spent managing the meet-up group left her leery of taking on even more work. She offered to help me with the group like I helped her with her meet-ups. I also recruited several new friends with decades of experience to help round out our team.

For nearly a solid year, I worked hard to insure that we had at least one investigation set up every weekend. We investigated state parks, inns, hotels and abandoned buildings, along with some of the famous haunted venues in our area. We shied away from doing very many private homes during this period. I wanted the team to become stronger and more experienced first, knowing the damage that could be inflicted by an ineffective investigation.

I saw other teams freely investigating private homes and it made me angry. Unless they were capable of making the issue better, they often left the homeowners in a worse predicament. They would pick and poke at the resident ghosts, making them volatile and angry. I always made sure Leesa was able to attend the few home cases we did take on.

When Leesa could swing it, she would join us for the public venues, as well. Those types of events were far easier to navigate. The ghosts at the location had already been identified, so we didn't need to worry as much about running into a negative presence that might follow one of us home. It also gave us a chance to hone our skills. Sandy and I were always excited when Leesa could attend. We took turns asking her to validate our impressions.

"What are you feeling, Leesa?" became a common question for us.

If the information we picked up matched what she saw, we felt as though we won the metaphysical jackpot. She also helped us develop other gifts.

When Sandy and I began seeing mind pictures, she explained to us that we were opening up our clairvoyant skills. By focusing on the initial trigger, we found that we could pull more information. We just had to trust our instincts.

That was the most difficult part for me. Having an active imagination often worked against me more than it worked for me.

When a ghost roamed into the room and I honed in on it, my mind went in a hundred directions.

The ghost might initially appear in my mind's eye as a female with blond hair, but then I would question my impression based on information I already knew. If someone told me that the facility was haunted by an apparition with dark hair, I would dismiss my initial impression.

"Your first impression is usually correct," she told us. "Just because someone else felt something different doesn't mean you're wrong. There could be two ghosts there and you're both picking up on different ghosts."

We began working in earnest to hone our skills and had a great chance to test our abilities at the Colonial Inn in Concord, Massachusetts.

(Above) The Concord Colonial Inn.
Photo credit: VisitingNewEngland.com

The inn was built in 1716 and was used as a storehouse for ammunition in 1775 during the Revolutionary War. It was located less than a mile from the North Bridge, where the "Shot Heard Around the World" started the war.

From 1835 until 1837 American author Henry David Thoreau resided there while attending college at Harvard. In the mid 1800's the inn was turned into a boarding house and was named

The Thoreau House, after Henry's aunts, who were referred to as "The Thoreau Girls."

The location had been investigated several times by other paranormal teams and was once featured on the SyFy Channel's paranormal television show *Ghost Hunters.*

We invited the members of Sandy's meet-up group, as well as the entire paranormal team from two states. Nearly two dozen people showed up, which made it difficult to organize.

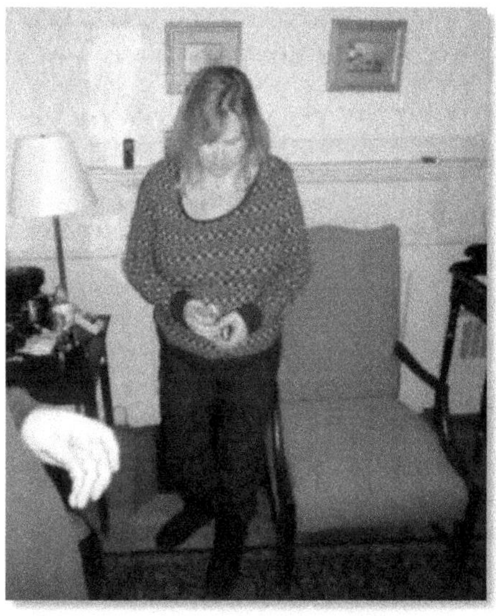

(Left) Joni during the investigation

During paranormal investigations, we typically tried to keep the amount of investigators limited to five or six. If the location would support more, we would add them based on need. This was a different type of event though. The Colonial Inn was more of a fun investigation at a notable location. We knew going into it that our evidence would be limited.

When too many people are involved, the evidence often becomes contaminated. Investigator's stomachs often rumbled or someone would shift on a squeaky floor. People walking around from room to room often forgot about the investigators in the rooms and spoke loudly during transit, which would be caught on our digital recorders. Multiply this by seven or eight people in the same room and the odds of getting an EVP that we could trust diminished tremendously.

Thankfully, the hotel was accommodating. Not only did they allow us to investigate the two rooms we had booked for the night, but they also allowed us to explore the kitchen, restaurant and even the attic area. This gave us a better chance to spread out.

My group consisted of five people and we claimed Room 24 as our first location.

(Above) Joni and Sandy doing a baseline sweep in Room 24 prior to the investigation

People who stayed in that room sometimes reported feeling cold spots and shadows at the foot of the bed. Several people also witnessed two separate apparitions in the room. One was a Revolutionary soldier, while the other was a woman. We hoped we would have the chance to experience at least one of them.

We settled into the rooms and turned on our equipment.

"We come in peace. We mean you no harm and no disrespect. We only wish to communicate with you," I said, as I usually do. I then introduce myself to the invisible residents and ask the other participants to follow suit.

I consider it a goodwill gesture. You wouldn't walk into someone's home and just start looking around and asking questions. You would introduce yourself and explain why you were there. Just because we couldn't see the people who lived there didn't give us the right to be rude.

I wasn't nervous at this point. I knew the hotel booked that particular room on a frequent basis and, as far as I knew, most of them got out alive afterwards. I was just worried about the overall experience.

Many times when we investigated, the location was unpredictable. Sometimes the activity would be astounding and we'd walk away elated by what we discovered. Other times, it was like talking to the walls. When we had quiet nights, it didn't mean there weren't any ghosts. It just meant that they didn't feel the need to talk to us.

Another factor that impacted our findings was the members we had on our team. I believe that ghosts often follow the strongest medium, knowing that will garner them the biggest bang for their buck. After all, why hang around a group of sensitives who may or may not be able to communicate with you when there's a psychic medium in the other room?

This was what happened to us. We had virtually no activity until Leesa decided to join us. Once she walked into the room, everything changed.

There were three budding mediums in our group, so I made sure that we all wrote down our impressions instead of blurting them out.

Not long after Leesa came in, something walked in behind her. I heard the buzzing tone that signified a male presence. It was lower in tone and had a static resonance to it. When I honed in on it, I saw a soldier, dressed in grey with sandy blond hair in my mind's eye. As I focused on him, I saw bandages around his mid-section and another bloody bandage on his head. He wandered to the middle of the room and just stood there for a moment. I quickly wrote this down in my notebook and looked up to see Sandy scribbling away, as well.

Having the opportunity to get a glimpse of the other side was both exhilarating and terrifying at the same time. It reminded me of the movie *13 Ghosts* where the investigator donned a pair of glasses and could actually see the invisible entities in front of him. My view of the spirit world wasn't nearly as profound, but it was still quite tantalizing. My only concern was whether it was real or not.

Was I expecting to see a Revolutionary War soldier and then conjured that image in my mind? Or was this truly a clairvoyant moment? I wanted to ask Leesa what she was feeling, but didn't want to ruin it for everyone else who was still attempting to pull information. Instead, I watched her closely.

Leesa was very good at keeping her impressions to herself, but sometimes the questions she asked gave her away.

"Were you in the war?" she asked.

I gasped. My impression was accurate. She was picking up on a solider too.

"Did something happen to your head?" she asked.

I was nearly jumping up and down in my chair at that point. I was seeing the same thing the psychic medium was seeing. I couldn't have been happier.

The session ended not long afterwards. We didn't record any EVPs, but that didn't matter. When the three of us compared our notes, we had all written down the same thing: soldier, sandy blond hair, head wound.

It was the validation that Sandy and I had been looking for.

CHAPTER 12

THE GHOST NEAR PURPLE HEAD BRIDGE

One of the most dangerous things you can do in the paranormal world is to become comfortable. Once you let your guard down, you put yourself directly in the high beams of trouble. I know this firsthand, because it's what happened to me.

Even though I had encountered a few negative ghosts, the majority of the souls I came across in recent months had been far more passive. In some ways, I think I believed that the worst was behind me. The truth of the matter was: I hadn't even scratched the surface yet.

The next negative encounter came during a trip back to Indiana to visit my family.

My entire family, outside of my children, resided in the mid-western state, scattered mostly in the southern tip. When I returned for a visit, there was almost always a ghost hunt set up and waiting for me.

Initially my family and friends were taken back by my ghost hunting, but after hearing about my adventures and sampling some of my tantalizing EVPs, they wanted to experience it for themselves. Because of this, I've gotten to investigate at several locations I would have never dreamed of pursuing on my own. The Purple Head Bridge is a good example.

The Purple Head Bridge is a narrow one lane bridge that connects Indiana to Illinois, spanning the Wabash River near Vincennes, Indiana, with barely a hope and a prayer. Driving across it is decisively precarious. While it's structurally sound, it's also only one lane wide. Drivers alert one another by flashing their headlights from the other side and then take turns going over it.

It's also incredibly haunted.

(Above) A photo of the bridge dating back to the early 1940's

Ghost stories abound, but pinning the legend down to just one story is difficult. It depends on who you ask. Some say that a man tried to commit suicide there, but something went horribly wrong. When he jumped from the bridge with a noose around his neck, he inadvertently decapitated himself. The sight of his floating "purple head" can be seen bobbing around the bridge. Others say Ku Klux Klan activity from the 1960's causes the disturbances. Some blame it on fierce Native American battles as they defended their land. I'm not certain what the cause is, but the area was definitely creepy.

Our group was fairly small, consisting of my younger sister, Leah, my old high-school friend, John, and his wife, Melinda. Leah had been ghost hunting with me before, but it was John and Melinda's first time. While Melinda was a firm believer in the paranormal, John was a true skeptic. He had to see it to believe it, which was something I could appreciate.

It was a muggy summer evening. The humidity was so thick, you could nearly part it with your breath, making the cool breeze from the Wabash River a welcome relief. We had made several wrong turns to find the bridge, but getting there was worth the effort. We stopped at the end and took it all in.

By all accounts, it looked like an old train bridge, but my sister assured me that it saw plenty of traffic since it was the only bridge in the area linking the two states.

In order to experience the ghost, she said we were supposed to drive out to the middle of the bridge and turn off the headlights. If we were lucky, we'd see the purple head floating somewhere near the bridge.

As it turned out, it was nearly impossible and actually quite dangerous to accomplish that feat. As soon as we drove out onto the bridge, a car appeared at the other end, waiting its turn to cross. Sitting in the middle with no headlights would be a very good way to get rear-ended by an unsuspecting vehicle. So, we moved onto Plan B.

We decided to park on the other side and hike down to the river's edge. Surely, if the head floated near the bridge, we would see it from our vantage point below. The only problem was plethora of people sitting around a bonfire at the edge of the bridge. Apparently the bridge was a local hang-out for teenagers in the area. So, we moved onto Plan C.

My sister knew of a location just ahead where a single-grave cemetery was located. She didn't know if it was haunted or not, but it was worth a shot.

We continued down the narrow road. The trees grew in a canopy across the black-top, providing a dark tunnel for us to navigate through. As we drove, the moon winked through the trees, setting the mood.

We found the area and pulled off the side of the road to park. We couldn't have picked a spookier location. It was something we all felt.

Something lingered in the air with the promise of enormity. It was the same feeling I got after watching a scary movie or when I came home late at night to an empty house.

We pulled out our flashlights and shined them around the dark parking area until we found the sign. I was curious why a memorial would be set up for one grave and the sign was helpful in filling in the details.

The memorial park was set up for a man named James Johnston, a Lieutenant Colonel in the Pennsylvania Militia, who served in the Revolutionary War. He apparently survived the battle and lived out his final years in the Indiana/Illinois area. A sign directed us towards a long dark pathway, which would lead us to the memorial park.

The dirt path wound deep into the forest, providing a chilling backdrop to what we would soon experience. We walked single-file down the trail, absorbing the enormity of the surroundings. My breath caught in my throat several times as twigs snapped in the darkness.

Somewhere in the back of my mind, warning lights began flashing. This would be the perfect place for a murder. Someone could leap from the bushes and we would be helpless for the encounter. The only people within yelling distance were the teenagers near the bridge, but they were more than a quarter of a mile away. By the time they got to us, our fate would already be sealed.

The light from our flashlights bobbed out ahead of us, illuminating swatches of the deep underbrush and the slip of trail that parted between it. A cadence of crickets and cicadas chirped from the depths of the darkness. An occasional car whished past on the main road, just to our right, making us giggle nervously with thoughts of people calling in reports of strange lights in the forest near the haunted bridge. Our smiles soon faded as we reached the end of the path.

The area was no larger than a standard-sized living room. It consisted of a park bench and a single grave, surrounded on all sides by the deep, dark woods. The first thing I noticed was how quiet it was. The trees barely stirred in the breeze and even the crickets quieted down as we arrived. It was as though the forest was holding its breath, waiting to witness what would happen next.

I sat down on the bench, while the others stood nearby.

"I'm going to do an EVP session, so I need everyone to stand very still," I said. "I'll ask a few questions and then wait for a response. Then I'll turn it over to the next person," I told them. Through the meet-up investigations, I learned that the best way to do an efficient EVP session was to establish guidelines in advance. The first person would ask a question, before the person on their left had a turn. By taking turns, we never talked over one another, and it gave everyone a chance to participate.

I was also careful to notate odd noises during the audio session. If someone coughed or their stomach growled, I would say "cough" or "stomach" to mark it. Otherwise, when I listened back, I might mistake the sound for a ghost. I turned on my recorder and started the session.

Before I could begin to speak, a cold chill washed over me and then my ears began ringing with an intensity I had never felt before. The tone was male and the emotion behind it was seething with anger.

I started to get up when I heard a man's voice. It almost sounded like it popped through the air right in front of me, despite the fact that no one was there.

"I hear voices. Does anyone else hear that?" I asked.

I wouldn't know it until later, but during this moment, I recorded a very chilling EVP. A ghostly voice said, "I hear *annoyed*."

To listen to the EVP, type the following information into your computer's browser:

https://soundcloud.com/jonimayhan/vincennes-revolutionary-1

We all sat quietly for a minute, but couldn't hear anything. After a while, I pulled out my flashlight.

On several prior investigations with Sandy's group, she used a flashlight to communicate with the dead. She would turn a flashlight to the setting in-between on and off and then ask the ghosts to turn the flashlight on to answer questions.

While I'm not a huge fan of using a flashlight as an investigating tool due to its propensity for error, I will admit that it has its advantages. It gives everyone in the group something to focus on during the session, keeping them both entertained and quiet as they watched the light.

"If there is anyone here with us, can you turn on the light?" I asked.

Almost immediately, I felt something whoosh in from the forest behind me. It felt like a small comet of cold air, blowing into me with a force that sent my hair flying in front of my face. I jumped up from the bench, startled. As everyone goggled at me, I laughed, embarrassed to be so easily alarmed. Some fearless ghost hunter I was.

"Was that a bug?" my friend Melinda asked.

"No, I just heard something behind me," I said, ashamed at my jumpiness. What I didn't realize, was that I had a very good reason to jump from my seat. The whoosh I felt wasn't a cold breeze, it was a ghost. And he had a message for us that I heard later that night when I reviewed my audio recordings.

"Go away!" he hissed, right before I jumped up from the bench.

Had I known about the angry entity, I would have led the group back down the path to our cars, but I didn't. I stood there for a moment and listened to the night. The tone seemed to be gone. Whatever was there appeared to have left.

After composing myself again, I sat back down and asked a few more questions, which went unanswered. I turned it over to the next person in the group, and sat quietly until everyone had a chance to take a turn. No more EVPs were recorded until we moved to the grave.

The energy felt different near the grave. It gave me a chance to catch my breath and calm down my rapidly beating heart.

As I stood there, my ears began ringing again. This tone was male, but had a gentler feel to it than the one near the bench. It felt inquisitive and friendly. The soul it belonged to would have had an openness about him, the kind of man who would stop to help someone in trouble. Returning the favor seemed like the right thing to do.

I knew that when people died, they were supposed to move into a white light that took them to Heaven. Sometimes people faltered in front of the light, fearful of where it would lead. If they did something in life they were ashamed of, they often worried that the light would bring them to Hell instead of Heaven. Others chose to remain earth-bound to look after family members or property and found themselves stranded. After my experience with Captain Sibley, I always spent a few moments counseling them. If they would cross over into the light, their pain and sorrow would come to an end.

(Left) the grave of James Johnston

As I allowed myself to tune into the tone, I saw a picture in my mind's eye of a ginger-haired man in his mid to late 50's. He was wearing a plaid shirt with suspenders.

Was it possible that I was talking to the Revolutionary War soldier?

I began telling him about the white light. I explained how the light was a doorway that led to a place where he would find peace and love.

"Your family is waiting for you inside of it with open arms. Just look up and see them, calling to you. If you cross through it, you'll find the solace and redemption you deserve."

As I finished, I promptly stepped backwards and nearly fell in a hole.

When I'm nervous, I can't always count on my emotions to follow the rules. Sometimes I laugh when I'm afraid, and this was one of these times. As I giggled, you can hear a very distinct response. The most interesting thing about it is the accent. It sounds like it comes from someone with a very strong Southern dialect.

"I'm gonna get the light," he says.

We spent a few more minutes there, paying our respects to the fallen soldier before heading back up the path to our cars. The full surprise of what we witnessed wouldn't present itself until I listened to the EVPs later.

I think there were two distinct entities in the woods that night. One wasn't happy we were there. He swooped in from the very woods to deliver two messages he hoped would chase us away. The other was from a very kindly voiced man, who we hope took our advice and moved into the light.

We didn't linger at the area for long. Tired from our experiences, we made our way back to the car and headed back to town. Since I was staying at my sister's house, John and Melinda dropped us off.

"I'm kind of tired, so I think I'm going to call it a night," I told my sister as I retreated to the guest room behind her detached garage.

The room was perfect for my yearly visits. It gave me a sense of privacy and room to relax. I quickly changed into my night clothes and then rooted through my equipment bag until I found my digital recorder.

I always tried to listen to my audio recordings shortly after the investigation ended. If I waited too long, I would forget essential details that happened. If someone stepped on a stick and I forgot to mark it on the audio, I might mistake it as an EVP later.

I plugged the recorder into my laptop, put on my headphones and then settled in to review the audio.

The sessions were short so it didn't take me long to find the ghost voices. I pulled my headphones off and stared off into space, stunned by what I heard.

While I was elated at the last EVP, I found the other two frightening. Why hadn't I listened to my gut reactions?

When we first got to the area, I heard the angry tone and felt uneasy. The last time I heard a tone with that much venom, the ghost had followed me home. I had to learn how to trust my instincts.

As I sat there, thinking about it, I began to hear the same tone manifest in the room. The sound was unnerving. Had he followed me?

I thought about our car-ride home, how we chatted mindlessly during the fifteen minute drive. Had there been an extra passenger in the backseat with me? Or had he just followed the trail of my energy back to my sister's house.

I thought about her three young children who were soundly sleeping inside the house. I didn't know what this ghost was capable of, but I certainly didn't want it anywhere near my nieces.

"You need to go back to where you came from!" I said in my angriest voice. "You are NOT welcome here!"

The sound buzzed even louder and was followed by a bang as a picture fell off the wall. I jolted around, feeling fear latch onto my heart with a vice-like grip.

Having had success with smudging before, I went to my bag and dug around until I found my stick of sage. With trembling fingers, I lit it with a match and then walked around the room, allowing the smoke to fill every inch of the space.

"I fill this space with love and light. I'm asking my guardian angels and spirit guides to help me banish all negative energy from this space," I repeated over and over again.

By the time I finished, the room felt lighter, but the tone remained. I wasn't sure what it meant, but it didn't leave me with a good feeling.

When I finally fell asleep, my dreams were filled with nightmares. I awoke the following morning feeling restless and edgy, which wasn't good considering I had a 17 hour drive ahead of me.

I made the trek back to Massachusetts with a ghost in the passenger seat. When I got home, my entire life would take a downward shift, something I'm fairly certain he had a hand in orchestrating.

CHAPTER 13

THE SOUL COLLECTOR

For many years, I teased myself with the notion that I would be fine being alone.

During my divorce, my husband told me, "I need someone who also needs me too, but you…you don't need anyone." I took those words to heart for five years after my divorce.

I had my writing and my pets. I worked on home projects and had a very demanding job to keep me occupied. I also had my ghost hunting and the new friends that came with it, but something was still missing from my life.

In 2010, I began the search for a man.

One of my friends convinced me to try online dating, so I set up a profile and responded to the messages that came through. After quite a few hits and misses, I met a man I thought I would spend the rest of my life with.

I've changed a lot of the names in this book and will do so with this person, as well. People sometimes don't like having their stories told and it gives me the opportunity to tell it like it happened without omitting some of the details.

Jacob seemed like a good match for me. He had a good sense of humor, a steady job, a neatly kept apartment and a strong connection to family. We settled into the relationship slowly, allowing ourselves to get to know each other on a deeper level. It didn't take long before we were fully intertwined in each other's lives.

After two years together, I was getting antsy. My ex-husband had remarried two years earlier and I wanted some sense of stability of my own. I didn't necessarily want marriage yet, but it seemed silly for both of us to have separate residences considering we usually divided our time between houses.

I began to have daydreams about sharing a house together. I could see us living out a happily-ever-after scenario. I would work from home all day and he would come home after a long day at the office to find a savory meal on the table. We would sip wine in the evenings as we watched TV, spending the weekends exploring New England together.

When I first brought up the idea, he seemed genuinely excited about the prospects and began earnestly searching for houses. We looked at a few, but he always seemed to find something wrong with them. We decided to continue looking and just left it at that.

Even though he had gone back to Indiana with me the previous trip, he had been unable to make the last trip due to his work schedule. When I returned from my trip, I was excited about picking up where we left off, but something was off.

He was initially happy to see me, but his attention seemed to wane day by day. Two weeks later, it was all over with and he was swiftly removed from my life.

He had never been a big fan of my ghost hunting. He didn't understand my mediumistic abilities and remained a true skeptic throughout my spiritual evolution. Truthfully, I think the entire concept scared him and challenged his church-based beliefs. Cutting me out of his life allowed him to continue his life without having to confront my realities.

"Give up the ghost hunting or I'm leaving," he basically told me.

I bristled at his words. How could anyone tell someone what they *could* or *couldn't* do? Part of being in a relationship involved compromise. There were things that he did that I wasn't crazy about, but I learned to live with them. Furthermore, this wasn't something I could give up.

Being a medium meant that I would be involved in the paranormal world for the rest of my life. Once I opened myself up to the energy, there was no going back. For better or for worse, this was my life.

I took the news hard. It made me feel like a failure. Maybe my ex-husband was right. Maybe I didn't need anybody, but that didn't mean I wanted to be alone either.

I sunk into a deep dark depression, seldom leaving the house unless I was forced to. I had since taken a promotion at work that allowed me to work from home, managing several training programs and I made it a point to stick close to my home base.

Sandy and several of my other ghost hunting friends grew worried about me, trying to lure me out of my house frequently, but I always resisted. In some ways, I had given up on life. I thought the best parts were in my past and all I was doing was basically waiting to die.

By November, my couch had a permanent indent on it from my steady nights of watching TV. If I had ghosts around me, I wasn't aware of them. The dark one that followed me home from the Indiana cemetery must have lurked in the shadows, enjoying the show, but I somehow blocked him out entirely.

In hindsight, I realize that he might have had something to do with Jacob's emotions. Ghosts can and will affect the living. They whisper in our ears and worm into our thoughts, changing one emotion into another without suspicion.

If he was trying to punish me for invading his space, he found the very best method. He made me vulnerable and despondent, putting me into a dark hole that I couldn't find my way out of.

By November, I was in a bad place. Hoping to get me out of the house, one of my friends asked me if I wanted to go ghost hunting. I looked around at the four walls I had locked myself away in and decided to go.

I'd like to say this was the worst mistake I've ever made, but I can't. Most things in our lives happen for a reason. The encounter

I had at the Rutland Prison Camps in November of 2011 would be a pivotal point in my life.

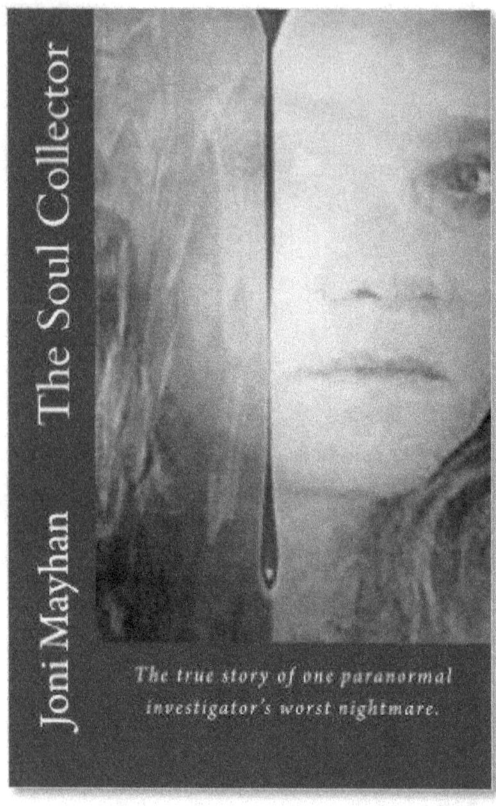

The Soul Collector
Joni Mayhan
The true story of one paranormal investigator's worst nightmare.

Excerpt from *The Soul Collector*

The Prison Camp is located in a remote area, far from the nearest human inhabitant. The road leading to it was overgrown and rutted, but the stars above us shone brighter and clearer than I'd ever witnessed before. It was our favorite place to investigate.

Built in the early nineteen hundreds, it was a working prison that housed prisoners serving moderate sentences for minor offenses. Photos from the time period show men working the fields and caring for the many animals.

(Above) 1934 photo of the prison camp taken from the root cellar

(Above) The root cellar present day

(Above) The root cellar in 1934

Besides the actual prison itself, there were many other buildings to explore. There was a dormitory, dairy barn, and sawmill, as well as a root cellar built into the side of a hill. While it was active, prisoners worked the one-hundred-fifty acre farm, producing enough milk, beef, and vegetables to sustain the prison without the need for additional funding.

Years later, during the outbreak of tuberculosis, they added a thirty-bed hospital down the road, bringing in sick patients from all over the state. Not all of these later prisoners were of the milder variety. Many were shipped in from local prisons, where they were serving time for much more serious crimes.

The Prison Camp was abandoned in 1934, because the property was located on the drainage area of a water supply that fed into a local reservoir being built. The property now stands in ruins.

After finding maps on the Internet earlier in the summer, my ghost hunting friends and I spent months exploring the overgrowth, while trying to find each building on the map. Most of the buildings were reduced down to stone foundations. We were able to locate most of them, intrigued at the way time had deteriorated the mammoth structures down to mere footprints.

We brought our friends to see it, conducting dozens of investigations over the course of the summer.

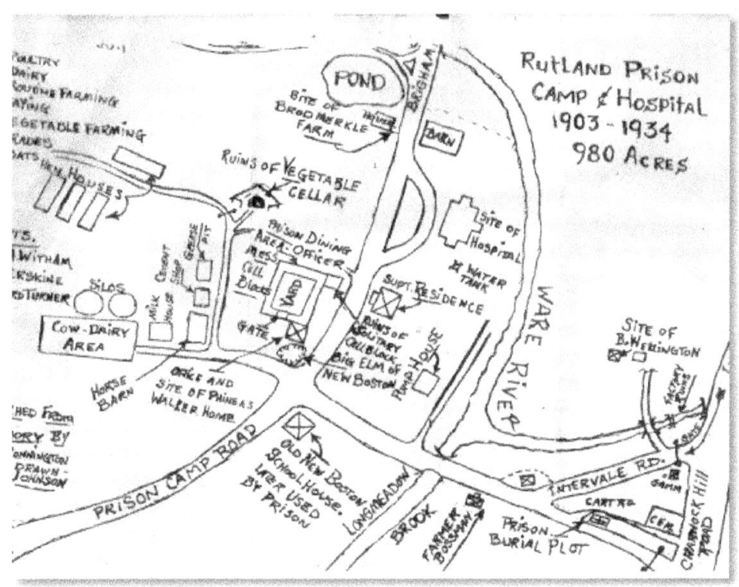

(Above) A hand drawn map of the prison camps

(Above) Photo of the old Tuberculosis Hospital in the 1930's

(Above) Joni standing inside the ruins of the old Tuberculosis Hospital modern da. Photo by Tina Aube

While the farmland and prison camp area seemed fairly benign, we had a different experience at the foundation of the old TB hospital. It had a somber feeling to it. You could stand there in the middle of it, and just feel the past vibrating under your feet. We quickly took out our recorders, and began our attempts to talk to the dead.

Over the period of a few months, we became well versed on the property's history. During the Revolutionary War, the property had also served as a prisoner of war camp. Both British and German prisoners of war were kept there, many of whom were forced to march a long distance just to get there.

I marveled at what they went through, asking them what it was like to finally get to the camp after such a horrific journey, where many of them died in transit.

"It must have been like Heaven, after everything you went through to get here," I said.

The response was appropriate. "Don't it," a ghostly presence answered.

Who were the people who lingered here? Were they once prisoners of war, or were they the men who had to work off a sentence for public intoxication?

We asked, but weren't sure of the answer. They simply said no.

The response only elicited more questions. So, who then? And, what were they feeling? Did they feel sad? Were they feeling as cold as we were?

One thing was certain: there was plenty of activity there. We spent a lot of time walking around the TB hospital ruins, dodging the thick undergrowth and prickly thorns, hoping for a paranormal experience. At one point, my EMF meter rose to 2.4. This was pretty astounding to us considering there were no electrical sources within five miles of the location. We watched it rise and then fall again, only to increase a few more times before returning to zero. A normal reading for the Prison Camp would have been zero, so this was interesting for us.

We found an old ceramic-coated bowl sitting on a post. One of the investigators pulled it off to look at it. Apparently, this wasn't something the resident ghosts appreciated.

"Hey, put it back," they told us.

This particular night, things just seemed different. It was a feeling all of us had. The entire mood of the camp had changed. It felt darker and more menacing. I kept looking over my shoulder, getting the distinct feeling someone was following us.

As we sat in the root cellar, doing an EVP session, we kept seeing shadows move across the walls.

"Did you see that?" my friend, Tina said, pointing towards a dark wall. The entire root cellar was like a cave. While the walls were made of cement, the entire structure had been built into the side of a hill. The only light we could see came from the opening, which was nearly obscured with vines and brush.

I looked to where she was pointing. The air seemed to be swirling and churning. If I stared hard enough, I could see the movement she was talking about. We weren't alone, and we all knew it.

As the night grew late, the air developed a definite chill to it. The ghosts seemed to grow a little edgier, as well.

One of them agreed with us about the temperature. She told us that it was cold in there.

We continued another EVP session at the TB hospital foundation, quickly finding a spirit who wanted to talk with us.

"What do you want us to do?" I asked.

"Fall," was the answer. It wasn't very reassuring.

"What are you doing here?" I asked again.

The answer came swiftly: "Following."

After about nine p.m., the activity died down, as it often did at that location. We always wondered about this. Why would they settle down every night at the same time? Was it the time when the prison turned the lights out for the night? Or, was there somewhere else they needed to be? We weren't sure. All we knew was that the place literally emptied out every evening and we would be lucky to get even a single hit on our equipment.

This was one of the last EVPs I captured there. The male voice was familiar, since he'd been speaking to me in several other audio captures. The whispery voice sounds like he's saying "Can't stop breathing," then something else I can't understand.

I left the Prison Camp that night with an uneasy feeling. My ears were ringing all the way home, which wasn't a very comforting sensation. It usually meant that someone was still with me.

I stopped the car in the middle of the dirt road.

"Whoever you are, you need to go back to where you came from. You are forbidden to follow me," I demanded.

I pulled out a bundle of sage I carried in my equipment bag, and lit it with trembling fingers. The sweet smell of sage rose into the air, the wisps of smoke looking like apparitions in the clear, dark night. By the time I got home, the ringing was softer, but I wasn't convinced I was truly alone.

This would be when it would all begin, when my life took a hellish turn.

***

I ended up with the worst attachment imaginable. Unlike the others, this one had demonic roots and had latched onto me to a point where I couldn't shake him off.

He was a soul collector, an entity that had amassed an extensive collection of human souls that he used to fuel his evil intents. He took their energy and used it to grow more powerful. It was the closest I've ever come to death. It made me seriously reconsider the prospects of delving into a darkness I didn't fully understand.

A friend who was training with the Catholic Church to assist in exorcisms did a layman's version of an exorcism on me, but it didn't work. I ended up turning to Leesa for help and she eventually did remove it, but not without leaving scars behind. By the grace of God, I survived and lived to tell my story.

Although the book eventually launched my prolific writing career, it rocked me to the core of my existence. Because of that experience, I will never be the same.

(EVPs available on Soundcloud.com/Jonimayhan)

CHAPTER 14

SURVIVING THE SOUL COLLECTOR

No one can ever fully understand the level of anxiety I felt the morning after the Soul Collector was mercifully yanked out of my life.

I awoke at six to the shrill shrieking of my alarm. I jolted up in bed, certain the sound came from the howling of banshees and not the electronic ring tone on my cell phone. Once my vision focused, my bedroom came into view. It was the same bedroom where I had suffered at the hands of a demon, the same room that had once been my sanctuary but was now my own personal hell.

My sweet brown tabby Gatorbug lifted his head from the end of the bed where he usually slept. He gave me a slow green blink, which seemed normal and natural. Just the fact that he was in my bedroom was a relief.

Even though my cats had always slept at the foot of my bed, having a demon in the room was more than they could bear. They silently began retreating to the living room where the energy was softer. Only the dog held her ground and remained by my side. I heard her tail thump the ground several times in acknowledgment of my awakening.

"Good girl, Ripley," I whispered, my voice sounding horse and faint, as though I'd spent the night screaming. She looked up at me with her brown loving eyes and watched me expectantly, hoping the next words to come out of my mouth might be, "wanna go outside?"

It was a slice of normal that I truly needed. If my pets were relaxed and content, then I knew the room was safe. I often watched them, using them like barometers to assess the safety of the room. If they were edgy and anxious, then I was too. Animals tend to see and feel more than we do. This was something I knew well.

I rose from bed, my gaze darting around the room as though I expected to see something amiss. Even though I tried not to, I found myself listening for the tone he made when he was in the room with me. The room was silent.

It was a Thursday and my son was at his father's house, giving me a respite from his morning routine. I wouldn't have to pry him out of his bed, feed him and then drive him to school. I'd have a few minutes to myself to process everything that had happened to me over the past several months.

As I walked into my home office, which was little more than a spare bedroom with a desk and futon in it, my ears began ringing again.

I went into a near panic. Normally, if I wanted to talk to Leesa, I messaged her and then waited for her to call. This time, I skipped the formalities and called her directly.

She answered on the fifth ring, her voice thick with sleep.

"I think he's still here!" I said without even bothering to say hello first. This was so unlike me. I normally hated calling anyone to begin with, never mind screaming in their ear at the crack of dawn.

"No, he's gone," she told me. "That's our ancestors. Several of us who did the banishing ritual sent our spirit guides to stay with you for the next few days."

I did manage to thank her before I hung up, but I would call her several more times over the course of the next few weeks until she finally clued me in.

"Honey, you're a ghost magnet. They're drawn to your light. You have an aura that is very bright, much brighter than most sensitives. They see that and want to be close to you," she said.

"I feel more like a bug lamp that's missing its zapper," I said sorely.

She laughed. "It's not a bad thing. You just have to learn how to control it. I'll send you some stuff later," she said.

The promised information never came, but that didn't mean I didn't wear Google out with my searches for anything relating to ghost magnets. What I found was both astonishing and depressing.

Ghosts tend to recognize people who are aware of their presence. We stand out to them in some way. When they see us, they are drawn to us for a variety of reasons. Some want help, while others want companionship. That left the ones with a darker intent.

Leesa was the one who explained this to me.

"Ghosts need energy to function and sometimes they pull it from the living. Most people's energy is the equivalent of drinking a power drink. Yours is like guzzling high octane rocket fuel."

This made no sense to me because it wasn't exactly something I could feel. I certainly didn't have a plethora of energy. I was as lazy as the next couch potato. If my energy was so potent, then why wasn't I zipping around like a loose balloon?

"It's your inner light. You shine very brightly and they see that," she said. "The dark ones see it too, which might be why you're attracting so many of them. They don't want you around for some reason," she said. She paused for a moment. "Maybe you have a gift that hasn't emerged yet. Maybe they know that and are just waiting for you to discover it."

"Awesome," I said with a heavy dose of sarcasm. I couldn't imagine a worse gift to have. It was one that would make my life miserable until I learned how to deal with it.

A month later, I convinced Leesa to come to my house to check it out. I was feeling more and more ghosts every day. Even when I didn't leave the house, a new ghost seemed to appear. I felt like I was living in a ghost hotel, something that was becoming increasingly terrifying.

(Left) New kitten George spent a lot of time in my bedroom, trying to catch the ghosts

She walked through my house and stopped in each room, staring into the air and shaking her head. By the time she finished, I was a basket case.

"Well, we got rid of all the ones you had here when we took care of the Soul Collector, but you have at least five new ones now."

I wasn't as shocked as I should have been. I'd been feeling them for a while.

"Where did they come from?" I asked.

She stared off into space again before speaking. "One is a boy who drowned in a body of water. Do you have a quarry nearby?" she asked.

I gasped. Directly behind my house was an old quarry. The water wasn't more than a few feet deep, but a drowning wouldn't be out of the question. After I told her this, she nodded.

"That makes sense. I see him wading in and getting stuck or something." She paused and studied the air again. "You also have an old man here. I think you picked him up while you were walking. And there's an old woman here too. I think she lived in the neighborhood. There's a younger woman with her, but I don't think they're connected. I think they just hang out together," she said.

She lit a sage stick and was getting ready to do a house cleansing when it dawned on me that she only told me about four of them.

"What about the other one? You said there were five here."

She blew out the match. "Yes. You have one that belongs to the house. I think he lived here. He's going to be tough to remove. You might have to just put up with him as long as he doesn't bother you," she said.

I shuddered with the thought. Living with unseen entities wasn't my idea of fun. If I couldn't get rid of him, that meant that he'd always be there watching me.

She continued with the cleansing and declared me "all set, except for the guy who belongs to the house," and then she left me there with him.

I wasn't sure what I was going to do, but I was beyond nervous.

***

I couldn't stop thinking about the Soul Collector, even days after Leesa cleansed my house. I thought about him every time I walked into a dark room. His memory followed me into the shadowed hallways of my dreams and came to me in quiet moments, like a whisper in the wind. I was the victim of an extreme haunting.

In many ways, I imagined it was similar to what people felt after they've survived an avalanche, a house fire or a near death experience. The symptoms of Post-Traumatic Stress were very similar. My heart raced and my self-defense mechanisms kicked in every time my ears began to ring. All I wanted to do was to take flight and bolt from the room, even though I knew it was something I couldn't run from.

I stopped attending paranormal investigations unless Leesa was there to keep me protected. Even then, I was nervous.

I became a dedicated student on paranormal protection. I read more books, watched more online videos and searched for a mentor who was more reliable than my current one.

I hoped to have learned more from her, but she lived too far away and led a hectic life. I'd try to make plans to drive to Maine to spend time with her, but our plans were often cancelled. During paranormal events, I had a hard time getting close to her to learn more about my own abilities. She was always busy.

She did help me with the Soul Collector. I have to give her full credit for that, but I also have to wonder why she filled my head full of horrific images and then turned me loose to deal with him until she was free to help me. In some ways, she probably made the haunting worse because she fed me fears that I in turn handed over to him.

Fear made him more powerful and only served to tighten his already rock-solid grip on me. By the time I was released from his hold, I was nothing more than a shell of the person I once was.

Gone was my sense of adventure and absolute courage. Not only did I avoid haunted locations, I couldn't even walk into a dark room without turning on a light ahead of me. At night, I slept with lights blazing. It took me a long time to get even a fraction of my nerve back.

With that said, I didn't necessarily regret any of the decisions I made because they led me to a place where I needed to be. I began to see the reason for my experience after releasing *The Soul Collector*. People began flocking to me, sharing similar experiences. It was when I learned that I wasn't alone.

Being a sensitive isn't an easy life, something I never considered when I began expanding my abilities. If they once hovered at the edge of my existence, they now quickly inserted themselves into my life like extended family members.

I didn't understand my vulnerabilities when I first began investigating. I just walked out into an invisible playing field, armed with a little bit of information, which was just enough to make me dangerous to myself.

I was intrigued by the way I could detect ghosts. The information I pulled from them also helped me ask meaningful questions during EVP sessions, as well. What I didn't count on was the fact that they might start following me home.

"What do you want from me?" I would shout at the walls, but never got an answer.

If they thought they could pass a message to me, they were sadly mistaken. I could feel them and get a sense of what they looked like, but I seemed to be missing a key component to spiritual communication. It was like trying to talk to someone on a telephone with a bad receiver. I wasn't getting anything, even if they shouted at the top of their lungs.

Another bad side effect of being a sensitive was not knowing the ghost's intentions. I couldn't consistently distinguish between positive and negative entities. I would hear a tone and often got an impression, but this wasn't always the case. Sometimes I just knew a ghost was in the room. I didn't always know if their intentions were good or bad. This made them unpredictable and sometimes dangerous, like toying with dynamite.

After having an extremely malevolent attachment, I became leery about allowing anything paranormal to get too close to me. The ghosts didn't seem to mind though. They just followed me anyway.

***

I began working with Sandy in earnest to learn the practice of using my own body's energy to construct a shield.

I knew about shielding from some of the books I read, but I had a difficult time imagining the bubble of white light I was supposed to surround myself with. Despite being a creative person, I truly struggled with the process of visualization.

In order to incorporate the process, I had to not only visualize the bubble, but I had to put all my faith behind its effectiveness. Because I've always been such a skeptic, this was especially difficult for me. If I can't see it, feel it, touch it, hear it, taste it, smell it or sense it with my extra sensory perceptions, I couldn't embrace it as being real.

Being someone with metaphysical gifts, this overt skepticism will probably shock some people. After all, I believe in ghosts, but can't perceive them with my normal five senses. Why couldn't I latch onto the idea of using my own body's energy to keep myself protected? An encounter with a fellow member of the paranormal team would come when I needed it most.

Kaden Mattinson *(shown left)* attended some of our events and investigations, lending his skills as a talented psychic medium whenever possible.

I watched him during investigations, marveling at the depth of information he was able to literally pull out of thin air. He was especially helpful in assisting me with energy work.

He invited Sandy and me over to his house for training.

One of the first things he did was teach us about our spirit guides. I knew from my research that we all have at least one spiritual assistant who follows us through our lives, helping and guiding us when we need it. Because I was still new to the concept of spirituality, I hadn't connected to mine yet.

Being a paranormal investigator and being a spiritualist are distinctively different. Most investigators I knew believed that people become ghosts when they refuse to cross over into the light. Their souls simply remain earthbound after they became disconnected from their physical bodies.

If you take that concept one step deeper and realize that we are the ghosts inside of us, then you begin to delve into spiritualism. Our bodies are nothing more than temporary homes, almost like hermit crabs that move into new shells once their old ones become too small.

Once we leave this physical body, we are supposed to move into the white light where we go to Heaven, or whatever you want to call it, and begin the transition towards assuming a new body and a new life.

Reincarnation isn't universally accepted. People with strong religious beliefs believe that Heaven is the final step and we stay there for all eternity. I believe we are reborn into new bodies.

Each new life presents us with new opportunities for our souls to evolve to a new level. The more lives we live, the better our souls become. In one life, we might choose to work on humility and will find ourselves presented with scenarios to help us deflate our egos. Another life might provide us with the chance to enhance our ability to love deeply. We make these choices along with our spiritual advisors before we are reborn and then set forth a plan of action to make it happen.

Our spirit guides are members of our spiritual advisor team. They are with us through all of our incarnations. They know every one of our lives, inside and out, and are there to help us with each lifetime.

Most people aren't consciously aware of their guides. They might hear the advice as "that little voice in the back of my head" and attribute it to intuition, but they don't often understand where it's coming from.

Once Kaden helped me make the connection with my primary spirit guide, I began receiving more help from the other side.

I'll never forget the first time I met my guide Kira during a guided meditation. I was being led along a stream to an opening in the woods where I was told my guide would be. As I parted through the trees, I saw beams of golden white sunshine pouring through the treetops. I followed the rays of light to the clearing where I saw the most beautiful soul I've ever set eyes on. In my first encounter, she looked much like Glenda the Good Witch in *The Wizard of Oz*, something my mind probably manufactured to ease me along in the process. After all, Glenda was the closest thing to a spirit guide I knew of.

Over the course of time, I began seeing her in a more contemporary body, but the blond hair and petite stature remained the same. The clothing and hairstyle is just different.

He also explained that our bodies are surrounded by a field of energy. If we learn how to tap into that, we can use it to shield ourselves from unwanted paranormal advances. By pulling in pure white ethereal light, we can incorporate it within our energy field and create an impenetrable bubble of protection.

Since Kaden could actually see our energy fields, he could help us learn whether or not we were expanding our shields. This was extremely helpful for someone with visualization issues.

Unfortunately, I wasn't a quick student. Effective shielding would be something that would take me years to master. If I could have latched onto it earlier, it might have prevented me from the next bad thing that happened to me.

CHAPTER 15

THE GHOST AT PARSONSFIELD SEMINARY

(Above) The back of the Schoolhouse Building and Doe Hall in the background

I had a bad feeling as I led my group into the haunted dormitory building.

The sensation felt like iron butterflies in the pit of my stomach trying to break free. I glanced back at the group of people behind me, seeing the mixture of expectation and apprehension on their faces. Should I turn back now before anything bad could happen?

"Is everything okay, Joni?" one of them asked.

I guarded my expression, showing them nothing more than what they needed to see. If I expressed any emotion, it would impact their experience, and the last thing I wanted to do was to make them fearful.

If something negative was here, I certainly didn't want to fuel it up with pure nitro as we walked fearfully through the door. This was my first solo investigation without the protection of my mentor since enduring the Soul Collector and I really needed it to be a quiet one.

Built in 1832, Parsonsfield Seminary was originally founded by the Freewill Baptists to serve as a high school for local students. It functioned for 117 years until it finally ran out of funding and was turned over to the Consolidated School Board to use for various functions. By 1986, the school board moved to another location, leaving the building empty for the first time in its 154 year history. It was then purchased by a non-profit group who wanted to preserve the location.

On paper, there was no reason why the seminary should be haunted.

If you perused through the newspapers and historical documents, you wouldn't find one anomaly to suggest foul play. There weren't any mysterious deaths, no claims of abuse and no reports of wrongdoings whatsoever. The building should have been a happy place filled with glorious memories of a bygone day, but it wasn't. It's one of the most haunted locations I've ever investigated.

It took years before the people who cared for the seminary acknowledged the haunting. They were probably aware of it, but found ways to turn a blind eye when they encountered anything strange. The sound of footsteps in a vacant area could be explained as squirrels on the roof. Doors that closed themselves could be attributed to air pressure inside the old building. Voices drifting on the wind could be someone's imagination. It wasn't until a contractor began doing electrical work inside the dormitory building that the full extent of the haunting was brought to light.

The man was atop a ladder, rewiring the ancient electrical system when he heard the distinct crinkle of his lunch bag rattling below him. When he came back down the ladder moments later, the bag was gone. He searched the building, but discovered he was very much alone. After experiencing several other equally curious happenings, he contacted psychic medium Barbara Williams.

(Above) Barbara Williams

Barbara is well known in the Maine area for her exceptional mediumship skills. She teaches at a local retreat, as well as conducting private readings and investigations. She checked out the buildings and confirmed his suspicions. The seminary buildings were haunted. Over the course of the next few years, she did more studies, bringing in select investigators to research the facilities. As a favor to us, she allowed Sandy's meet-up group to come in to investigate.

(Above) The Schoolhouse Building

I had avoided haunted locations for the past year, unless my mentor was at my side, but I couldn't turn down this opportunity. Not only did the location offer all the intrigue and history I yearned for, it gave me access to another possible mentor. Still though, I couldn't shake the trepidation.

The building in front of me was called Doe Hall, named after a former administrator from the seminary's early years. Long and white, it was three stories tall with twin doorways situated at either ends of the building. The dark windows twinkled in the moonlight, telling me nothing.

I thought about turning around, but couldn't bring myself to do it. The meet-up group had paid good money for the pleasure of experiencing a paranormal investigation. I was supposed to be their group leader. They trusted me to be fearless and brave, not someone who ran away at the first sign of trouble. I took a deep cleansing breath, said a prayer and then moved on.

"Ready or not, here we come," I whispered under my breath.

I pushed open the door and felt the dead air caress my face. It smelled stagnant and stale, like air trapped inside a coffin. It wasn't difficult to imagine the souls of the dead whisking through the room, creeping closer to check us out. I repressed a shudder and crossed the foyer.

The interior of the building was impressive. Restored to its original glory, it was like taking a step back in time. The foyer was broad and square, with four rooms and a staircase branching off it. Intricately carved woodwork graced the cornices and moldings, while photos of former administrators lined the walls. Looking into their eyes reminded me of a scary Jesus picture from my childhood. No matter where I moved in the room, those eyes followed me.

We reached the mahogany staircase that would lead us to the second and third floors.

"What was this building used for?" one of the men asked, startling me out of my thoughts.

Thankfully, I recovered quickly, realizing I'd been standing on the bottom stair for more than a moment. I tucked my hair behind my ear and turned with a smile.

"This was the dormitory building where the children stayed. The bottom floor is mostly administration and public areas, but the second and third floors house the dorm rooms," I said.

I climbed the stairs to the third floor, making sure the trail of people was still behind me. I listened to them chatter amicably, excited about the prospects. Most of the people in my group had never been on a ghost hunt before and were quite excited.

Sandy took me aside.

"Are you okay? You seem a bit preoccupied?" she asked.

I took a deep breath and let it out in a sigh. "Yeah. I'm fine. I just keep getting a bad feeling, almost like a premonition," I told her.

She studied me for a moment. "We can always investigate another building and leave this one until later," she suggested.

I noticed the others in the group watching us. "No. I'm fine. It's probably nothing."

The truth was: there was negative energy in the building. We felt it years before when we investigated here, but it always kept its distance. I was probably just overreacting.

Our group included a woman in her late twenties named Carleen, a former Marine named Daryl and a contractor from nearby Salem named Jeff Legere. Of the three of them, only Jeff had been on an investigation before. The others were complete newbies.

"What do you think about this, Daryl?" I asked, knowing he'd never been on an investigation before.

"I don't believe in this stuff. I'm just here because my girlfriend made me go," he told us.

Sandy and I exchanged grins. Skeptics were often the first ones to have experiences at a haunted location. It was almost like throwing down a gauntlet to them. I only hoped they were gentle with him. I finished climbing the stairs and then paused on the third floor landing to give myself a chance to catch my breath. The air upstairs was distinctly cooler. Normally in a situation like this, the air would be warmer since heat has a tendency to rise, but this wasn't the case at the seminary. An icy chill hung in the August air as though blown into the building by an army of air conditioning units. Fluctuations in temperature, especially those as dramatic as this, were often a sign of paranormal activity. It's almost as though they suck all the warm air right out of the room.

"Okay, this is the third floor boy's dormitory area. We've had quite a few experiences here," I told them, thinking fondly of the numerous EVPs we recorded in the past. The ghosts in this location were downright chatty, whispering into our digital recorders as though it required little effort.

We once captured an EVP at Parsonsfield Seminary during an investigation. On it, you can hear me tell them to back off and speak to us one at a time because we were getting a rush of voices. The response was, "We're not going to behave."

The hallway was long and narrow, lit only by the hazy beams of our flashlights. As I walked down it, I glanced into the dorm rooms. Thanks to the efforts of the non-profit that purchased the buildings, the rooms were being renovated and staged with furniture to make them look much like they did a hundred years ago. Most of the small rooms had beds and dressers in them. Several had been decorated with pictures and decorative items. Sometimes, I caught sight of a face, smiling at me from a framed wall photo. I led the group all the way down the hallway to the last room on the right, the room we nicknamed "The Wheelchair Room" due to an old wheelchair that sat in the corner.

We found seats in the room and got to work. I've always had good luck with my spirit box, so I set it up in the middle of the room. As soon as I turned it on, it began scanning through the radio stations, providing white noise that the ghosts could use to communicate. We started the session by introducing ourselves and were astounded when one of the ghosts immediately responded.

After Carleen introduced herself, the spirit box said, "Hi Carleen!"

"Oh wow, that's crazy!" Jeff said.

"Are you sure that wasn't just radio interference?" Daryl asked.

"You never know, Daryl. Let's see what else we get," I told him, trying to keep the sense of aggravation out of my voice. Having a skeptic in the group was often a downer. If he was anything like the other skeptics I'd experienced, I would spend half the night defending everything we discovered.

"Maybe the ghosts will school him for us," Sandy whispered in my ear, making me smile.

"We should be so lucky," I told her.

After twenty minutes in the Wheelchair Room, we moved down the hallway and checked out a few more rooms, not finding anything overly exciting. The spirit box had grown quiet, which didn't surprise me. Sometimes we tend to wear them out after a productive session.

"Let's try the girl's side of the dormitory," Sandy suggested.

I arched my eyebrows at her. "Are you sure?" I asked. The last time we were there, we felt a sense of negative energy lingering on the girl's side of the building. Barbara thought it might be a former schoolmaster.

"We'll be fine. If we run into any problems, we can always find Barbara," she said, which was reassuring. Barbara was the strongest psychic medium I knew. She could help us if we had any issues.

"Sounds like a plan," I said, trying to quiet my inner nerves.

Nothing bad was going to happen.

I chanted those words in my head as we walked back down the narrow hallway to a room I always thought of as the Gateway Room. It must have originally been used as a dormitory room, but a doorway had been cut into the other side of it, linking the boy's side to the girl's side.

When the seminary was in operation, the boys and girls were separated to prevent any hanky-panky among the students. However, when renovations were started, a small doorway was discovered in the Gateway Room's closet, allowing them secretive access to one another. It was something that usually made people chuckle. The secret doorway was only one of the mysteries surrounding the dormitory building. The other dealt with the negative energy.

Why would a seminary with such a tragedy-free history be so haunted?

After investigating there several times, I knew there was more to the buildings than what was being discussed. People of wealth and power have a great deal of affluence in their towns, especially back in the nineteenth century. It wouldn't be difficult to hide incidents from the public. After all, children back then didn't have any rights. If they talked about abuse, would anyone truly listen to them?

Suppose one of the schoolmasters had a dark hobby that required the participation of unwilling children? Where else would he work but at a facility that provided him with ample opportunities? We see it in modern days with child predators posing as scout leaders and daycare teachers. It made sense that it could have happened back then too.

Barbara Williams confirmed that something was amiss. Chris Bouchers, who was a member of her paranormal group, left a digital recorder in the attic for an hour while they visited the schoolhouse building. When they came back and listened to it, they were astounded. The recording included a thirty minute account of a child pleading with someone. "I'm so sorry. I've never done anything like that before. Please, please. I've never done anything like that before," it said over and over again between the continuous sobs.

It certainly supported the theory behind the haunting. The dead often linger when they've met tragic endings. It also lent a sense of credibility to the presence of the negative entity. If someone had abused the children, the abuser might fear the repercussions he would face on the other side of the white light. Considering the location, he might have been a person of faith. If that were the case, he would have worried that his passage into the afterlife might bring him to a place of fire and brimstone instead of angels and harps. Good people went to Heaven. Bad people went to Hell. It would present a scenario where the lost souls were trapped in a never-ending hell with their abuser, repeating the history over and over again.

"Here goes nothing," I whispered to myself.

As we crossed over into the girl's dormitory area, the vibe changed immediately. The air sizzled with energy, as though thousands of souls zipped around the room. The sensation of being watched was so strong, I swiveled around several times, fully expecting to find a wayward soul watching me from the doorway of an empty room. My ears rang with so many tones, they overlapped one another.

"It feels different over here," Jeff commented.

I couldn't agree more. Was this the reason for my earlier apprehension?

I wasn't sure, but I led them to the first room I came to.

"Let's go in here," I suggested, directing the beam of my flashlight around the long narrow room.

In the center of the room was an old barber chair. It was missing a portion of the seat and couldn't be used for seating, so we pushed it against the wall and found spots surrounding it. Sandy turned on her spirit box and we began asking questions.

At first the responses seemed to come from a child. We began structuring our questions around the child, hoping to gather more information. I especially wanted to know why he had remained earthbound, but he refused to answer. Sometimes, the best way to uncover the history of a haunted location was to ask the ghosts themselves, but they frequently wouldn't answer the questions we wanted answers to. They would tell us their favorite colors and the names of their pets, but kept the important details to themselves. It always made me wonder if there were rules on the other side. Were they not allowed to talk about some things?

(Above) The Barber Chair Room

"Why are we getting boys responding on the girl's side of the dormitory?" Carleen asked.

It was a good question. Logically, we should only be hearing from girls.

"Maybe they followed us over?" Sandy suggested.

"Or maybe they crawled through that secret passage in the Gateway Room," Jeff said, which made far more sense to me. We settled in, hoping for answers that would never come.

As suddenly as it began, the responses stopped. The air grew impossibly colder as a gush of energy rushed into the room, feeling like a tidal wave of negative emotion. Every hair on my arms stood at attention as the tone of a negative male rang in my ears.

"What was that? Somebody just came in here," Jeff said. It was apparent that Jeff also possessed some mediumship abilities because he was feeling the exact same sensation I felt. Sandy must have felt it too because she directed her next question towards the new energy.

"Who just joined us? Can you tell us your name?" she asked.

Immediately a voice come through and began spurting vile profanity.

We had been collectively leaning forward, listening intently for the response. As soon as we heard it, we simultaneously shifted backwards, stunned looks on our faces.

"Did that just say what I thought it said?" Daryl asked.

"Sounded like the f-word," Jeff said. Carleen had grown very quiet. I could barely make her out in the corner of the room. If anything else happened, I knew I needed to get the group out of the room. We were slated to sleep in the dorm rooms overnight. If we had a negative experience, we were going to be in a difficult situation considering we were hours away from the nearest hotel.

"I'm not sure what I just heard, but that was unexpected. That's not very nice. Is there somebody else with us? Is a man with us now?" Sandy asked. Red-headed and often fiery, she was the mother of our group, the one who often stepped forward to take care of everyone. "If you're going to talk like that, we aren't going to continue communicating with you," she said adamantly. As though challenged, the voice on the spirit box repeated the litany of profanity.

"Those aren't words they're allowed to use on the radio," Daryl commented, his voice trembling ever so slightly.

"I don't like the way this feels," Carleen added.

"Me neither," I said, standing up. Every cell in my body screamed at me to get out of that room. It was so strong, I could hear the words echoing through my head. If there had been doubt before, it was long gone. This was the reason for my earlier anxiety. If I didn't get them out, something bad was going to happen. "Let's get out of here."

While Sandy retrieved her spirit box from the floor, I turned on my flashlight and picked my way around the old barber chair to the front of the room. When my fingers touched the door, a sense of panic spiked through me.

There was no doorknob on the door.

"Oh my God," I whispered under my breath, trying to wedge my fingers in between the door and the frame, but it was shut tightly. The last person who came into the room must have pushed it closed, not realizing it was missing the doorknob.

As an experienced investigator, I knew to control my emotions, but there was no stopping the absolute horror that ran hot and wild through my body. The energy in the room continued to build, making the air pressure almost unbearable. It felt like we were in the heart of a tornado.

Dear God. What was happening?

Something made a tremendous crash at the far end of the room, which was followed by another wall pound in the mad darkness on my right. Invisible fingers trailed along the bare skin on my arm, nearly sending me skyward.

"There's no doorknob!" I finally managed to say.

The others pushed against me, like a mobbing crowd.

We needed to get out now!

As another crash boomed from behind us, Daryl yanked a ring of keys out of his pocket and shoved one into the locking mechanism, trying to get the clasp to release. After a few harried seconds of fumbling fingers, the lock finally disengaged and the door swung inward. We nearly trampled one another in our efforts to leave the space.

My first instinct was based on pure survival. I wanted out. I yearned to race down the stairs, taking them two at a time, but I held myself in check. We could not flee the building.

Running away would only empower the negative entity, giving him a blueprint to work with. If he knew he could scare us, he would do it to others too. I also didn't want the group to lose their nerve. If I allowed them to flee, the only thing they would remember was the fear.

I stopped them in the hallway.

"Let's just stand here for a moment before we do anything else. The last thing we want to do is run away." I saw their pale faces staring at me from the shadows. Their eyes were wide as they moved closer.

"Why don't we just head down the hallway to another room?" Sandy suggested.

I heaved a sigh of relief. "That sounds like a great idea. Let's try the room on the end where someone smelled lilacs earlier," I suggested. I saw several nods, so I led them down another narrow hallway.

This hallway was shorter than the others, with two doorways on each side. The first two rooms were used for storage, but the room on the end to the left was staged with a bed and dresser. Earlier in the evening as we were doing a walk-through of the building, another investigator had smelled lilacs. Knowing that the dead often send us scents as a sign of their presence, I took comfort in that. Anyone who would send us the smell of flowers couldn't be bad, right? I envisioned an old lady, possibly a school marm who took care of the children. I practically bolted down the hallway.

I paused in the doorway as I came to the room and shined my flashlight around it. I don't know what I was looking for. It wasn't as though the specter of an evil schoolmaster would show himself, but I wanted to make sure nonetheless. The room looked as benign as any of the other rooms.

It wasn't staged as nicely though. The sagging bed was pushed up against the wall, the stained blue and white striped mattress bare of any dressings. A small dresser was parked just inside the doorway, but was void of decorations. Several folding chairs were placed around the room, possibly placed there by another group of investigators, so we quickly took our seats.

As Sandy came in the room last, I gestured towards the spirit box in her hand.

"Why don't you turn that on and make sure he didn't follow us," I said.

"Good idea," she said.

I sat on the edge of the bed, keeping my eyes locked on the dark doorway. My senses were on heightened alert as I tried to calm down my thumping heart. If we heard the same male voice come across the spirit box, we would have no choice but to leave the building. We weren't a group of spiritual warriors. We were a mixture of newbies and budding mediums. This wouldn't be our battle to fight.

I've always been a firm believer in knowing your limitations, especially in the paranormal field. If you encounter something that wigs you out, you can stand and face it or you can find someone who is better prepared to deal with it. This was something Barbara should handle.

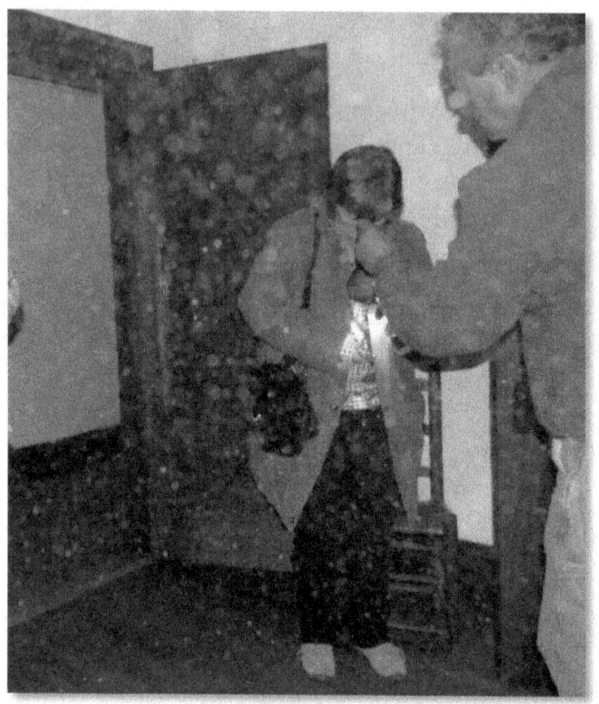

(Above) Sandy coming into the room to place her Spirit Box on the ground while Jeff Legere assisted with a flashlight

Sandy bent down to place the spirit box on the ground. As soon as she turned it on, the male voice blasted from the speakers, again saying the same foul words. Thankfully, I still had my digital recorder running because I captured an EVP at that moment that set my hair on end later when I listened to my audio.

The moment when Sandy bent over, the same male voice said, "Bend over."

I sprang to my feet.

"Let's get out of here," I said. Nobody protested as we hurried towards the door.

I led them down the stairs to the first floor, trying to keep my pace slow and steady so no one tripped and fell in their rush to vacate the building. By the time we made it to the front porch, we were running high on adrenaline.

"What was that?" Jeff asked.

"Nothing good," I said, taking a deep breath as Daryl pushed past me. The tough-as-nails former Marine and skeptic paused only to collect his girlfriend before he scrambled to his car, never to return. His first paranormal encounter would probably also be his last.

The rest of us found couches and cots on the second floor, spending a sleepless night staring at the shadows, waiting for the malevolent schoolmaster to find us. As dawn hovered over the horizon, it sent spears of golden light through the windows, chasing away the threatening shadows. We rose from our beds, shoved our belongings into our bags and left for home, feeling as though we survived something monumental.

The negative schoolmaster had won, for now.

EVPs available on Soundcloud.com/Jonimayhan

(Above) The Schoolhouse Building

Chapter 16

Taking Back My Power

The connection Sandy and I made with Jeff Legere seemed important, something we felt we should pay better attention to. I often listened to my gut reactions when I met new people and this one was telling me that he would be an essential part of our progress as mediums.

I once read a quote that said, "In life, you will realize there is a role for everyone you meet. Some will test you, some will use you, some will love you and some will teach you." That little voice in the back of my head was urging me to pay attention. This person would play some role in my journey.

I needed help in the worst way. The negative schoolmaster had managed to steal some of the courage I'd built up over the past year and it bothered me that I had given it to him so willingly. Sandy and I began making plans with Jeff to return to Parsonsfield Seminary, so we could do something about it.

We returned to the seminary several months later with a distinct agenda. We weren't necessarily going to bully the bully, but we were going to let him know that it wasn't okay to push people around like he had.

It was fully dark by the time we made our way into Doe Hall. As we passed through the lobby and headed towards the mahogany staircase, I felt the dead drift curiously in our direction.

It's possible they already knew what we were planning to do. Had they read our thoughts and were aware of our intentions? I wasn't certain, but there was no question that we had a full audience.

As we walked down the narrow hallway, I glanced into some of the rooms, catching the movement of shadows. If I tried to focus on them, they dissipated like ashes in the wind.

(Left: Sandy with Jeff Legere)

I could almost hear them whispering amongst themselves, wildly elated that someone was finally confronting the one they all feared. It was clear from our previous investigations that the schoolmaster ruled with an iron fist and most of them didn't agree with his methods.

We climbed the dark stairs to the second floor and then walked down the hallway to the third floor staircase, leading a parade of dead people behind us. I could hear their tones swooping in and out of one another's, like a hoard of bees circling a hive. Each tone was distinctive and unique. There were so many, I couldn't even begin to count them. It was as though the entire ghost population followed us to see what would transpire.

While the majority of the dormitory building was filled with ghosts, something we could feel as mediums, the closer we got to the schoolmaster's lair the more they faded away. It felt as though they were trying to distance themselves from him, as though they were just as fearful of him as we were. By the time we made it to the girl's side of the dormitory, we were completely alone. I could almost feel them lingering at the doorway, straining to see what we were doing.

We went directly to the Barber Chair room, the site of our last encounter. The room looked a little different than it had the last time we were there. The barber chair had been moved to the left of the doorway and an odd assortment of cast-off furniture had been pushed into the room, using it for storage.

It seemed odd to me that they wouldn't know the importance of this room. It was the core of the haunting, the throne where the self-crowned leader held camp, but was being used as a storage room instead.

We pulled chairs off of the piles and situated them near the end of the room by the window. I peered through the window and looked down at the front walkway below, taking in the circle of amber light that trailed down the stone stairs, leaving the rest of the world shadowed in darkness.

I closed my eyes for a moment and tried to visualize my own amber circle that surrounded me with protection. I imagined filling it with a light that was so bright, it would blind me if I tried to stare at it.

Jeff cleared his throat from across the room, bringing me back to the moment.

I turned on my EMF meter, which gave the room a bit more light. Jeff was settled into his chair, but Sandy was still moving about.

It always seemed to take Sandy a while to get situated. While I sat and waited, she dug through her bag, looking for the equipment she wanted to use and then messed with it for an eternity until she was finally satisfied. My impatience was growing alongside my anxiety.

"Are you ready?" I asked her in a voice that was a bit too sharp and condescending.

She could have responded in kind, but she took the high road like she usually did, replying in her normal, everyday voice, despite the situation.

"I'm ready."

I skipped my normal speech about coming in peace and meaning them no harm. Instead, I got right down to business. Patience has never been one of my virtues.

"We've come to talk with the schoolmaster," I said and then waited until his familiar tone came into the room.

"The last time we were in this room with you, you made it a point to chase us out, which wasn't very nice of you," Sandy said. "Can you tell us why you did what you did?"

The silence rang heavy around us. Besides the steady ringing in my ears, I couldn't hear another sound. It was as though the entire seminary was holding its breath, waiting to see what would happen next.

"We didn't appreciate it very much," Jeff added. "What you did was wrong. There's no reason to scare people like that."

I felt the schoolmaster's energy change. It wasn't something I could easily explain, but it felt as though he was actually considering our words. Some of his anger was sloughing off and was replaced by curiosity.

(Left) Looking down one of the long dark hallways

"If we worked together, we might be able to help you," I said. "I know that something happened to you during your life that made you the way you now are, but you can let that go and move on," I said, remembering the way my words had an impact on Captain Sibley. If we could work with the schoolmaster in the same way, we might be able to help him find some peace, as well.

If he had been curious and complacent for a moment, all that changed instantly. He nearly roared at us.

"He didn't like that," Sandy said.

"No, he didn't." Jeff agreed.

Without warning, the schoolmaster lunged at me. I could feel his energy break through the shield I had created as though it was nothing more than tissue paper. His cold fingers latched onto my throat as his energy spiked into me with a tremendous force.

My world quickly melted away. In its place were images of death and destruction, of bloody limbs and fiery pits. I couldn't latch onto one image before it was replaced with another equally gruesome one. I felt myself being pulled down, down, down.

"Help me! He's getting to me," I managed to say as my fingers clawed into the metal seat of my chair.

Sandy and Jeff jumped from their chairs and moved closer to me, until they were on either side of me.

"Surround her with your shield," Sandy said to Jeff.

I immediately felt the schoolmaster withdraw. The images faded from my mind's eye and I was able to open my eyes and see the disheveled room in front of me.

I took a deep breath and let it out with a sigh.

"That's better, but he's still here."

I could feel him lingering at the edge of our energy boundaries, waiting for another opportunity to attack me.

"We need to push him out," Jeff said. "Let's try linking our energy together."

It's difficult to explain what happened in that moment, but it was perhaps one of the most amazing experiences I've ever lived through.

Before then, I didn't know that our energy has color. But as I felt Jeff's energy connect with mine, I saw it in my mind's eye as a bolt of deep yellow light. As it merged with mine, I saw my energy as the shade of blue, beaming from my body to find Sandy. Once it connected with Sandy, a bright orange light shot from her body and connected to Jeff. The triangle of energy was complete.

Like a circuit of electricity, once the connection was made, it zipped through all of us like a live wire of current. My breath was instantly swept away as I felt the combined energies rush through me. All of my thoughts and feelings were erased in a second. The energy utterly consumed me.

"Now, push that energy outward," Jeff said and I felt the energy grow larger.

The moment was epic and indescribable. I could see the light in my mind's eye, circulating between the three of us like a rainbow of commanding light. It spun faster and faster, picking up speed and power until it radiated outwards, filling the room with intensity.

If we had kept it going and allowed it to grow even larger, it might have filled the building and then the town, and maybe even the entire world, but we couldn't hold it in place for longer than a minute.

"Okay, that's enough. He's gone," Sandy said as the energy fell down around us like a curtain. I felt Jeff's yellow light retreat at the same time Sandy's orange light faded away.

As I came back to myself, I felt as though I was awaking from a dream. My entire body tingled. Every cell and nerve ending in my body was on fire.

I stood up and stretched, then looked around the room.

The schoolmaster was gone.

I couldn't feel his energy or hear the sound he normally made.

"Oh my God! We did it!" I said.

The elation I felt in that moment was immense. Even though I couldn't fully comprehend what we did, I felt it like a mark on my soul.

If we could link energy with one another, it would make us all stronger.

Despite everything I had learned in the past few years, that moment in the Barber Chair Room was the most impactful experience I'd ever had.

I learned that forces beyond our comprehension can touch us in ways that we never imagined. It left me speechless and humbled, giving me the smallest of glimpses into the unknown world that surrounded me.

It also gave me hope.

(Above) The Schoolhouse building viewed through the attic window in Doe Hall

CHAPTER 17

THE SCENE OF THE CRIME

It was apparent to us that Jeff Legere had more abilities than he alluded to during our first investigation together. This became even clearer during the following year.

Besides being clairvoyant, he was also able to utilize his body's energy field more readily than either of us was able to do. He could tap into his own etheric layers and push the energy outwards, sending ghosts flying. It was an ability I both admired and envied.

We began meeting up frequently with him and his brother Mark, who was also a paranormal investigator. Mark had access to an old warehouse that was filled to the brim with ghosts. We spent frequent weekend evenings there, learning as much as we could about the location and the ghosts inside.

In the same way that we once shared energy with one another, we began sharing our impressions. Instead of writing them down this time, we bounced them off of each other.

"I feel a male," one of us would say, which would prompt the connection for me. I would then get a picture in my mind's eye.

"He has dark hair and is very tall," I would say, and then Sandy would chip in her impressions.

"And he is wearing a dark jacket and pants."

"I see a hat on his head...and a mustache," Jeff would say, allowing the layers to fall into place.

I wasn't fully convinced that we were just feeding each other information, but tried to remain open minded. If I was honest with myself, it didn't feel forced or connived. It felt as though we were all contributing individual pieces of the puzzle and were helping each other see the parts that were missing to us.

Jeff was also becoming even better at pushing ghosts away.

Once, while we stood on the sidewalk at a haunted establishment, I could both feel and hear a ghost lingering close to us. Fear latched its icy cold fingers around my heart, sweeping away what little courage I had gathered.

"You are not allowed to follow us!" I said.

Sandy made a hum of agreement. "It's a female. I think it was the woman from the last room," she said, which was something that resonated with me. A mind image instantly popped into my head of a young blond woman. The last thing I wanted to do was to add her to my collection. It had become a standing joke in our group that they never had to worry about getting a ghostly attachment as long as I was with them. If it was going to follow anyone, it would follow me.

"You need to go back inside," Sandy added, but Jeff shook his head.

"She's not going to listen to you. She already has her hooks set into Joni. Give me a second," he said, staring at the front of the building.

As he continued to stare, the most amazing thing happened. I began to hear the buzzing tone fade. It was almost as though someone had turned down the volume. After a moment, the sound was gone completely.

"She's back inside," Jeff said. "Let's take off before she has a chance to come back."

We heeded his advice and got into our cars, shouting our goodbyes over our shoulders. Since Sandy and I lived so close to one another, we often shared a ride. We weren't two miles down the road before I heard the same buzzing tone appear in the car with us.

"She's back," Sandy said before I could verbally acknowledge it.

"Dear Lord. How did she find me?" I said, not really expecting an answer. Our drive home was only fifteen minutes, but I didn't want to take any chances. I called Jeff on my cell phone and filled him in.

"Okay, give me a second," he said.

I pulled over to the side of the road and put on my hazard lights. I wasn't sure what he was going to do, but I wasn't going to be driving a vehicle while he was doing it.

"Let's help him by expanding our own shields," Sandy suggested.

I still wasn't very good at shielding, but I closed my eyes and tried to envision the white light surrounding me. Being a physical person, it helped me to hold my hands up as though I was feeling the inside of my bubble. Once I had the image of the shield locked in my head, I pushed my hands outwards and made my bubble larger.

Since linking energy with Sandy and Jeff, I learned that I could reach out and borrow some of their energy too when I needed it. I would construct my bubble then pull in Sandy's orange energy. It felt like rubber, so I coated my bubble with it before reaching out for Jeff's yellow energy. When I tried to fill my bubble with Jeff's energy, it wouldn't stay inside the bubble. It shot outwards like a starburst.

Sandy didn't need to hold her hands outwards. She just closed her eyes and concentrated. After a moment, the buzzing sound retreated, just like it did before on the sidewalk.

"Okay, she's gone now," I told Jeff.

"Good. Let me know if she comes back and I'll do my best to help you," he said. I thanked him and hung up.

I looked at Sandy and arched my eyebrows. "Well, that was easy."

"It was almost too easy," she said, echoing my thoughts.

I drove her home and let her out in her driveway without any further encounters from the paranormal world. As I watched her walk up her driveway, I felt a sense of elation.

Was it really that easy?

Did we really just push a ghost away on our own? Or did Jeff do it all by himself? It made me feel a bit like the water boy on the football team.

As the one year anniversary of my encounter with the Soul Collector approached, we began talking about returning to the Rutland Prison Camps. Since this was the location where the Soul Collector found me, I was understandingly apprehensive about returning. Even though I'd been reassured that the Soul Collector was long gone, I worried about picking up something else. What if there were more just like him there?

The paranormal group was anxious to investigate though, so I set up the investigation for a Saturday. Leesa promised to attend as well, which gave me another measure of comfort. If something was there, she could take care of it.

Sandy was vehemently against returning to the scene of the crime. She felt that the ground was tainted with negative energy and that no good could come from investigating there. As it turns out, her suspicions were right.

***

I watched the calendar with a nervous eye, worrying about what I might find when I got to the prison camps. A big part of me wanted to just put it all behind me and move in a more positive direction, but something kept niggling at me. I needed to take my power back.

I looked at that parcel of land like it was home to the devil himself. By fortifying it with such reverence, I was giving it even more power. I needed to go back and prove to myself that it was nothing more than earth and trees.

A few days before the event, my nerves got the better of me. I called my psychic medium friend Kaden Mattison.

"Will you come out to the prison camp with me and see if there's anything bad there still?" I asked. If Kaden looked it over and found something negative, I'd cancel the event.

Kaden paused and I could hear paper flipping in the background as he looked through his calendar.

"How about Tuesday? I can be at your house at five," he said. I had plans for that night, but knew this was far more important.

"Tuesday sounds perfect," I said and scratched it on my own calendar.

***

Kaden showed up Tuesday night with his girlfriend Allie in tow. She was also a sensitive and had a warm, bubbly personality.

As we drove the ten miles to the prison camps, Allie sat up front with me, while Kaden sat in the backseat.

"That's so funny," he said out of the blue.

I met his eyes in the rear view mirror. "What's funny?"

"Oh nothing really. I just saw your energy reach out and combine with Allie's energy. Do you feel anything?" he asked.

Sometimes some of the metaphysical stuff went a bit too far for me to readily latch onto, but I did feel differently. Just before Kaden said something, I felt a lightening in my mood. I had been tense for the majority of the drive, but suddenly felt almost giddy.

"Yeah, I did feel something," I said with a nervous laugh. "I felt kind of bubbly for a moment."

"That's because you were tapping into Allie's energy."

"You can see that?" I asked. I knew that Kaden could see other people's energy field, but it still seemed like a strange concept to me.

"Oh yeah. Your energy reached over and kind of merged with her energy for a minute. It was pretty cool," he said.

We drove the final few miles in silence as the scenery opened up to us.

The Rutland State Park was beautiful. Endless grassy fields and rolling hills melted off into the distance with a perfect blue sky above us.

(Above: the road leading into the prison camps

A rutted one lane path led through the area. I navigated it carefully, trying not to get stuck in any of the ruts. Finally, we came to the road that led to the prison camps. I pulled up near one of the old ruins and stopped my car.

The prison camps were quiet. Every time I used to come up there, I could always count on crossing paths with a few hikers or dog walkers, but the area was vacant.

We started with the old root cellar, which looked like a cave dug into the side of the hill. Inside, the walls floors and ceilings were fortified with cement, which had been covered with graffiti over the years.

"There's a woman here. I don't think she's connected to the camp, but she follows people around," Kaden said.

This resonated with me. We spent almost a full summer here last year, exploring the area and picked up on a woman several times and even got her voice on a few EVPs.

"Nobody else though," he said as we moved along to the solitary confinement cells.

The old cells looked like ghosts rising out of the tall weeds. The square building was once part of a larger structure, but was the only standing structure that still remained. Just like the root cellar, it was covered inside and out with graffiti.

As we walked along, Kaden began picking up on something else.

(Above: the inside of the root cellar)

"There's a man here. I think he was a warden or a guard here back when it was an active prison," he said and then shook his head. "I don't like him. I think he might have dabbled in devil worshipping. I see him doing rituals and sacrifices," he said.

"Sacrifices?" I nearly screamed, imagining people being impaled with ceremonial daggers.

"Not people. I think he sacrificed animals. He wasn't a good person though. I think he did things to the prisoners here. Not good things either," he said.

I didn't like the sound of that. "Should I cancel the investigation?"

"I think you'll be fine as long as Leesa is here. She can keep them from following anybody home," he said.

While his words were less than comforting, I felt somewhat better about the investigation. If there was something nasty lingering at the prison camps, maybe Leesa could take care of it and move it along. I hated thinking about all those people who walked through the area on a daily basis. If Leesa could move it along then the area would be cleansed.

As the day of the event approached, many of the people who pushed me to set up the investigation cancelled. Someone forgot about a birthday party, someone else came down with the flu, while another person landed free concert tickets and was unable to attend. The excuses and reasons began to pile up on top of one another like parade confetti.

"You should cancel the event," Sandy told me. "This might be a sign from your spirit guides."

I considered her words and then dismissed them. Something fierce and stubborn rose up inside of me. I wasn't backing down. The Soul Collector had taken enough from me during the past year. Even though the wounds were barely healed over, I wasn't going to allow him to dictate my life any further.

I received a further blow the day of the event. Leesa cancelled.

I sat there cradling the phone in my hands after hanging up with her. Leesa had been my safety net for the past year. Not having her there was terrifying.

By that time, it was too late to cancel. People were already in transit, heading to the prison camps. If I didn't show up, they would be standing there, wondering what happened to me. I had to go. My only solace was the fact that Jeff would be there. He had helped me before. Maybe he would help me again if I needed it.

It would have been nice if Sandy was there, at least. Then, I could bounce my impressions off both her and Jeff, but she dug in her heels about the investigation. She thought it was a bad idea and wouldn't attend.

When I pulled up in front of the prison camps, my heart fell. There were only three other cars there. That meant that out of the dozen or more people who pushed me to set up the investigation, only three of them bothered to show up.

It probably wasn't good to start the investigation in a foul mood, but I couldn't help it. I was beginning to feel like a cruise director for a group of kindergarteners instead of the director of a paranormal team.

It often took me hours to find locations for us to investigate and then spent another few hours, if not days, to research it before I even set it up. At that point, I would have to juggle all the people who were interested in attending. I'd have to answer questions about the location, as well as provide directions from different starting points and sometimes change the date because too many people couldn't attend. If I was getting paid to do this, it would have been one thing, but I wasn't. This was all coming out of my own free time and I seldom even got an acknowledgement for all the work I did, not even a thank you.

I grabbed my equipment bag off the passenger seat and glanced into all the cars, not finding any occupants. Instead of waiting for everyone to show up, they must have gone ahead inside to start investigating.

I tried to fend off the sense of agitation that was quickly seeping into my brain, but the train had already left the platform.

I could hear their voices inside the root cellar, so I ducked under the hanging vines that nearly covered the entrance and found them.

No one even looked up when I came in.

"Hey guys!" I said, trying to sound cheery. "I thought you were going to wait outside for everybody to show up before you got started," I said.

"Oh…we heard a noise inside and came in to see what it was?" someone said.

"And you brought your chairs, coolers and equipment with you?" I responded, the cheeriness leaching from my voice word by word.

"Stephen was already here. That was the noise we heard," someone said and I shone my light around in the darkness until I found Stephen.

"Oh…hi, Stephen," I said, taking in the scene ahead of me.

Stephen was an old friend and fellow investigator who often spent his summer evenings at the prison camp. He would come down for a few hours and attempt communication and then leave. Similar to how other people might go out to see a movie, Stephen went to find ghosts.

He was a jovial guy with an endless supply of interesting equipment. The lights from several devices shone brightly in the darkness like ornaments on a creepy Christmas display. In the center of it all was a big brown teddy bear.

"What's that?" I asked, pointing to the bear.

"Oh, that's a Trigger Bear. It's wired with EMF detectors. If something gets close to it, the lights will flash," he said.

"Cool. Has it gone off yet?" I asked, trying to find a spot where I could sit. I finally settled on a large rock, which wasn't nearly as comfortable as I first thought it would be.

"Yeah. A few times," he said and then continued on with the session that was obviously already in progress.

I pulled myself off the rock and walked back outside to retrieve my folding lawn chair. Even though I had just stubbed one out as I pulled up, I lit another cigarette.

As I leaned against my car, smoking, I saw the silhouette of someone emerging from the root cellar. It wasn't until he got almost halfway to my car that I could pick out his features. It was Jeff.

"Sorry about that. They were already inside when I pulled up, so I went in to see what was going on. Crazy place, huh?" he said.

I blew a stream of smoke above my head. "Very crazy. Are you picking anything up?"

"Yeah, a little bit. It kind of feels like they're hiding. When I first pulled up, they were talking about hearing footsteps going up the hill, but they didn't see anybody."

As we started to go back in, we heard a man's voice. It sounded like it came from behind the root cellar area.

"Did you hear that?" Jeff asked.

"Yeah, but it's not a place where people can easily get to. The root cellar hill is steep and is covered with prickly bushes," I said.

"Hmmmm…" Jeff said, staring at the front of the cellar. "Wanna go up there?" he asked, but I shook my head.

"Not in a million years. I don't care if the ghosts are lined up shoulder to shoulder. That area is covered in bramble. We'd need stitches afterwards," I said.

Jeff laughed and we headed back into the root cellar to join the others.

Stephen was still attempting to engage the ghosts.

"Can you tell us the date of the last newspaper you read?" Stephen asked, which I always considered to be a great question.

(Above) The Superintendent's House in 1934

(Above) inside the Superintendent's house, sitting on the front wall of the foundation, present day

If they answered it, we would get a better timeline of when they died.

As soon as Stephen stopped talking, I began hearing a bird warbling just outside the cellar.

"Can you make that bird stop singing?" I asked playfully, not really expecting anything to change.

The bird stopped singing mid-warble.

Several people in the group gasped. We sat there in the near darkness, waiting for it to start singing again, but it remained silent for several minutes.

"Can you make it start singing again?" I asked.

The bird started right up again. None of us wanted to consider the experience paranormal, but it was very strange.

We went through our other standard questions, asking how many souls were with us and if any of them wanted to talk to us. We didn't get any responses. After a while, we drifted off to the other areas of the prison camps.

The entire camp was spread out over a three or four acre area inside the state park. Miles of empty fields and forests surrounded us on all sides.

I found myself relaxing a little bit and tried to simply enjoy the investigation.

A big part of me really missed investigating. It was far more than just attempting to communicate with the dead. It was also a social endeavor. I got to spend time with like-minded people and enjoy myself.

As the night progressed, people starting leaving, one by one. Soon, Jeff was the only person left. I still wanted to investigate the foundation of the old superintendent's house, so we decided to stay for a bit longer.

The foundation was located across the dirt road from the prison camp and had once been a beautiful home, complete with a manicured lawn that sloped gently down the hill. Now, it was nothing more than a stone foundation. If you stood in the middle of it, you could almost envision where the house would have sat, but the area had become overgrown with trees and bushes. Evident by the scattering of old beer cans, it was also a popular hangout for the party crowd.

As we walked over, I began getting a strange feeling. I glance behind me, as if expecting to see someone following me.

"Are you getting the feeling you're being watched?" Jeff asked.

I suppressed a shudder. "Yeah. Definitely. It feels like someone is walking right behind us, but I can't hear any tones because of the wind and crickets," I said. My ability came with a definite disability. If the area wasn't quiet, I couldn't pick up on the tones. There could be a dozen ghosts behind me and I wouldn't hear them.

"I'm feeling it too. Maybe they just didn't like the big group of people," he said, which made sense. I wasn't crazy about crowds either. If I were a ghost, I'd wait until the pack thinned out a bit too.

We got settled on the foundation and I started an EVP session.

"Is there anybody who wants to come out and talk? There's only two of us now." I said.

Jeff fumbled around in his bag, searching for his recorder for a minute until he found it.

"Anybody here with us?" he asked, finally.

We didn't hear anything except for the crickets chirping in the background. It was a beautiful July night and the stars were out in abundance. The bright moon allowed us to see across the overgrown yard to the road out front. Behind us was another field that led to a bank of woods, but we couldn't see it from our vantage point on the foundation due to the overgrowth of trees that grew from the center of the home's former location.

"I'd say make a noise, but it would probably be pointless," I said. Since we were outdoors, the sounds of the night would make it difficult to interpret whether it was natural or paranormal.

That feeling of being watched came over me strongly again and I shifted around to peer into the darkness. Something was definitely there. I could feel it and I didn't like it one bit. It felt dark and conniving, the kind of ghost I usually attempted to avoid.

Without warning, we both heard a growling noise. It sounded like it was directly behind the foundation in the grassy field behind us.

"What the hell was that?" I asked.

"I don't know. It sounded like a growl," Jeff said.

We sat and listened intently to the night. It was conceivable that it could have been a black bear. They were known to live in the area.

"We're the only two in this park. How does that make you feel?" Jeff said with a laugh. While it was spoken jokingly, there was a sense of truth behind his words. The park was over 300 acres large and we were miles away from the nearest person, should we need help.

"Well, all you'd have to do is outrun me," I said, which caused Jeff to laugh.

I got an instant image of us running for our lives across the field with a huge bear directly behind us. There was no doubt that Jeff would outrun me, leaving me as a snack for the hungry bear.

"That's a cheery thought," I said.

As we sat there still chuckling, heavy branches began breaking in the same spot where we heard the growling. If we needed more confirmation that something large was prowling nearby, we got it.

"Okay, this is getting kind of creepy," Jeff said, swiveling around to try to peer through the branches behind us.

"I'm suddenly not afraid of anything paranormal anymore," I said, feeling the words ring true. A negative entity could latch onto me and follow me home, but a bear could actually kill me.

We sat there for a few more minutes and then decided to leave.

"I don't get a good feeling," Jeff said, which was something I had to agree with. Besides the entire paranormal aspect, we were nearly a quarter of a mile from our cars, which was far too great a distance to travel with a bear behind us.

As we walked past the solitary confinement cells, which were close to the area where we parked our cars, we decided to do one more EVP session. I can't explain our reluctance to leave, but it was there nonetheless.

We stood in the cell and just chatted for a minute about how we've been using our energy to help each other. After a few minutes, we began hearing a rumbling noise. We peered outside to check and heard the crunch of tires on gravel as a pickup truck headed down the long lane towards us.

"I think it's time to take off," Jeff said, echoing my own thoughts. The last thing we wanted was to find ourselves in the middle of a group of rowdy partiers.

We said our hurried goodbyes and got into our cars. Since Jeff wasn't as familiar with the maze of roads leading to the prison camps as I was, I led us out of there.

The roads were narrow and unpaved, consisting of long hardened ruts and massive potholes. The night seemed to close in on me as I followed the beams of my headlights along the turns. By the time I reached the main gate to the state park, I realized I wasn't alone. Even worse, the tone sounded exactly like the Soul Collector.

(Above) The Solitary Confinement cells present day

Chapter 18

The Prison Camp Hitchhiker

After enduring the worse paranormal attachment of my life, the last thing I wanted to do was pick up another one. I stopped my car at the entrance and got out. Was it the prison guard that Kaden had picked up on?

This was strange to me on several accounts. None of us had felt anything even remotely negative the entire night. Furthermore, this was the first time I picked up on this specific tone. I felt the woman earlier, but hadn't really tapped into anything else all night. Had he been somehow cloaking himself?

Jeff rolled down his window and peered at me curiously.

"Is everything okay?" he asked.

"Something is with me. Can you help get it out of my car?" I asked, my voice rising in pitch.

Jeff put his car in park, his face showing the exhaustion we both felt. He probably wanted nothing more but to drive home, pop the lid on a cold beer and then sink into a dreamless abyss, but he couldn't since my car was blocking his escape route. "Yeah, give me a second."

As I watched him, a sinking sensation settled into my stomach. I should have known better than to come back to the prison camps. Even though it looked like a simple state park, it was far more than that. The land was somehow tainted with negativity, allowing darker entities to gain a foothold. It's possible that not even Leesa could have protected me.

What had I done?

I watched Jeff as he closed his eyes to concentrate. The last time he had pushed off a ghost, it went quickly. It didn't seem to be working this time. I could still hear the tone clearly as if the entity was standing right beside me.

Finally, he opened his eyes and shook his head.

"I can't budge it. Maybe try getting away from this place and I'll try again when I get home," he suggested.

Disappointment settled deep into my soul. If Jeff wasn't able to get rid of it here, he probably wouldn't be able to evict it later either.

"I want to sage me and my car before I leave," I said, feeling the hopelessness growing stronger. If Jeff wasn't able to pull it off, sage would probably be a waste of time as well, but I had to try.

Jeff got out of his car as I lit the sage.

The moon gazed down at us from behind the tree cover, lighting up the sky above us, but barely touching the land. Our headlights beamed straight ahead, picking out random bits of details in the heavy underbrush, but did nothing to make me feel safer.

As I held my arms outwards, he moved the smoking bundle of sage around me until I had been thoroughly bathed in the smoke. I did the same for him and then we smudged both of our cars too.

When I first started investigating, people told me that sage was a way to eliminate ghosts from the area, but I was quickly finding out that it wasn't the case. It seemed to help with weaker ghosts, making them temporarily disoriented while we made a hasty get-away. On stronger entities, it was like blowing raspberries in their faces. They just brushed it off with a laugh and continued on.

I hated the idea of parting ways with Jeff, but there wasn't much else he could do. I could have asked him to try again, but the effort seemed fruitless. Besides, this wasn't really his battle to endure. He wasn't the ghost magnet.

We got into our cars and drove away, following the dark road through the deep forest until we got to the highway and went our separate ways.

Sorrow quickly took over the space where disappointment had settled in. Was my life going to always be this way? Would I have one attachment after another until I just couldn't take it anymore?

I recognized the sense of depression as something the Soul Collector once did to me. It was a tool from his bag of tricks that he used quite effectively. He made me feel hopeless and dejected, removing all possibility of escape.

It gave me a better understanding about what people with disabilities endured. Despite the fact that I looked normal and appeared to live a fairly conventional lifestyle, I was internally crippled with a fear I couldn't escape.

It was something my ex-boyfriend couldn't wrap his mind around.

"Just stop ghost hunting," he once told me, which was a laughable solution.

Ghosts found me in the grocery store and at restaurants. They latched onto me at Wal-Mart and when I went to visit friends at their homes. Ghost hunting was the only way for me to learn more and hopefully find some sort of solution for my problem. Even though it looked like fun and games, it was research on how to one day make my life more livable.

As I passed the sign that welcomed me to Barre, the tone was still buzzing directly in my ear. Whatever had latched onto me at the prison camps was still firmly in place. I didn't want to go home, because I knew he'd just dig his talons in and refuse to budge, but I had nowhere else to go. I pulled into my driveway and sat out in front of my empty dark house, and the familiarity didn't escape me. It felt exactly like it had with the Soul Collector.

I remember all those dark nights well. I would pull up in front of my house, dreading the night ahead of me. Once they got into my house, they became even stronger and were capable of invading my thoughts easier. My home was supposed to be my sanctuary, the one place in the entire world where I felt safe, but mine was nothing more than a torture chamber.

I came inside and began turning on lights until every illuminated device in my entire house was ablaze. It didn't help me push away the nasty entity, but it felt better to chase the darkness away with light.

I somehow managed to fall asleep, but awoke the next morning feeling as though I wasn't alone.

For reasons I couldn't understand, my bedroom seemed to be the hotspot for the activity. When I walked through the doorway, the energy felt different. It was heavier and filled with some sort of static electricity. All of the hairs on my arms would rise as my ears rang loudly.

From my experience as an investigator, I knew that sometimes electrical malfunctions could impact a haunting. In several cases, faulty wiring created a false sense of ghostly activity.

Electromagnetic energy (EMF) wasn't something to mess with. Most people didn't realize that electronic and electric devices that emitted high levels of EMF energy could impact their health and well-being. People who were sensitive to the energy might feel uneasy, as though they were being watched, and could even develop headaches and hallucinations if the EMF levels were high enough. EMF energy has also been linked to serious health concerns, including cancer, birth defects, Alzheimer's and depression, just to name a few.

(Above) Joni's bedroom in the Barre house

Common items that frequently emit high levels of EMF waves include digital alarm clocks, refrigerators, microwave ovens and even Wi-Fi units. It has also been connected to issues with depression and even suicide.

I pulled out my EMF meter and did a thorough sweep of the room, dismayed when I didn't find anything out of the ordinary.

When I first purchased my EMF meter, I was ecstatic. Other people in the paranormal world touted them as a good way to determine if a ghost was present. I wasn't finding that to be the case. I came to realize that it was a tool, just like all the other useless tools I carried around in my equipment bag. If the ghosts wanted to use it, they would. If they preferred to remain hidden, they simply ignored it.

I put a call into Jeff.

"I have a house full of ghosts. Can you help me?" I asked.

"Is that guy from the prison camps still with you?"

"Oh yeah. Him and about a dozen of his new friends," I said, the dismay in my voice unmistakable.

"Let me see if I can blast him out of there," he said.

I sat down on my bed and waited as patiently as possible. My bed was a rumpled mess, so I began straightening out the sheets and comforter. I was normally a devout bed-maker. I couldn't start my day without leaving my bed looking like something out of a *Better Homes and Gardens* magazine layout, but I hadn't even bothered in the past few days.

After I finished, I sat back down and tried to tune into the room.

The sounds of ghosts buzzed around the room. There were so many of them, I only caught a brief snippet of a tone before it zipped away and another replaced it. How many ghosts did I have in my house? I couldn't even fathom a guess.

"Wow. You have a lot of them. What are you doing, collecting them?" he asked.

Knowing that our friendship was strongly based in sarcasm, I didn't bother to answer. He knew very well what I was dealing with.

After a few more minutes, the noise in the room abated somewhat. It was apparent that he hadn't been able to remove all of them, but he had definitely weeded through them.

"Is that better?" he asked.

I sighed. "Yeah, somewhat. I still have quite a few of them here." I wasn't sure what I was going to do about it. The ones Jeff removed would probably be replaced in a matter of days. Short of having Jeff on stand-by, I didn't have many other options.

"Why do you think you're suddenly drawing so many of them in?" he asked.

"I don't know," I said.

"Maybe you're opening up more and they're becoming more aware of you. You need to learn how to focus your energy. It just goes everywhere," he said.

We had that same conversation at the prison camps while we were in the solitary confinement cell doing an EVP session. Like Kaden, Jeff was able to see people's energy and he didn't like what he saw with mine.

"How do you suggest I do that?" I toyed with the edge of the comforter, my mind a million miles away.

"I don't know. Maybe try meditating more," he suggested.

I got up off my bed and walked to my dresser where I had several meditation DVDs stored. I fingered through them, feeling the same sense of displeasure I always felt with them.

I knew meditation was good. In fact, I often preached the merits of it to others in my group, but I had a difficult time doing it myself. There was something about sitting still for a half hour that went against the grain of my existence. By nature, I was an antsy person. I couldn't even sit through a half-hour television show without getting up every few minutes. Even if I did try to sit through a program, I found myself toying with my phone, playing Solitaire or checking social media.

I even had a hard time during EVP sessions. After about ten minutes, I was ready to move to another room. He was probably right about my erratic energy field. Sometimes I felt like a spinning vortex with a tornado in the center.

"I'll try," I finally told him.

I hated bothering him so much with my issues. I knew that he had a life and his own issues to deal with. The last thing he needed was another Joni call to pull him out of his life.

I started to end the call, but he surprised me with one more kernel of information.

"Hey, I'm worried about Sandy. I checked in on her earlier and her energy is really down. It's like she has these black things in her energy field that need to come out. I've been sending her energy, but it doesn't seem to do anything. Is she okay?" he asked.

Sadly, I was so caught up with my own drama, it had been a few days since I last touched base with her.

"I'll check on her," I told him and then ended the call.

As it turned out, Sandy had her own issues she was contending with.

CHAPTER 19

SANDY

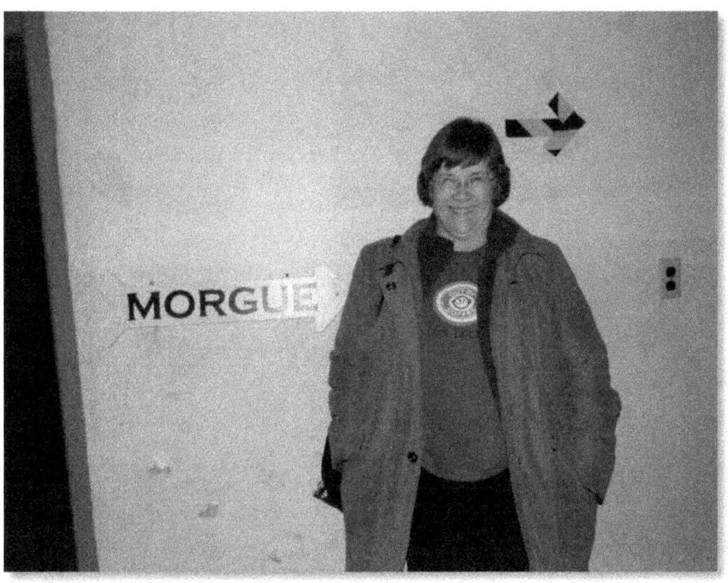

(Above) Sandy at Rolling Hills Asylum, one of the many places we investigated together

On the surface, Sandy seemed like a kind, calm person, someone you could always count on to be there. People often thought of her as being solid as a rock, but nothing could have been further from the truth. Inside, Sandy was a myriad of competing emotions.

She confided to me that she suffered from depression and a host of other issues that made her life far more complex than mine.

Until I got to know her, I didn't truly understand the depths of depression. There were a few times when I might have grazed the surface of it, but it was like comparing a common headache to a migraine. There was no comparison between the two.

Sandy's depression could be triggered by a number of things, but it always seemed to be the worst in the winter months, when she was already dealing with a lack of sunlight from our northern skies.

Her bouts would last anywhere from a few weeks to a few months and she suffered through every moment of them.

"Let's go get some pie," I suggested early on, knowing of her love for the delectable treat. Somewhere in my mind, I connected her issue with nothing more than sadness. Surely pie would cheer her up. As it turns out, I had a lot to learn.

Depression is like a vast pit of despair. When people look down into it, they only see what is on the surface. They can't see down into all the layers and depths of it. When someone is having an especially dark bout of depression, they might be swimming between the layers you can't see from the top. Pie certainly wasn't going to change anything.

When Sandy's depression was in full swing, she almost always attempted to retreat from the world. She would hole herself up in her nineteenth-century farmhouse and would spend days on the sofa, not having the mental or physical energy to function in the outside world.

Being someone with abilities compounded this.

Besides dealing with the depression, Sandy was an empath. She felt other people's energy and often absorbed it. When she went out into the world, she was like a sponge, pulling in everything around her. If someone was angry, that went into the sponge, as did sadness, hatred, anxiety and depression. Even a few minutes out in the world was overwhelming and often caused her to sink down further into her pit.

After a few definite hits and misses, I learned how to navigate around her a little better. I didn't necessarily walk on eggshells because I had too much respect for her to treat her gingerly, but I did learn to edit my words a bit. If she made me angry over something she said or did, I first considered the pitfalls she lives with before responding negatively…usually.

I like to think of myself as a fairly easy-going person. I often roll with the punches, but that doesn't mean I'm immune to negative emotions. In some ways, I think Sandy deals with these in the same way that I deal with hers. She takes into account my background and my own situation and gives me the benefit of the doubt.

Coming into her metaphysical abilities was a mixed bag for her. While it was exciting to learn that she too had a superpower, as we jokingly referred to it, she was also saddled with the responsibilities that came along with it. When she suffered a dark bout of depression, she could no longer hole herself in her house and wait it out by herself. She now had an entire flock of ghosts hovering around her, vying for her attention. In some ways she had it worse than me. What she lacked in volume, she made up for with intensity.

The dead often feed from our energy and Sandy's was very strong, despite her depression. In some ways, I believe she was born with a stronger energy field, but in other ways, I think she fortified it due to necessity from a less than stellar childhood.

Instinctively, she knew that in order to fend off the ghostly masses, she would need to push them off with her energy field, similar to what Jeff did. That wasn't always easy to accomplish. When she was deep in her pit of depression, the energy she needed was a rubber duck floating on the top. She would have to find her way to the surface to get to it, which left her vulnerable in the meantime.

Thankfully, Sandy wasn't getting the sheer amount of ghosts that I was getting. If I had six or seven in my house, she might have one or two.

We spent a fair amount of time trying to figure it all out.

"Why do you think they're following us like this?" I asked while we had a quiet dinner together at a diner, one of Sandy's favorite guilty pleasures.

Sandy took another bite of her salad. Besides having issues with depression, she was also lactose intolerant and suffered from Celiac Disease, a condition that prevented her from eating anything wheat-based without causing her intense stomach pains. While I chewed on my bacon cheeseburger, she ate salad.

"I really think it goes back to the point where we opened ourselves up," she said, setting down her fork. "I once read something a famous medium wrote about how she went through her own spiritual awakening. She said that once she opened that door and embraced her abilities, she was in it for the long haul. She had to learn how to close herself down so she didn't attract so many ghosts."

I knew where she was going with that line of conversation because we had discussed it before. Most people are literally closed down, which is why they don't experience anything paranormal. Once you open yourself up, you become aware.

Sandy already knew quite a bit about the chakra system, but I was still learning. What I knew at that point was that the body had several energy centers which governed the internal functions of the organs that were located near them and were connected with our emotional well-being.

The seven primary chakras were almost like the electrical circuits of our bodies. They spun in a circular motion, keeping all of our processes moving smoothly. If one was out of balance or was closed off entirely, it not only affected that area of the body, but also interfered with the chakras nearby it.

I made it a point to learn as much as I could about the chakra system, since it seemed to play such a large role in my life.

While the first five chakras were essential, the sixth and seventh chakras were the ones we focused on for spiritual growth.

The seventh chakra was called the Crown Chakra and was located on the top of my head. It was thought to be the doorway to divine connection. Once you opened it, you had a better chance of communicating with your spirit guides and guardian angels.

Sandy once took a class on chakras and the instructor walked them through how to open and close it.

"Imagine it like a lotus flower, opening and closing," Sandy told me, but the mental image didn't resonate with me. Instead, I imagined mine to be a large steel lid that I could open and then close.

The sixth chakra was the one that interested me the most because it was the one most connected to my mediumship gifts.

When I touched the space on my forehead, between my eyes, I could feel the energy behind my Third-Eye Chakra. Everything I did seemed to come from that one spot. If I attempted to use my body's energy to push a ghost away or tried to pull more information from it, this spot tingled.

Some people believed it was connected to the pineal gland, a rice-sized endocrine gland located in the center of the brain that is thought to be the seat of the soul.

The pineal gland is responsible for producing melatonin, a hormone that helps regulate our sleep patterns. In animals, this gland plays a major role in hibernation, sexual development and breeding, as well as metabolism.

Unfortunately, as the brain ages, it begins to calcify as it collects mineral deposits such as calcium, fluoride, and phosphorous. This causes the pineal gland to become unreliable, resulting in lack of sleep, as well as closing you down psychically. Research has also shown that patients with Alzheimer's disease have pineal glands with a higher rate of calcification.

Sandy and I talked about this at length. According to the reports, the biggest culprit for the calcification of the pineal gland was fluoride, which wasn't an easy thing to avoid. It was pumped into our water and inserted into our toothpaste. It could be found in processed meats and in foods like lettuce and grapes that were sprayed with fluoride pesticides.

We began brushing our teeth with fluoride-free toothpaste and started filtering our water. Chances were, the damage had already been done, but we hoped to minimize further consumption as much as possible.

"Why though? Why are we different from most people?" Sandy asked.

It was an interesting question and one I didn't really have an answer for.

"We were just lucky, I guess," I said with more than a trace of sarcasm, but I couldn't get the thought out of my head.

When I don't understand something, my typical behavior is to research the hell out of it. Thanks to the Internet, I now had unlimited information available to me and I took full advantage of it.

I learned that people with mediumistic or psychic gifts often inherited their abilities from their parents or grandparents. Sometimes the gift seemed to skip a generation, but if you searched far enough back, you could see a pattern in place.

Strong psychic mediums like Leesa came from families with gifts. It was a little harder for me to track my lineage. Neither of my parents seemed to have any abilities and all of my grandparents were deceased, so I couldn't question them.

"Do you think that sometimes people might have gifts that they aren't aware of?" Sandy asked.

It was an interesting concept. If they never opened themselves up, they might not have full access to everything they were capable of.

This seemed to be the case for me and Sandy. We were born with these gifts, but kept them somewhat dormant for most of our lives. Once we made the decision to open them, we found ourselves in a world we never dreamed was possible.

When we additionally opened our Crown Chakras, we basically became beacons. We could not only pull information from the dead, but were also receiving information from our spirit guides and spiritual allies.

"I think you're a little different. Maybe you opened yourself up a little bit as a child and then really blew the gate open later," Sandy suggested.

It made sense, but it brought up an even bigger point.

"I wish there was some way of closing it down, even for a little while," I said. Having this ability was like being on-duty 24/7 for a job you didn't really like to begin with.

"I think there is. I heard a story that I thought was interesting," Sandy said. "This other famous psychic medium – I can't remember her name – but at any rate, she would always wear a hat when she didn't want to communicate with dead people. It helped her remember to close down her Third-Eye and her Crown Chakras," she said.

I had to laugh. "What about tinfoil hats?" I asked, thinking about how in bygone days people with paranoia issues wore them to prevent mind control and to protect them from EMF energy.

She surprised me by arching an eyebrow. "You never know. It might work. Make us a few of them and we can try them."

I truly hate to admit it, but I did try it. Every night as I tried to go to sleep, the dead hovered close to me, often giving me horrific nightmares. One night, I inserted a tinfoil lining into a sock hat to see if it helped, but it didn't. I could almost hear the laughter as they watched me attempt my little science project.

"We have to keep trying things until we find something that works," she said.

"Yup." It was a frequent conversation with us. We tried new protection stones, new amulets, new prayers and new types of sage, but nothing seemed to work for us.

Tinfoil hats weren't going to touch what was in store for both of us.

(Above) Sandy on top of the light house at Rose Island in Rhode Island

CHAPTER 20

GHOST OF THE WEEK CLUB

I felt as though I had been enrolled in the Ghost of the Week club. Every day there seemed to be an addition to my already growing household. Some people collected cats. It appeared that I was now collecting ghosts.

The new guy from the prison camps was becoming unbearable and the fear he was instilling me was nearly pushing me over the edge.

There wasn't a single night that I didn't flee from my bedroom and end up on my couch. The fear was wearing me down mentally and physically. I was losing sleep, which was impacting my work day as well. If something didn't happen soon, I feared that my entire life would begin crumbling around me.

Jeff did what he could to push them away for me, but it was clear that I needed other resources as well. I reached out to Kaden again and asked him to come out to my house.

He walked through my house, staring into space like Leesa had done before. After he finished his evaluation, he shook his head gravely.

"You have a number of ghosts here. I'm picking up on a tall thin man with dark hair. I think you picked him up at a restaurant," he said.

I gasped. "Sandy and I had dinner at a Chinese restaurant the other night and we felt him come up to the table. Why did he follow us?"

Kaden arched his eyebrows. "I think you reminded him of someone. I'm not sure, but I can send him along easily enough."

(Above: Kaden Mattison)

Unlike Leesa, who primarily communicated with the ghosts telepathically, Kaden talked out loud to them.

"No, you need to leave," he told the man. "She's not who you think she is," he said, shaking his head. "No, you can't. Now go!"

It was strange watching him interact with someone I couldn't see. It was almost like watching someone on the telephone. I could only hear one side of the conversation.

Finally, Kaden turned to look at me.

"Okay, he's gone," he said.

I was both thrilled and curious about the process. "What did you do? Where did he go?"

"I just gave him a little nudge and he went back to the restaurant," he said casually, as though this wasn't one of the most amazing things I'd ever seen. He made it look far too easy.

"God, I wish I could do that."

"Oh, you will. You just need to focus your energy," he said. "You have a few others here, but I can send them on their way," he said and closed his eyes.

When he opened them, he seemed surprised. "I got rid of several of them but there are two males here that I can't budge. I think one of them belongs to the house and the other might have followed you from the prison camps," he said, much to my dismay.

He asked to check out the basement, so I led him down the narrow stairs to the space. The temperature dropped by at least twenty degrees by the time we made it to the bottom and the smell of mildew assaulted our noses.

"You should get a dehumidifier down here," he commented.

I laughed. "It's not like I want to spend any time down here," I told him. The basement truly creeped me out. It made me think about all those dark stains I found on the wall that looked like blood. I didn't say anything to Kaden about it, curious what he would pick up.

He walked directly to the wall and studied it for a moment, something that made my heart race.

"What are you picking up?" I asked nervously.

"I don't know. Something bad happened down here. I don't think it's attached to the man who's here, but maybe a family member, a boy?" he said.

This made perfect sense to me. Since moving into the house, I learned more information about the last people who lived there and the news hadn't been comforting.

My neighbors described the previous tenants as "train wrecks." The mother was slovenly and was probably mentally unstable, walking around the yard bra-less in a stained white t-shirt most of the time. They said that you could barely see the grass due to all the trash they threw there. After her husband died, she seemed to lose complete control of her kids.

I knew very little about the husband, only that he was burly and gruff. He apparently had as little concern about cleanliness as his wife did because the back yard was consistently littered with old lawn mowers that he repaired and refurbished. This information was supported by the buckets full of screws, bolts and odd bits of machinery I found while mowing the yard.

The two of them had two children: a son and a daughter. The girl was a few years younger than the boy and appeared to be the normal one in the family. The boy was a different story altogether.

He was a juvenile delinquent in the making since childhood, often breaking into the neighbor's homes and stealing their prized possessions. His family had a small shack on the property that the neighbors referred to as "the cat house" because it was filled to the rafters with meowing cats. One neighbor once saw him driving one of his father's lawn mowers across the lawn, dragging a cat on a rope behind him. His antics eventually led him to incarceration at a local boy's detention area. Knowing what I did about him, it wouldn't have surprised me if he had killed some of the cats in the basement. The thought gave me a shudder.

To my surprise, Kaden walked to the edge of the wall and began searching the top of the support board. When he pulled his hand back out, it contained a knife.

"Oh my God! What's that?" I asked moving closer to get a better look. The knife was the sort that people use for hunting.

"It's a gutting knife. Hunters use it to gut the animals they kill," Kaden said, holding the knife out for me to see.

It was about eight inches long with a hook at one end. The handle was made of worn wood that had seen many years of service. What shook me to the core was the brown residue that covered the end of the blade. It was the exact same color as the stains I found on the walls when I first moved in.

"Is that blood?" I asked, my heart hammering.

"That's what it looks like to me," Kaden said, turning it over in his hands. "Let's get this knife out of the house. It might be holding onto residual energy."

We walked out into my back yard and sat down around my large round table. The top of the table was made of glass. When Kaden set the knife down, it made a clinking sound that made me jump a little.

"I'd recommend getting that off the property," he said.

I agreed wholeheartedly. It wasn't exactly my idea of a keepsake.

After Kaden left, the house felt supercharged. I couldn't put my finger on it, but the energy level just felt magnified. I wasn't as adept at interpreting the invisible forces at work inside my house as Kaden was, but it set me on edge.

***

I didn't have a lot of options. I no longer considered Leesa a resource. Her busy schedule made it nearly impossible. That left me with Kaden and Jeff.

While both of them were good at getting rid of most of the ghosts in my house, I still had two I had to deal with. I only felt the man who was attached to the house on occasion. He seemed like he was content just being there and didn't bother me very often. The real problem was the prison camp ghost.

It got to a point where I simply dreaded going into my bedroom. I'd stand in the doorway and look longingly at my bed, remembering days when it was my sanctuary. I would look forward to the moment when I could climb in with a good book and just read until I got sleepy. Now, it was the last place I wanted to be.

I wasn't sure why it felt worse in my bedroom. I turned over several theories in my mind, but dismissed most of them. The only thing that felt possible was because it was the place where I felt the most comfortable, in some ways making it the heart of the house. My energy was the strongest there because it had once been my sanctuary. They knew they could do the most damage by hitting me in my soft spot.

I stood in the doorway and studied my bedroom. It looked just like it normally did, with the soft terra cotta colored walls and dark metal framed bed, but it felt far different. My ears began ringing loudly as a sense of fear blasted me back out of the doorway.

I retreated back to the living room, where the glow of the TV gave the room a blue cast. I quickly flipped on several lights to chase away the rest of the gloom and settled down on the couch.

I had to work in the morning and really needed my sleep. My job was becoming more intense than ever and I needed every one of my brain cells active to get through it.

My cats were parked on the arms of my sofa, sleeping soundly, which gave me a sense of contentment. If the cats were sleeping, the paranormal activity was low. They were my unofficial barometer, but they were often effective. The fact that they weren't sleeping in my bedroom didn't escape me. They didn't like ghosts any more than I did.

I typed out a quick text message to Jeff, telling him what Kaden discovered and waited for a response that never came. In the back of my mind, I had hoped that he would respond quickly and I could ask him to try to push it out one more time, hopefully piggy-backing on what Kaden had already done. If Kaden had weakened it, Jeff might be able to push it out this time, but he didn't respond.

The last few times he attempted to move it out, he said that he saw it leave.

"Just believe it's gone and let it go," he would tell me, but that was all but impossible considering I was still hearing the sound it made. My ears rang as loud as before.

I knew I was becoming a pest. I was burning through my psychic medium friends far too quickly with my urgent pleas. I wasn't sure what else to do though. Nothing else was working.

I glanced up at the clock. It was already midnight. I needed to get up in six hours to start my day.

"I need to get to sleep," I groaned.

Sandy also had a difficult time sleeping and used a sleep-aid remedy that worked miracles for her. It consisted of taking one melatonin tablet, combined with a Benadryl tablet. She swore that the combination of the two always knocked her out, so I gave it a try.

I took the pills and then sat on the couch, watching mindless television programs until I began to feel sleepy. Then I practically launched myself into my bed, hoping to fall asleep quickly.

I did, but awoke hours later as a dark shadow raced across my room.

CHAPTER 21

THE PRISON CAMP GHOST

The next morning, I awoke on the sofa, groggy and stiff. I pulled myself up and stretched, trying to work out some of the kinks that had settled into my muscles, but it was a useless effort.

I sat for a moment and listened to the house. I could hear the faint ticking of the refrigerator, followed by the soft lapping of a cat drinking from the water bowl. A car whooshed past on the road outside, but there weren't any other sounds. If the ghost was there, he was remaining quiet.

I showered and got ready for work, glancing into my bedroom as I passed it. Evidence of my restless night greeted me. The covers were thrown from the bed and the nightstand lamp was still on.

Memories of the sheer terror returned to me. There were times in my life when I would see something I was uncertain of. Shadows were tricky things. Sometimes they could be explained. A car could pull into the driveway next door and cast a shadow on the wall. Even a cat walking past the nightstand lamp could create a shadow. This shadow was different. It had arms and legs and a head.

When it raced across the room, it almost seemed separated from the wall. It moved so quickly, I didn't get more than a two-second look, but I'd swear on my own life that it wasn't just a shadow.

It was easy to fall into a pity party and that was usually my first inclination after a horrible night.

Why me? Seriously. Why me?

Other people had normal lives and didn't have to cope with this stuff. They could go on believing that ghosts were just the product of imaginative minds and spend their time worrying about playdates for their children or which resort to visit on their next vacation. My life was a constant nightmare. With a sigh, I continued down the hall.

I walked into my home office and sat my cup of coffee on my desk and stared out my window at the street in front of my house, not really seeing anything beyond my own thoughts.

I wanted to think that I was a strong person. I didn't allow anything to hamper my life. If something bad was thrown at me, I stepped over it and moved on. A sense of inner resolve usually kicked in and I tried to use the experience as a learning opportunity. This time was no different. I had to find a way to stop all this madness or at least slow it down a bit.

I returned to my bedroom. Maybe if I opened the curtains and blinds, the sunlight would at least make the room look cheerier.

I made the bed, turned off the lamp and then set about flooding the room with sunlight. As an extra measure, I turned on the radio and tuned it into an oldies channel that played light music.

I wasn't sure if I actually made any headway, but the room felt distinctly lighter. As I settled into my day, I realized that I hadn't heard the tone of the prison camp ghost all day.

I got up from my desk and walked around the house, trying to get a feel for the energy. Everything actually felt better, but I wasn't sure why.

Had the simple act of opening the blinds helped?

I needed a break, so I carried my cell phone into the living room and called Sandy. She answered on the fifth ring, sounding like she had been revived from death.

"Are you okay?" I asked after hearing her tired greeting.

"I'm just tired. I didn't get much sleep last night," she said. "I've had my own ghosts keeping me up."

I filled her in on Kaden's findings and then told her about the shadow figure that raced across the room.

"That's not good. Shadow people are usually associated with negative entities. Do you think it would help if I came over tonight and we combined energies and tried a house cleansing? I'd be happy to," she said. "A little while ago I tried pulling some pure white energy and surrounding myself in a bubble of it. So far, I haven't been touched. Maybe if we tried something like that, just to protect your bedroom, it would help."

"That sounds like a good plan," I told her. Even though things felt momentarily better, there was no guarantee it would remain that way. If Sandy came over and we combined forces, we might be able to give it the final nudge it needed to move along.

She arrived later that evening with chicken-topped salads from the local pizza shop. The succulent scent of oven roasted chicken and melted cheese filled the room and made my mouth water. We ate in the living room and decided on a game plan.

We would do a smudging of the entire house and then we would go into my bedroom and attempt to fill it with white light. There was no definite rhyme or reason for what we did. We just followed our instincts and did what we felt was right. After filling every room with the aromatic smoke from the sage stick, we returned to my bedroom.

"I suggest that we hold hands and link our energy," Sandy said.

I felt a little odd, standing in my bedroom and holding my friend's hands, but I was willing to try almost anything at that point. Once our hands were joined, Sandy instructed me to help her build a bubble of white light.

As we worked to construct the shield, I felt the energy in the room grow lighter and brighter. Even though I had my eyes closed, I could see the light filling the backsides of my eyelids. A cold chill climbed my spine as I realized this was the first time I'd been able to hold the visualization in my mind long enough for it to fully take shape.

"Now, push it outwards so it encompasses the entire house," Sandy said. After a few minutes, she released my hands. "Okay, I think we're done here."

I turned my head in both directions, trying to see if I could hear him, but couldn't.

"I don't hear him. I think we're good," I said, feeling better than I had in a long while. If we had somehow stumbled upon a method of eradicating ghosts on our own, we wouldn't need to keep pestering other people to help us.

As I knew from the past though, the proof was in the pudding. I wouldn't know for certain if he was gone or not until I went to bed later. That's when they usually found me.

Sandy left, so I decided to take Ripley for a quick walk in the park across the street before it got dark. Children were playing softball in one of the fields and their cheers made me smile, remembering when my own children played team sports.

My daughter was in her final year of college, pursuing an engineering degree and my son was in his junior year of high school. He still came to stay with me four days every week, but I now had to share him with his girlfriend.

When he visited, I tried to keep everything paranormal to a minimum. Since he wasn't sensitive to the activity, he wasn't usually aware that anything was going on unless he came in and smelled sage in the air.

"Smoking that wacky weed again?" he would say with a grin.

I always played my part in the game by protesting that "it was just sage!" and we'd laugh some more. I was just thankful that none of the activity had touched him.

After he read *Soul Collector*, he had a better understanding of what I had been dealing with years ago. It also served to educate him on how close he had been to the activity without knowing about it. It was the last of my paranormal books he would read. If I wrote something that was fictional, he would read it, but he had no interest in knowing about my paranormal encounters from that point on.

I wasn't sure if it scared him or bored him. It's something we tended to steer clear of. It wasn't necessarily a taboo topic, but we both knew our boundaries and that was a definite one.

My daughter, on the other hand, was intrigued by the paranormal to an extent. She attended several investigations with me and actually participated in the EVP sessions. If she possessed any metaphysical gifts, they hadn't emerged yet. It was one of those things that time would unravel if that were the case.

I made it back home, feeling recharged and refreshed, like I usually did after a walk. I came through the door, fully expecting to hear the give-away tone of the prison camp ghost, but the house was quiet. The only thing I could hear was the softer tone of the female ghost I called Carla. She had been hanging around for several months and wasn't an issue. She just liked being with me.

Sandy had been having activity in her house too. She felt a male presence there from time to time, along with a woman. The woman was similar to my Carla. She was quiet and reclusive, making an appearance several times a day. The only time she truly bothered Sandy was when she came into her bedroom with her.

"This is my space! You need to get out!" she would shout and the ghost would scamper back out again. The male wasn't as cordial. He often sat on the side of her bed and touched her cheek as she attempted to drift off to sleep, which was more than a bit unnerving for her.

My evening routine was fairly simple. I would spend a few hours on the couch, watching TV. I plopped down on my sofa with a bag of microwave popcorn when I heard the tone return for the first time that day. I felt my shoulders slouch. So much for our spiritual boundary. He just went somewhere else for a while and then came back.

The feeling of having him there was eerie. I could feel his eyes boring into me. Even if I got up to move to another room, he seemed to follow me. I walked into the bathroom with a dire need to empty my bladder and he trailed along right behind me. That was when I hit my limit.

"Enough! You need to leave my house NOW! You aren't welcome here!" I shouted, sending my cats flying. I didn't yell very often, so they weren't used to it.

He didn't budge.

If nothing else, he moved close enough to hand me the toilet paper.

I went through my evening, but my heart wasn't into anything I attempted. If I turned on the TV, all I focused on was the shadow near the doorway that seemed to move when I looked away.

I wasn't sure how much of this I could take.

I knew that ghosts could actually hurt the living. They could mess with the electrical systems or turn on the burner on a gas stove. They could knock photos off the wall or heave heavy objects off shelves. They could also pin you to your bed and hover over you while you fell into a deep panic. Some of them could even influence your thoughts and change your mindset. None of those things were very comforting realizations.

I tried hard not to spend much time thinking about them. I knew from watching Leesa that they could communicate telepathically. They knew what scared us and often used it against us.

Finally, as bedtime approached, I swallowed Sandy's sleep remedy and waited until I felt sleepy. Then, I ran into my bedroom and fell asleep as quickly as possible.

The next thing I knew, sunlight was shining though my windows.

It was another work day, so I had no choice but to get ready for my day. I showered, let the dog out in the backyard, made coffee and then carried my mug into my home office.

I hated taking the sleep meds because they left me feeling groggy and grainy the next morning. I wasn't coherent until I made my way to the bottom of my second cup of coffee.

I didn't want to ruin Sandy's day like the ghost had ruined mine, but she needed to know that he came back. As soon as it was reasonably late enough, I called Sandy. She answered with a sleep deprived voice that was very similar to mine.

"What time did you go to sleep last night?" she asked me.

I had to think for a minute. "I believe I finally dozed off at about eleven, why?"

"Because that's when your ghost came to me," she said, sending a chill down my spine.

My ghost had jumped to her.

We were now sharing it.

Chapter 22

The Baron of the Cemetery

Sandy and I continued to track the ghost. We kept logs, documenting when we felt him come into our space. The results were fairly astounding. When he wasn't with me, he was with Sandy seconds later.

How could he do that? It wasn't as if Sandy came over and he hitched a ride with her. He was finding her without her physical presence.

Both of us also felt him in a way that we'd never felt a ghost before, which we found to be a bit unnerving. Sandy still got a tingling in her scalp and my ears still buzzed, but we also felt a sense of his physical presence. When he popped in, the air was displaced, as though something swooped in like a giant bat. I could feel the sensation as though I was picking him up on some sort of internal radar. The feeling was so strong, I often flinched when it happened.

"Are we getting stronger or is he just more powerful than what we've dealt with before?" Sandy asked me.

"I think it's a combination of both," I said, sadly. Whatever the case, we needed it to end. It was affecting my sleep and my overall wellbeing. I was becoming jumpy and nervous.

I hated bothering Kaden and Jeff with my continuing paranormal issues, especially since neither of them had been able to push this ghost off. I needed a new mentor.

Sandy and I met for breakfast at the Blue Moon Diner, which was in nearby Gardner, Massachusetts. As we came through the door, we were hit with a wall of delicious food smells. Bacon, eggs and hash browns fried on the cooktop, while coffee brewed on the counter. Waitresses bustled past with plates teaming with pancakes and omelets. We found an empty booth and slid in, only giving the menu a cursory glance before placing our orders.

Sandy got some sort of strange omelet with ingredients in it that I'd never consider paring with eggs, while I went for the Eggs Benedict, something I couldn't easily make at home.

While we waited for our food to arrive, we sipped our boiling hot coffee and chatted.

"It's clear that he's hopping back and forth between us, so what do we do?" she asked.

"I don't know. Neither Jeff nor Kaden has been able to do much about him. We need a new mentor, someone who can budge him off," I said. I took a sip of my coffee and burnt off all my taste buds. "This is really hot, so be careful," I told my friend.

"I like it hot. The hotter, the better," she said, pouring cream from a little plastic container into her steaming brew. I watched her take a sip and then recoil, feeling an I-told-you-so threaten to escape, but I kept that snarky remark to myself. Sandy was one of my few friends who put up with my snide sense of humor, but even she had her limits.

She sat her cup back down and straightened her flat wear.

"I did a bit of research last night on the computer and found a psychic medium in Sturbridge we might want to check out. She's offering psychic medium development courses. I think the first one is in a few days," she said.

"Do you know anything about her?" I asked.

"No. Just what I saw online. I'll stop by her shop tomorrow and find out more information."

Our food arrived to the table, sending clouds of wonderful aromas into my face, so we quieted down and ate.

Several days later, Sandy called to tell me about the shop.

"It's a little metaphysical shop. She sells all the normal stuff. I picked up some sage while I was there," she said.

"Hmmm…" I said, noncommittedly.

I really wanted her to be the real deal, someone who could finally help us, but I didn't have much faith in the prospects. Owning a metaphysical shop didn't make her a good psychic medium. The two didn't always go together.

"Her classes start Tuesday. I'm going to call and sign up. Do you want me to add you too?" she asked. "I think it's forty dollars for a two hour class," she added.

Forty dollars was essentially half of my grocery money for the week. Parting with it was an expense I truly didn't need at the moment, but what else was I going to do?

"Yeah sure. Sign me up," I said.

We showed up for the class the following Tuesday.

The shop was located in a long strip mall in the historic town of Sturbridge, Massachusetts. The town was best known for Old Sturbridge Village, a living museum that depicted a town from the late 1700's. I brought my kids there several times to watch the farmers plow the field with a team of horses and to see handcrafters create candles out of bees wax. Sandy and I went to Sturbridge on occasion to walk around the antique shops.

The smell of sage was strong inside the shop. A string of bells jingled as we pushed through the glass door. The woman at the counter was busy with a customer, so we walked around and checked out the shop.

It was similar to most of the other metaphysical/new-age shops I'd been to with Sandy. She often dragged me to them in her pursuit of a special semi-precious gemstone or for Wiccan supplies. This shop had all of those wares, plus a few things I wasn't familiar with.

"What's Florida Water?" I asked, showing her a bottle I pulled from a shelf. I popped the cap and was treated to a strong citrus smell.

She took the bottle from me and sniffed it, closing her eyes as though she had just caught a whiff of bacon and coffee instead.

"It's used in Hoodoo, Voodoo and Santeria," she said with the same casual tone that she might use to tell me that my shirt was on inside-out.

I was ready to bolt from the store. Santeria? Voodoo and Hoodoo? I considered myself to be fairly open-minded about all the metaphysical stuff she'd been introducing me to, but I wasn't going to start sacrificing chickens any time soon.

The look on my face must have been priceless because Sandy was quick to explain.

"I think the shop owner practices Santeria. I don't know as much about it as I should, but it's basically a Caribbean religion that was brought over with the slaves. It's sort of like a combination of Voodoo and Catholicism," she said.

"But, don't they do animal sacrifices?" I whispered, keeping a closer eye on the now-evil shop owner.

"I think so, but I can't imagine her doing anything like that in this class. I'm sure she'll just stick to the psychic medium end of things," she said.

Sandy was far calmer about all this business than I was. Having been born and raised in southern Indiana, I was a bit out of my league here. Most of my knowledge about religions like Voodoo and Santeria came from movies where people chanted around a blazing bonfire, dangling dead chickens and cutting the throats of frightened goats. I didn't want anything to do with any of it.

"Let's just see what she shows us in the first class," Sandy said, watching my expression. I glanced at the door, marking its placement in my mind like I would if I was on an airplane, listening to the flight attendant announcements.

At that moment, our conversation was interrupted by the shop owner.

"Okay, everyone who is here for the class needs to come back here," she said ushering us into a small room at the back of the store.

The room was filled with statues of gods and goddesses, candles and bells on strings, similar to the one on the front door. An altar of some sort was set up at the front of the room. Having hung around Sandy and her Wiccan friends, I recognized some of the components, but it was all still a little strange for me.

"Is she Wiccan too?" I whispered to Sandy as everyone started filing into the room.

"I think so. A lot of practitioners pick and choose between various religions. They use what resonates with them, even if it doesn't fall into their particular faith," she said. I knew some of this already. Wiccans were as diverse as many of the other belief systems. While they all believed in a god and goddess, some still also believed in the same god as in many other traditional faiths. I didn't even try to understand it. I just accepted it as something out of my range of knowledge.

As Sandy predicted, the class was largely dedicated to psychic medium development. The teacher touched on all the same topics I was already familiar with, including spirit guides, soul mates and cleansing a space with sage. As the class ended, Sandy took the woman aside and told her about our specific situation.

"He can't follow you in here. I have wards set up outside the shop," she said.

I held little faith in wards. While enduring the Soul Collector, another psychic medium had buried St. Benedict medallions at the four corners of my property that were supposed to stop ghosts from being able to come into my yard, but it hadn't been effective.

Part of me believed that the ability to successfully ward a property came from the person who lived there to begin with. If you were able to use your energy to build a spiritual barrier, the details didn't matter much. You could bury whatever you wanted and it would be successful. For someone like me, with very few gifts, nothing would work. I could hire priests to stand outside my house and the ghosts would still come in.

I was beyond frustrated by the people who told me, "Just tell them to leave and they'll leave." If that worked for me, I wouldn't have an issue to begin with. Telling them to leave just didn't cut it. It also made me a bit angry, as though the person was challenging my intelligence a bit. Asking them to leave was the first thing I did. I was a thousand steps past that point by now.

"Have you asked the Baron of the Cemetery to remove it?" the teacher asked with all seriousness.

Baron of the Cemetery?

I pictured a wizened old man sitting at the gates of the cemetery, guarding the property. It actually wasn't far from the truth, her truth anyway, with the exception that he was a bit more than wizened. He was dead.

In Voodoo, Baron Samade, the Baron of the Cemetery, was a spirit of the dead who stood sentry at cemeteries, protecting the graves.

"Take an egg and rub it all over yourself to trap the spirit inside of it. Then go to the nearest older cemetery and ask the Baron to accept it. You will need to leave a payment of eleven cents," she said in all seriousness.

"What do we do then?" Sandy asked.

"You throw the egg over your shoulder and leave. Make sure you don't look back, not even to see where the egg lands. Otherwise, the spirit might follow you back out," she said.

She handed me a small container. "Use this too. Rub it on your feet and it will prevent other ghosts from following you," she said.

I turned the container over in my hands. The white powdery substance looked like thick flour full of bone fragments.

"What is it?" I asked.

"It's a mixture of ingredients, but is mostly egg shells," she told me.

I somehow suppressed the need to roll my eyes and made a bee-line for the door.

My life was strange. I lived with a sense of weirdness that most people wouldn't grasp, but this was over the top, even for me. It was like being asked to leap over the Great Wall of China on a pogo stick with a unicorn on my back.

Sandy was willing to try it though. The next day, she called to tell me that she found fresh organic eggs at a farm stand. According to the teacher, the requirements for the eggs were specific. They had to be brown and it must have been laid before noon on the day of the ceremony.

"Meet me at my house at seven and we'll walk to the cemetery down the road from me," she told me.

The September night was cold and dark by the time I pulled into Sandy's driveway. The waning moon was nothing more than a smudge in the cloudy night sky. Thunder rumbled in the distance, which wasn't a good sign for what we were about to undertake.

I grabbed an old black hooded sweatshirt from the trunk of my car and shook it out, trying to dislodge some of the cat hair that was plastered all over it. My ex-boyfriend had always hated the cat hair that clung to my clothing, calling me "messy," but I had bigger fish to fry. Having cat hair on my hoody was the least of my problems.

Sandy came out of her house minutes later and walked down the long dark lane where my car was parked.

"Hey!" she said, obviously excited about our upcoming adventure. She was far more enthusiastic than I was. I was missing an episode of *Survivor* to be there. My couch had a way of calling to me sometimes and this was one of those moments.

She had the largest stick of sage in her hand that I'd ever seen. It must have been at least ten inches long and was the width of a roll of quarters.

"I brought my sage stick along. I thought it might help," she said. I arched my eyebrows but didn't comment. The entire scenario was getting weirder by the moment. The only thing missing was our tinfoil hats.

(Above) Rural Glen Cemetery. Photo credit: us.geoview.info

We got into my car and drove the quarter mile drive to the end of her road. I parked in the narrow lot beside the lake. People often parked there to go fishing, but tonight the lot was empty. As soon as we got out of the car, the skies above us opened up and it started pouring rain.

"Ugh!" I said. "Maybe we should do this another night," I suggested.

"No. We have to do it tonight because of the moon phase. You always do banishing rituals during the waning moon and it will be over by the end of the week," she said.

"Well, what about tomorrow night or the night after?"

"I can't. I have my Wiccan class tomorrow night and the next night I'm having dinner with Don," she said.

Sandy's schedule was usually busy, so I didn't push the issue any further. We'd just deal with it. If we got a little wet in the process, then we'd dry off later. Thankfully, I didn't have a husband or boyfriend to explain it to later when I came home looking like a drowned rat.

"Okay, then. Let's go," I said, but Sandy was still fumbling around for something in her pockets and hadn't left the car. I pulled the hood up on my sweatshirt and shoved my hands in my pockets in my attempt to stay as dry as possible.

"I want to light my sage stick first. Somehow, that seems important. It resonates with me," she said.

Any prompting for her to hurry up wouldn't have been met with a positive light, so I just bit my tongue and waited it out. With most people, my overwhelming sense of impatience would have reared its ugly head, causing me to say something I might later regret, but I was much better at suppressing it with Sandy. She had that way about her. I trusted her judgment more than I trusted most people. If she was doing it, it was for a reason and who was I to question her? After a few failed attempts, she finally got the sage lit and we were on our way.

"Here's your egg," she said, handing me the tiniest egg I'd ever seen. It looked like a wild bird egg. "They were really small. I'm not sure why."

"What are we supposed to do with them?" I asked, inspecting the egg.

"Rub it all over your body. It's supposed to capture the spirit inside," she said in all seriousness.

I watched while she proceeded to rub the egg all over her body and then grudgingly followed suit, feeling more than a bit silly. Her saving grace was the fact that the parking area was in a secluded area with very little traffic passing by. If there had been even the slightest chance that someone was watching, I would have abandoned the metaphysical mission in a heartbeat.

"How do you know when you've trapped the ghost?" I asked.

"I don't know. I think you just have to believe it happened," she said. Belief came up a lot in mediumship training. If you put your intent behind something, you empowered it. As soon as you stopped believing, you remove all chance of anything happening.

"All right. Let's go," I said to Sandy, eyeing the rain that was coming down. My cotton jacket was already soaked. I knew that within five minutes of walking alongside the highway, my shoes would be in similar shape.

Sandy took off ahead of me with her stick of sage sending plumes of smoke behind her. As the wind picked up, it began fanning the burning stick, making it glow a bright red.

Cars zipped past us, slowing slightly to gape at the sight of us, probably thinking we'd lost our minds. It wasn't a road that people typically walked alongside, especially in the pouring rain.

Each time a car passed, Sandy attempted to hide the sage stick under her jacket, but wasn't overly successful in her attempts.

"I probably look like I'm carrying the world's largest doo-bee," Sandy said, which sent me right off the edge. I started laughing so hard, I nearly peed my pants.

By the time we made the quarter mile walk to the cemetery, my face was wet with a mixture of rain and tears from laughing so hard. I had to stop several times because laughing that hard and walking were impossible for me to do at the same time. Every time a car drove past and slowed down to gawk at us, it sent me right over the edge again.

We found a bit of reprise from the rain beneath the towering trees at the cemetery entrance. Sandy pulled the eleven cents from her pocket and put it on the curb just inside the entrance.

"We call on the Baron of the Cemetery. Please take this negative entity from us and prevent him from harming anyone else," she bellowed loudly, her voice momentarily rising above the roar of the pelting rain.

With that, she turned around and lobbed the egg over her shoulder. I followed suit and we headed back out of the cemetery.

"I just hope Don is ready with the bail money after we get arrested for egging a cemetery," I said, which sent us into more peals of laughter.

As we walked, a part of me held onto the hope that what we did had an impact. I felt like a swimmer drowning in a lake, hoping for a lifeguard. I really needed this to work.

We were soaked to the bone by the time we made it back to my car. As I slipped inside the dry enclosure, I realized it was all for naught. The prison camp ghost was waiting on us. I could hear his tone.

"What now?" Sandy asked, picking up on him too.

"I don't know. This was Plan B," I said, feeling all traces of humor slip away from me.

CHAPTER 23

BARBARA WILLIAMS

Sandy and I often had what we called "out and about" days. I'd pick her up and we would just drive, following the roads until we came to something interesting. Sometimes, we just explored nearby towns and other times we went a bit further down the road. If we saw an antique store, we would stop and play our favorite game: Find the Haunted Item.

We would split up as soon as we entered the store, going into separate rooms. We then walked around the room and felt the energy that radiated off the items inside.

Most people who purchase antiques probably aren't aware that furniture and keep-sakes can come with ghostly attachments. The dead will often have a strong attachment to something they once owned and will hang around to watch over it. I've found this to be especially true with toys, tools, furniture and jewelry. People often bring home more than what they counted on.

In one particular instance, I discovered that I didn't even need to purchase the item. I skipped the preamble and just brought the ghost home instead.

I heard the buzzing sound as soon as we got into the car. Sandy must have picked up on it too because she stiffened up in her seat.

"You can't follow us! You need to go!" she stated in a voice that would have caused me to tuck tail and run, had I been the entity in question.

"Is it the guy from the tool area?" I asked, seeing a picture appear in my mind of a haggard looking man with wild grey hair and a long shaggy beard who was dressed in old fashioned denim overalls. One strap was unfastened and dangled down in front of him. Beneath it, he wore a faded white sleeveless t-shirt that we now refer to as a "wife beater" but probably had a different name back in his day. I had encountered him in a room that was filled with old tools.

"Yup. White beard and a dirty white t-shirt. He worked with machinery. I see grease under his fingernails," she said, adding in another layer of information that resonated with me.

We pulled over at the first parking lot we came to and Sandy hauled out her enormous phallic looking sage stick. While Sandy saged the interior of the car, I tried to push my energy outwards to create a bubble of protection.

Ten minutes later, he was still there.

"What now?" Sandy asked.

That was a very good question. We had already burned through all of our resources. I couldn't bring myself to trouble them again after all the other times I had asked for help.

"What about Barbara Williams?" I asked.

"We could try her, but I hate bothering her with this."

Sandy was right. Besides being one of the over-seers of Parsonsfield Seminary, Barbara was also a full time nurse with real life obligations. We had worked with her at Parsonsfield several times and found her to be amazingly gifted, but something about her always held us back from reaching out to her.

"You can contact her," I said to Sandy. "She intimidates me more than a little."

"I would, but I'm busy the next three days. It will be Thursday before I can find the time," Sandy said.

I sighed.

Some people have an essence of prominence about them. When you meet them, you simply know that you're in the presence of someone essential. Your hands might sweat and your heart might pound as you worry about saying the wrong thing. Barbara Williams was one of those people to me.

She was stoic and reserved, someone who chose her words carefully before speaking. I wouldn't hesitate in going to her with a demonic infestation because I knew she could handle it, but troubling her with a mere ghostly attachment seemed beneath her, somehow.

(Left) Barbara Williams and Joni

With her long blond hair and her piercing green eyes, she was more than just a witch with psychic powers. She almost seemed other-worldly to me. In some ways, she didn't seem human. But living with an attachment wasn't a pleasant thought. I needed to put aside my fear. When choosing between the rock and the hard place, I chose the rock.

"I'll reach out to her tonight," I said, reluctantly.

I dropped Sandy off at her house and continued home with the ghost in tow. It was beginning to feel like a familiar process. I could all but see him in the backseat, stretched out with his arms across the top of the seats, glaring at me.

The impression I got from him was that he followed me because I reminded him of someone he knew in life. I wasn't sure if it was his wife, daughter or some other woman who apparently did something to disturb his Zen, but he didn't like me. Not even a little bit.

While the attachments were disturbing, I was learning a great deal about the paranormal world. Not all ghosts were created equally.

Some had abilities, while others just buzzed in my ear, trying to get my attention or intimidate me with their presence.

From my research, I knew that it took a great deal of effort for the dead to communicate with us. Having been separated from their human body, they no longer had vocal cords to talk through or a physical body to touch with. They basically had to learn how to interconnect with the living all over again, using other forms of interaction.

In the same way that Sandy and I used our energy to create a bubble of protection, they used their energy to manipulate the physical environment. Some managed to make tapping noises on walls, while stronger ones could push an entire sofa across the room. It just depended on how much they had learned.

I seemed to be picking up ghosts in the moderate range, with the exception of the ghost from the prison camp. They had learned enough to make an impact, but not enough to do serious damage. This one was no different.

As soon as I got home, I began hearing strange taps in the other room. Being a woman who lived alone, I couldn't just dismiss every sound I heard as being paranormal in origin. I needed to check it out to insure it wasn't actually someone trying to break into my home.

Every time I would walk into the room to look, I'd find my cats staring into a corner.

"You need to leave. I'm not the woman you think I am. My name is Joni Mayhan and I was born nearly a hundred years after you died," I would say to no avail.

I turned on the light in the living room only to find it turned back off moments later.

"Nice trick, but I bet I can turn it back on much easier than you turned it off," I said, angrily snapping the switch back on. The light went off again before I could even drop my hand.

Seconds later, I felt a sharp pain in my stomach. It nearly bowled me over with its intensity. Did the ghost do this too? Could they make people ill? The question only led to more questions. If they could make me physically sick, could they also do more serious damage?

I took a deep breath and blew it out in a sigh, something I was now prone to doing on a regular basis. It was obviously time to contact Barbara Williams.

I knew her phone number, but couldn't quite bring myself to actually call her. Instead, I messaged her on Facebook, telling her about my situation. Twenty minutes later my phone rang. I was shocked to see that it was Barbara calling.

"He's gone now," she said, making me realize that I was no longer hearing the buzzing sound. I heard it so frequently; I sometimes tuned it out.

"Oh wow…thank you!" I said, practically gushing. "Who was he?"

"Just some guy attached to a tool. Were you at an antique shop today? That's where I'm picking up that you got him," she said.

I was astounded. I hadn't posted anything about our excursion on social media. There was no way she could have known that. Then, she said something that completely knocked me for a loop.

"I also took care of your stomach issue," she said.

I looked down at my stomach, realizing that the pain was now gone as well. How could she have known that?

"Oh my God! Wow! Thank you!"

"You should also make sure you cut your cords. Do it when you leave places like that so they can't follow your energy trail," she said.

During one of our investigations at Parsonsfield, she told us this. It was something I found interesting. According to Barbara, we connect ourselves to both the living and the dead with cords of energy. With the living, this causes us to often feel the other person's thoughts and emotions. This is also true for the dead, with the added ability to track us down, as well. They used it like an ethereal highway.

I had two options on cutting the cords. I could either call on Archangel Michael and ask him to do it for me, or I could do it myself. Sometimes, I even did both, just to be assured it was done. Unfortunately, it was something I often forgot to do.

I thanked Barbara for her help and we ended the call.

I tried to use her several more times after that, but often had a difficult time getting a hold of her. Due to her busy schedule, she wasn't on social media frequently and my calls went to voice mail. She always responded, but by the time she got back to me, I had usually already found another solution.

"I wish she lived closer. We could just jump in the car and drive to her house. Maybe she could teach us how to take care of this ourselves," Sandy said on more than one occasion.

"Yeah, I know." Barbara lived in Maine, which was nearly three hours away.

This time was different, though. The prison guard attachment was actively jumping back and forth between the two of us. By the time several weeks had passed, I was at my wits end.

"He's doing something to me to make my body vibrate," I told Sandy. I couldn't fully explain how it felt, but the sensation was similar to lying on one of those old-fashioned "magic finger" beds you used to see in motel rooms. You would plug in a quarter and the bed would vibrate. That was happening to me without benefit of the massage.

The experience was horrifying, usually happening when I went to bed at night.

My bedroom was already a horror chamber, but now it was even worse. As soon as I would rest my head on my pillow, the buzzing sound would grow louder as he came closer. I could feel the shape of him, almost as though he was blocking out the air in the room, creating a void. Then, the vibrations would start.

It sent me into a full panic because I didn't know what it meant. Was he trying to get inside of me?

I raced from my bedroom and curled up on the couch, watching the doorway in terror. I tried burning sage and spraying myself with holy water. I put various protective stones in my pocket and wore crucifixes around my neck. I recited the Lord's Prayer so many times, I could say it without thinking about the words. I even started reciting the Prayer to Michael the Archangel, asking him to protect me. Nothing worked. The vibrations continued.

I reached out to Sandy, who confirmed she was still getting visitations as well. "He's only coming to me now at night after you go to bed, but I'm not getting that vibrational thing. Maybe it's just getting too close to you and you're feeling its vibration," Sandy offered.

I knew that ghosts vibrated at a different frequency than the living and that ghosts needed to sometimes raise their vibrational rate in order to communicate with us, but I wasn't convinced this was what was happening. It felt more intrusive, more like being raped without the sexual aspects.

"Try shielding yourself and see if you can push it away with your energy," she said.

I tried it that night and found that I was able to push him off for several seconds at a time. I couldn't hold it for long though. After a few moments of relief, he was back again.

I tried to research it, but couldn't find a single article to explain what I was feeling.

By the time I finally broke down and messaged Barbara, I was an internal mess. I couldn't sleep. I couldn't focus during the day and

I was beginning to make mistakes at work. I began forgetting to fill in reports and often remembered conference calls minutes before they began, leaving me unprepared for my expected presentations. If this continued, I'd be out of a job.

My timing couldn't have been better. She called me almost immediately.

"Try pushing it out yourself," she said. "You're powerful enough to do this, Joni. Just give it a little nudge and send it on its way," she said.

I closed my eyes and sighed.

"I've tried that. I've tried a lot of things, but nothing works," I told her.

"Okay," she said, the tone in her voice filled with disappointment. "I'll see what I can do, but you should probably work on it on your end as well." She offered to send me a CD with a recording of Oms on it and told me to play it every night while saging my entire house. She explained that sound is also cleansing and the Oms often did more than the sage.

At that point, I didn't know an Om from an Ohm and took to the internet to research it. What I found was that Oms were a form of sacred meditation, with the words representing a myriad of elements. When chanted by Buddhist monks, they resonate through the universe like ripples on a lake. In my case, it was supposed to cleanse and calm down my space.

By the time I got the CD in the mail, I was nearly to my breaking point. The vibration sensation was worse and he seemed to be gaining energy from me, allowing him to perform even more ghostly tricks.

One night, I climbed into bed and watched as the covers were slowly pulled off me. They landed with a plop at the foot of my bed. I raced out of my room, feeling like I was trapped in a bizarre horror movie.

For someone like Barbara, exterminating this ghost would have been easy, but I wasn't nearly as gifted. It was like having someone with a V8 engine telling me to follow her up a steep hill on nothing but roller skates.

After I received the CD, I followed her instructions to the letter but didn't see any improvements in my situation. Nothing changed. I called Barbara after a week of it.

"Well, we have an event coming up at ParSem next month. Why don't you come to that and we'll see what we can do," she suggested.

Relief was in sight, but I wasn't sure I could make it that long.

Chapter 24

The Living Nightmare

A month was a long time to deal with a negative ghostly attachment, especially after having already lived with it for several months beforehand.

Every night was like being trapped inside of a nightmare I couldn't wake up from. His buzzing tone followed me everywhere I went and he took delight in frightening me at every opportunity. Light switches turned back off seconds after I turned them on, bangs pounded on walls as I walked past. It was as if he had full access to my internal data base and was fingering through my fears one by one.

When I climbed into bed, something often climbed in with me. I could feel the bed sink down and hear the springs squeak with weight. Invisible fingers often stroked my cheek or ran through my hair while I was absorbed in my work. I was being stalked by an invisible monster.

If this had been my first attachment, it would have been horrifying enough, but it wasn't. It only served to remind me of my terrifying months at the hand of the Soul Collector.

As I sat there at my keyboard, attempting to focus on a report I needed to complete for work, the similarities struck me like a slap against the side of my head.

This attachment came from the same place that the Soul Collector came from and was doing many of the same things.

Was it possible? Could this be the same entity?

My breath caught in my throat as the memories flooded my mind.

"No. It can't be him," I whispered to myself.

Leesa and her coven had bound and banished him. They sent him to a place where he could never hurt another soul.

But what if they didn't?

What if they only sent him back to the prison camps and I simply picked him back up again?

The thought was terrifying and put a brand new spin on my waking nightmare. I knew better than to allow myself to feel fear, but I couldn't help the onslaught of horror I felt. I wasn't sure I had the energy to fight him twice.

The first time had left me frail and weak. If this was him again, I wasn't sure I could survive it. Tears stung my eyes as I considered everything I was facing.

My email notification made a dinging sound, pulling me back to reality. I tried to shake off the apprehension and bring myself back to my work, but the thoughts were never far away.

As if hoping to capitalize on my realization, the entity continued to make noises in the other room. The minute I shoved the thoughts aside and focused on my work, he did something to remind me that he was still there.

My cell phone rang from inside my pocket and I nearly jumped out of my skin. I pulled it out and looked at it. It was Kaden.

"I'm just calling to check on you. Have things calmed down any?" he asked.

I wanted to tell him about my realization but held back, not wanting to empower this thing any more than I already had. Instead, I told him what Barbara said.

"That's a long time to wait," he said. "Why don't I come over again and see what I can do in the meantime," he offered.

I hated to get two mediums involved in the same issue, but waiting a month seemed like an eternity, especially if my suspicions were correct. I readily agreed.

***

I wasn't a very practiced hostess. I knew how to cook, but my introvert status prevented me from actually hosting or attending very many parties. The only experiences I had was from the family gatherings I had attended while I was married.

When I thought of those, I nearly froze with a brand new flavor of terror. My former mother-in-law would cook for days before presenting delectable trays of food that could have been featured on the cover of magazines. Never in a million years could I hope to pull something like that off. The best I could hope for was avoiding giving everyone food poisoning.

Still though, I decided to give it a try. I told Kaden that we would have a cook out when he came out. I put a quick call into Sandy and invited her to come over for moral support. She also brought the potato salad, which insured that there would be something edible at my party.

The results were predictable. I burnt the hamburgers and served baked beans that had gone cold by the time the burgers were charred, but nobody complained. They ate double helpings of Sandy's store-bought potato salad and smiled with fake pleasure. After we choked down our food, Kaden decided to walk through the house to see what he was feeling.

"He's been here with us since we sat down," he said, as he rose from the table.

"What do you feel? Is it the prison camp guard…or something else?" I asked, desperate for more details. I didn't want to sway him. If I told him that I suspected it was the Soul Collector, he might not be able to get a clear reading of his own.

"I don't think he's from the prison camps. I think he belongs to the house," he said, which went along with what Leesa had told me years ago. Maybe I was wrong. Maybe this was something different.

Entities sometimes tried to appear as something different, hoping to send you into a full blown anxiety attack. Then, they could feed off that fear and become even more powerful. If that was the case, then he could be attempting to dupe me. I felt myself relax a little.

"Is he an older guy with a beer gut?" I asked.

"No. I'm seeing a younger guy. Mid-twenties. Light brown hair and a t-shirt. Let me walk around a bit and see what else I can pull," he said.

I followed around behind him like an eager puppy looking for a head-scratch, hanging on his words. Sandy held back and stayed in the kitchen. When we returned, she nodded towards my basement door.

"You should have him check out your basement again," she suggested.

I wrinkled my nose. My basement was the worst part of my house. It was the last place I wanted to bring my guests.

The strong stinging odor of mold and mildew hit you as you descended the rickety stairs. By the time you hit ground zero, it became apparent that the basement wasn't hospitable for human life. Everything down there was damp to the touch, even the concrete walls. My efforts of turning one of the rooms into a home office had been quickly abandoned after I came down with a severe case of bronchitis. It was a curious space though.

On the floor in one of the rooms was a place where the floor had been patched. It looked like the doorway to a secret sub-basement room, something I found intriguing. As soon as we entered that room, I pointed towards it.

"What do you think about that?" I asked.

It didn't take Kaden long to respond. "I think a body was buried under there."

I probably gasped because that had been my initial thought too after I first moved into the house. I dismissed it because it was so outlandish, but the prospects returned to me every time I went in there.

"Is it the young guy you've been seeing?" I asked.

"I think so. I see an argument and possibly a fight. I think he was struck on the head and they panicked, not knowing what to do. So, they buried him here and then patched up the floor."

There were a lot of questions I could have asked, but none more important than the first one that rose in my mind. "Can you get rid of him?"

"I can try."

He closed his eyes and frowned, while Sandy and I watched him. He was boyishly young, looking nothing like what I would expect a psychic medium to resemble. Sandy caught my eye and arched her eyebrows. Could it really be this easy? Could he just move the ghost along?

I began fantasizing about actually going into my bedroom and sleeping without being molested by a ghost. I imagined changing into my sleep clothes and then lying there with a good book until I began feeling sleepy. It seemed like such a normal thing, but nothing was normal about my life. Simple pleasures were more elusive than lottery wins.

Kaden opened his eyes again and my dreams were swept away like fairy dust.

"He's not budging," he said, finally. "Maybe I can at least bind him to the basement. That way he can't bother you."

He closed his eyes again and worked his magic. When he opened them again, he nodded towards the stairs.

"Let's go on upstairs. I think he's bound down here now."

We climbed the stairs one by one, squinting at the brightness of the kitchen as we emerged from the dank shadows. Kaden didn't hang around long after that. He needed to get home to meet a friend, so we said our goodbyes.

An hour later, I received a phone call from Barbara Williams.

"Did you have Kaden out to your house?" she asked.

The question shouldn't have rocked me to my core after her phone call regarding my stomach issues, but I still found myself a bit flabbergasted.

"Yes," I mumbled, feeling the full weight of the situation. "He just left an hour ago."

"Why would you do that? Kaden just made him angry, trying to bind him to the basement," she told me, her stiletto words striking me like pellets. "The entity was feeding him misinformation in hopes of redirecting him. Now, he's going to be even harder to get rid of. He thinks that Kaden is too young and inexperienced. He only wants to communicate with you or with me."

The shame that came over me was enveloping and consuming, eating me from the inside out. Why did I do that? I had enlisted Barbara's help, but had allowed another medium in the middle of it. I felt like someone who had cheated on her spouse.

"I'm sorry. It's just been horrible, living with this and Kaden offered to come out…" I started, but she stopped me short.

"I'm going to try to set up a contract with him. I'll let you know how that goes," she said and we ended the call.

My life was quickly spinning out of control. I usually didn't let stress get the better of me. I always looked for the silver lining in situations and latched onto them with both hands until I managed to pull myself out. This was different. It was so far out of my league, it might have been a *Twilight Zone* episode. How did I get myself into these things?

Barbara's last comment rang in my head. She was going to set up a contract with him? I had no idea something like that was even feasible. What would keeping my end of the bargain entail?

I put my phone back in my pocket and tried to go on with my evening. The cats needed to be fed and the dog was begging for a walk.

Life went on, like it usually did. It didn't stop for anyone, especially with needy pets thrown into the mix. After feeding the felines, I slipped the leash around Ripley's neck and headed to the small park across the street.

The sun was sinking into the horizon, casting a rosy glow across the sky. A definite chill was in the air, reminding me that autumn was nearing an end with winter hanging on its shirttails. I needed to get rid of this attachment before the first flakes of snow fell from the sky. If I didn't, I wasn't sure I could survive a long cold winter with my invisible houseguest.

I was so mentally exhausted that I fell into a deep sleep and didn't wake until morning. Barbara's call came several hours after I woke up.

"He's agreed to a contract," she said matter-of-factly, as though we were discussing a business contract between the living and not an agreement with the dead.

"Okay…" I started to say, but she continued, obviously still peeved about what I did.

"He will leave you alone if you set a time and agree to communicate with him," she said.

Thoughts about the Soul Collector rose to my mind, but I pushed them back down. I had to trust her. Surely she wouldn't put me in a dangerous position.

"How do I communicate with him?" I asked. All he'd been doing so far was scaring me to the point where I nearly peed my pants every fifteen seconds. Now, he was going to talk to me?

"Telepathically. Just use your mind. You can do it, Joni. You have far more abilities than you give yourself credit for," she said in all seriousness. "What I want you to do is spend a few minutes in your room and tell him about your intentions. Set up a specific time to communicate with him and then do it."

I hung up the phone and stared into space for a moment, my head spinning with what she told me. Something about it felt very wrong. I wanted to distance myself from this beast, not try to befriend it. Running and screaming seemed like far better options, but I had to trust Barbara. I had to.

I had a conference call for work coming up in a half hour that I hadn't even started preparing for. I checked my schedule and saw a gap just after lunch.

"Okay, here goes nothing," I said to myself and pushed myself away from my desk.

I approached my bedroom like I was walking up on a coiled snake. I sat on the edge of my bed and stared at the corner where his tone radiated from.

"I will agree to communicate with you at one o'clock, but you need to back off and leave me alone," I said.

There wasn't a response, not that I expected any. I guess in the back of my mind, I had hoped for a tap on the wall or some sort of acknowledgement, but I didn't get it. I returned to my desk and tried hard to absorb myself in my job, but thoughts of the monster in my bedroom wouldn't leave me.

I imagined getting on my conference call and apologizing to everyone for my lack of preparation, telling them that the ghost in my room wouldn't let me work. It was the metaphysical equivalent to "the dog ate my homework," so I didn't bother.

I somehow got through the call without too many battle wounds and found myself parked in my bedroom at the agreed time.

"Okay. I'm here. What do you want to tell me?" I asked, hoping for something to come to me.

The buzzing grew closer, but no further information flooded my mind. I sat there for ten full minutes until I heard the distinct sound of my work phone ringing. I pulled myself off my bed to catch the call.

The rest of the day found me elbow deep in work issues. Thankfully, I was barely aware of the ghost for the remainder of the afternoon. More than likely, he hadn't backed off, but was prevented from fully gaining my attention due to my encompassing work issues. By evening, I was exhausted, both mentally and physically. When Barbara called, I was almost to a breaking point.

"He tried to communicate with you, but you weren't responding," she told me.

If I didn't respect, and possible fear Barbara so much, I probably would have chosen that moment to completely lose my shit. Instead, I took a deep breath and blew it out in a sigh.

"I tried, Barbara, but nothing came to me."

"You have to try harder. Open yourself up. You can do this, Joni," she said. "Are you still doing your Oms every night?"

"I am. Nothing seems to be helping. I need help, Barbara. I can't keep doing this. It's a complete and total nightmare for me. I'm not as gifted as you are. I can't do the things you can do."

This time it was her who sighed.

I expected another well-meant lecture, but she surprised me instead.

"Why don't you plan on coming out to ParSem next weekend. We'll set something up and have people out to investigate. Maybe we can help you there," she said.

Those were the words I was hoping for.

Now, I just had to get through the next ten days.

CHAPTER 25

THE EXTRACTION

I woke up the next morning with a brand new determination. I wasn't going to let this thing rule my life. If I could learn how to push it away, I could save myself from a lifetime of attachments. After all, what would happen once this one was gone?

I'd already experienced that answer, several times in fact. As soon as one left, another appeared. It was almost as though I had a deli number machine posted outside my house and they were just waiting their turns. I needed to learn how to take control of this before it pushed me over the edge.

I began working on pushing my energy in earnest. Whenever I felt his vibrations course through my body, I focused my energy and attempted to send it through my third-eye. After several attempts, I learned that I could actually hold him off for several minutes at a time.

The relief was immense. I could have won a Nobel Peace Prize and it wouldn't have felt any more rewarding.

The more I was successful at it, the stronger I became. Was it possible that I was disconnecting him from his energy source? When I felt that sensation, did it mean that he was pulling energy from me? The results were fairly staggering. The more I pushed him off, the less I began feeling him around.

Elated by this development, I tried to call Sandy to tell her, but my call went to voice mail. I tried again the next day, only to get the same results. This was troubling to me. Sandy almost always called me back, especially after what we'd been going through.

With her history of depression, there was always the possibility that she had hit another snag and was swimming in a pit of despair.

When she got that way, she often holed herself up inside her house and stopped communicating with everyone. If this was one of those cases, I felt a strong need to help her. I jumped in my car and drove to her house.

It was a quiet Saturday morning. The leaves were beginning their voyage into full autumn glory. As the sun shone through them, it created a kaleidoscope of color that beamed down onto the blacktop. I felt as though I was driving through a fairy land. By the time I pulled up in Sandy's driveway, my spirits were high. I hadn't found the cure for cancer or created world peace, but I might have found a way for us to live our lives with less fear and aggravation.

I pounded on the door for an eternity before Sandy finally answered. She looked exactly like death warmed over.

She wore an old bathrobe and her hair stood up in twenty different places, as though she just rolled out of bed. Even more disturbing was the expression in her eyes. She looked utterly hopeless.

"Are you okay?" I asked.

"No. I'm going through a rough spot," she said, glancing away from my gaze, as though the simple process of maintaining eye contact was too much for her.

"I'm sorry for just showing up, but I was worried about you when you didn't return my calls."

I would have done anything to pull her out of her funk, but I knew that this wasn't something I had any control over. A bright sunny day would be wasted on her when she was in this place.

"Come on in," she said and turned to go back inside.

I followed her up the narrow stairs to her kitchen door where I was greeted by the sight of fleeing cats.

Over the years, Sandy had coaxed several feral cats inside and made them pets. Even though they had seen me numerous times, they still ran away and hid. I always made it my goal to befriend them, despite their obvious reluctance. She led me into her sunroom.

"What's going on?" I asked.

"I think your attachment came to me. I've tried ordering it out of the house and calling on my spirit guides for help but nothing happened. I'm too depleted to try to push it out," she said.

I told her about my efforts at pushing him off and she shook her head.

"Maybe that's why he switched to me. You're getting stronger, and I'm pretty weak right now. If that's what happened, then I'm really screwed because I can't fight it at all."

The thought made me beyond angry. This attachment was an opportunist. He was jumping back and forth between us, finding the weaker link. Sometimes it was me and other times it was Sandy. We had to put a stop to him.

"Barbara Williams wants us to come out next weekend. She's going to set up an investigation at ParSem and is going to bring in some mediums to help us," I told her.

The news seemed to brighten her, at least a little bit, but we still had a week to wait it out. I stayed and chatted with her for a few more minutes, but it was apparent she wasn't up for company. I apologized for barging in and headed back home, feeling worse than I had when I left.

We had to do something about this ghost. If he continued attacking us, the results weren't going to be good. He seemed to be getting stronger and smarter, knowing where to land his blows. By attacking Sandy and sending her into another bout of depression, he was learning how to gain a foothold on her psyche. This went far beyond making taps on the walls and turning off light switches. He had found a place where he could actually inflict some real damage.

The similarities between this ghost and the Soul Collector were becoming clearer all the time. The Soul Collector got to me in a similar way, wearing me down and then attempting to take me over. My entire personality had started to change with thoughts of suicide penetrating into my normally optimistic mind. If we didn't stop him soon, I worried that the same thing would happen to Sandy.

I came through the door and patted Ripley on the head. The cats were sleeping in pools of sunlight on the back of the couch and barely opened their eyes to acknowledge me. I stood for a moment and just listened to the house.

The refrigerator hummed softly and the clock made a steady tick-tock as it marked the time. Somewhere in the neighborhood a chain saw roared to life, bringing to mind the upcoming winter season. I imagined someone cutting up a fallen tree into hunks they could later split for firewood. Everything seemed so normal it was a bit unnerving.

I walked around and listened for the tone of the prison guard, but couldn't hear him. Several of the other ghosts I had collected over the course of the past few years acknowledged me, but he wasn't there. Apparently, my efforts had paid off for me, but had backfired in the worst possible way.

I messaged Barbara and explained the situation. She promised to pull him off of us to give us a well needed breather.

During this same period of time, I had become involved with the Haunted Victorian Mansion in Gardner, Massachusetts, which would later become the subject of my book *Bones in the Basement – Surviving the S.K. Pierce Haunted Victorian Mansion*. Despite my issues with attachments, I was still intrigued by the mansion and found myself drawn there at every opportunity.

The house had already been on several paranormal television shows by that point and interest in the house was high. I loved having an inside perspective on the haunting and spent as much time there as possible to try to learn more.

(Above) Joni in front of the Haunted Victorian Mansion

Some of the activity there was concerning though. The ghosts were capable of doing things I didn't think were possible. Not only could they slam two-hundred pound doors, but they could also appear as apparitions, something that scared me more than a little. As a paranormal investigator, seeing a full body apparition was considered to be the Holy Grail. It was what we all longed for every time we walked into an investigation. Seeing one at my home wasn't my idea of fun though.

If ghosts could read our thoughts like Barbara said they could, then could they also use that information against us? I wasn't sure I could survive a visual sighting that popped up unexpectedly. Hearing them, seeing shadows and knowing they were there was one thing, but actually having a full color visual confirmation would be taking things a bit too far.

I tried to tuck that information away in a place he couldn't access, but it was hard keeping it in place. It rose to the surface every time I heard him pop in. I just continued to push my energy and force him back out, hoping he wasn't just jumping back to Sandy again.

By the time the weekend arrived, I was more than ready.

I pulled up to Sandy's house early that Saturday and found her with her back pressed against the giant oak tree in her front yard. She often used the tree to help her ground her energy, sending the excess into the ground where it could be recycled.

Over the years, I had really latched onto the concept of grounding too, but I did it in a different way than Sandy did. I used my breathing. I would imagine pure white light hovering above me. As I took a breath, I pulled it into the crown of my head and exhaled the negative gunk that bogged me down through my feet and into the ground.

"Grounding?" I asked as she opened her eyes.

"Yeah. I really needed it," she said, pulling herself away from the tree. She looked a little bit better than she did the last time I saw her, but it was always hard to read Sandy. She was a chameleon at adapting to her environment. She often hid her depression behind a smiling facade.

"Hopefully, Barbara can help us," I told her as she got in the car.

"I hope so," she said, her voice telling me more than her words had. We had clung to hope for so long that it was becoming an abstract concept. Help came frequently, but it didn't always live up to the expectation. Opportunities often just led to more disappointments.

We always loved taking road trips together because it gave us a large chunk of time to talk. We usually discussed the paranormal world and the information we had uncovered during our time away from one another. This time was no different.

"I read something you might find interesting," I told her. "We already know that ghosts follow us because they recognize us as someone they can possibly communicate with, but what if it goes even deeper?"

"How so?"

"What if Barbara is right about us? What if we are both more powerful than we realize? It could be something that's imprinted on our energy, something they can read."

"I talked to Barbara earlier in the week and she thinks the reason we're being so beset with spirits is that we've never learned to shut down our psychic ability. She was clear that she does want to teach us and work with us because she knows we need someone to teach us this stuff. I think she'll commit to that, just not on our timetable. She told me she works 15-hour days and has an hour commute each way, so she must be pretty tapped out at night."

"It's a lot to ask of her. I just don't know where else to turn at this point," I said.

Sandy and I had been tracking the entity for over a month, sending each other emails when we felt him come into our space. One time, I was at the movies and felt him there. As soon as I left, I lost track of him and later learned that he had jumped to Sandy at the exact time the movie let out.

"I guess the magnets didn't end up being helpful either," Sandy said, which made me laugh. She had read somewhere that the polarity of magnets could create an energy field that ghosts didn't like. We tried putting hematite magnets on our bedframes and even put them together north to south, which caused them to push away from one another. At first, the results were positive, but that soon wore off like everything else we tried. We joked about being old ladies sitting in our magnet-covered wheel chairs at the nursing home, wearing our tinfoil hats. Unfortunately, it was looking like a potential reality.

"No. They worked for a while, but they don't do anything now. I tried sleeping on my stomach and that helped keep him from making my body vibrate for two nights before it stopped working too," I said.

"This is becoming a nightmare," she said and we allowed her words to settle in for a while.

I kept going back to what I read earlier. If the ghosts realized we had some sort of undiscovered abilities, it would make sense that they would follow us. What could it be though?

"I talked about us possibly being gifted. What if they know that we can help them, but we don't know that yet?" I asked.

"Like how? Helping them cross over, maybe?"

That was a concept I hadn't considered. "Maybe Barbara can work with us on that," I suggested. We had watched Barbara cross over rooms filled with ghosts before, so I knew it could be done. I just wasn't sure I was capable of learning how to do it.

By the time we pulled up to Parsonsfield Seminary, we had nearly talked ourselves out. Circling around the unknown was like being caught in a never-ending cyclone. We just spun in circles, never making any headway.

We found Barbara inside the old schoolhouse building, chatting with several other people. I recognized them from previous investigations and was thrilled she had pulled in so many talented mediums.

One of Barbara's mediums was my friend Kaden. I was so happy to see him there, working with Barbara. I was worried that I had damaged his relationship with Barbara, but I could see that wasn't the case. He gave me a warm hug.

"We're going to finally get rid of this guy. Are you ready for this?" he asked, his eyes nearly sparkling with delight.

"I'm more than ready," I said, praying this would work.

Barbara parted from her group and made her way to us. She was dressed from head to toe in various shades of purple, which I knew was her signature color. Purple has immense metaphysical properties, something she used to help her in her work.

"Oh, there you are!" she said with a smile. She pulled us both in for hugs. "Has it been a rough week for you?"

Our groans served as our responses.

"Well, let's get to this before the investigation starts," she said and began corralling her mediums into a back room of the building.

Sandy and I exchanged weary glances. Could it really be this easy? After several months of torture, could we shake him off once and for all?

Barbara sat us in chairs with our backs together. The group of mediums surrounded us, locking their hands together.

"Left hand over right," she said to them and they readjusted their hands. "The left hand sends energy and the right hand receives it. It's important to remember this," she said. Her words served to remind me that we weren't the only people Barbara was helping. Despite her 15 hour work days and her long commute, she was also mentoring several budding mediums. She was collecting people just like we were collecting ghosts.

"I call on the guardians of the four corners. Archangel Michael in the south, Archangel Gabriel in the west, Archangel Uriel in the north and Archangel Raphael in the east. Please surround us with your protection," she said.

The room seemed to fill with impossibly bright energy. Even if I couldn't see the angels around us, I could feel the hairs on the back of my neck rise.

"Now, close your eyes and fill the circle with white light," Barbara said.

The mediums closed their eyes as the energy in the room built to an even higher level. Despite the chill in the air, sweat rose on several brows as they focused their energy.

The sound of the prison guard swirled around, as though trapped inside the circle. I could almost feel him bashing against the sides.

After a few minutes, nothing seemed to change. The energy fluctuated, rising and then falling as the mediums became drained.

"We're going to have to try something else," Barbara said, finally. "This isn't working."

"He's really determined," someone else commented.

"Let me call in something else. That should work," Barbara told them.

At that moment, it was as if the Heavens themselves opened up. I closed my eyes at the intensity of the moment. Energy swirled around us, churning and picking up speed as it rotated. My ears began ringing with a bell-like tone that sounded like metal striking a goblet. It was so loud, it nearly split my eardrums. I didn't know how much more I could take.

I added my energy to the group, pushing with all my might, hoping to nudge them off the edge and force the entity to release his foothold. Behind me, Sandy was doing the same. I could feel her orange-hued rays spiking out of her like fireworks.

The entity fought back with everything it had. I could feel its anger lashing out at us, clawing the sides of the energy field with invisible talons. Then, with a pop, the sound stopped and the energy faded.

I opened my eyes to a brand new world. I was so filled with love and light, I wanted to cry.

"Is it over?" I asked, praying for the answer I'd been seeking for so very long.

"Yes. He's gone," Barbara said. They broke the circle and collected themselves, looking like weary soldiers who had just returned from battle.

"That was so cool. It ate him!" Kaden said.

"It what?" I asked, sad that I hadn't been able to see the visual of what had transpired.

"The thing that Barbara called in swallowed him whole. That was so cool," he said.

I tried to get someone to elaborate on what Barbara had called in, but nobody would explain it to me, as though it was some big secret. Even though I was insanely curious about it, I let it go.

The group spent a few minutes hugging each other and talking about their experience. I found Sandy and gave her a hug.

"I can't believe he's gone," I said, feeling my eyes fill with tears. After months of living in that horrible nightmare, the prison guard was finally gone.

"Now, we just have to work on keeping others from attaching to us," she said, which kind of took the wind out of my sails. She was right though. This one was gone, which might just mean that a new spot was opened for another one to jump into.

Barbara parted through the group and touched both of our shoulders. I could feel her energy sink into my skin, reaffirming my belief that she was far more powerful than I had ever imagined. She then told me something that would nearly bring me to my knees.

"I didn't want to tell you this until it was gone, but that entity – the one that attached to both of you for the past few months – was the Soul Collector," she said.

Cold chills rippled up and down my arms.

"When Leesa bound and banished him, she simply stripped him of his collection of souls and sent him back to the prison camps. You picked him up again when you went back out there," she said.

The horrified expression on my face prompted her to continue.

"Don't worry. He's truly gone now. We took care of him," she said.

Sweeter words had never been spoken.

Unfortunately, Sandy was right in her assessment. Now that he was finally gone, it made room for the others that wanted in. Our battle was far from over. In fact, it had just begun.

I would swiftly move from ghosts to demons.

CHAPTER 26

ONTO THE NEXT

I'd been strangely drawn to the Haunted Victorian Mansion in Gardner, Massachusetts since the first time I saw it. I already knew that a house in Gardner had been on the paranormal television show, *Ghost Hunters,* but since I seldom visited the town, I didn't know where it was. Then as if by chance, I started dating a local guy who showed me a shortcut across town. It led me directly past the huge Second Empire Victorian Mansion.

The first time I set eyes on it, my breath was swept away.

That's the house, I thought to myself with a sense of awe.

I wanted more. I wanted to walk inside of it and see the beautiful architecture. I wanted to know if it was really haunted. I wanted to know why it was for sale. I kept my eye on it for several years, making excuses to drive past. When fate intervened again, I had an opportunity to investigate there through a public ghost hunt.

I was mesmerized by what I saw. The house was even more grandiose on the inside than I expected, especially considering the rapidly deteriorating exterior. The rooms inside were garnished with elaborate hand-carved woodwork. Every door was a work of art; every doorknob was a slice of history. I tried to imagine how many people had put their hand where my hand was, how many lives passed through these doors, and how many of them never left.

Over the course of a year, I would investigate there three more times. When I overheard the owners talking about a Halloween Haunted House tour, I quickly volunteered to help. I spent several evenings at the mansion, helping to decorate, and then fought a surprise October blizzard to be there for the seven hour tour. For the next few years, I would find ways to be there, whether it was to help with investigations and tours, or to help the caretaker shovel snow, or walk through periodically during the long winters when the mansion was closed. In all honesty, it became an obsession to me.

(Above) Joni on the grand staircase of the Haunted Victorian Mansion, her "home away from home"

Being intuitive, I had a deeper connection with the souls at the house than was probably healthy. I felt bad for them, having to go through investigation after investigation. I talked to them, explaining that the funds that we raised would be invested into well-needed house repairs. I began helping with fundraising events and connected the owners to a friend of mine who did websites. I found a contractor who promised to donate his time to do some of the repairs. I even blogged about my experiences and defended the owners when they were under attack from several members of the paranormal community. I never turned down a chance to be there.

Sandy noticed it and worried about me. "You need to make a break from that house. It has an unnatural hold on you," she told me.

I didn't disagree, but I was like an addict, needing a fix. "You are probably right," I'd tell her, and then make plans to be there the following weekend. Even after my friend MJ had a strange dream about me, I still couldn't pull myself away.

In the dream, she saw me working in the nursery, while a ghost in the room told her that I wasn't allowed to leave. He told her that I belonged to the house now. Most people would have listened to something as potentially prophetic as that, but not me.

One October afternoon, I promised MJ that I'd bring her to see the house. She'd always wanted to see the inside, but couldn't make it to the numerous investigations that were hosted there because she had small children at home. By this time, I was writing a book for the owners about their experiences, so I wanted to stop by for another interview.

The day started fine, but the closer I got to the house, things began happening to prevent me from arriving. It started with a migraine.

Normally, a migraine would knock me out for the entire day, but I managed to get rid of it by swallowing massive amounts of migraine relief tables. Even though I normally didn't get migraines in the mornings, I didn't think anything about it.

(Above) Mary-Jane O'Dou "MJ" with Joni at the Haunted Victorian Mansion

I got into my car and plugged MJ's address into my GPS, but it didn't recognize her address. I had to call her to get some old-fashioned directions. Even then, I found myself driving around in circles, trying to find the right road.

"What else can happen?" I mumbled to myself. Seconds later, my phone rang. It was the owner of the Victorian calling to tell me he was going to be late.

As soon as I hung up, I realized that I didn't have a key to the house. We would have to wait outside until he arrived, which could be hours after the agreed upon time, if past experiences were repeated. I then realized I was hearing the buzzing sound in my ears. Was something paranormal behind all the strange circumstances?

I had spent quite a few months working with Barbara Williams on honing my abilities. Through a lot of trial and error, I learned to differentiate between the sounds I was hearing.

I knew that a ghost made a tone that was similar in pitch and clarity to static or white noise. A spirit, someone who had crossed over into the white light, had a pure high pitch. The tone I was now hearing was high-pitched, making me wonder who was with me. Was it a spirit guide? A relative who had passed on? I didn't know, but it gave me the impression that it wasn't happy with me.

I've been told that we all have spirit guides or guardian angels that look after us. After working with Kaden, I knew that mine was young and inexperienced. She must have spent most of her time shaking her head at all the places I brought her.

When we finally arrived at the Victorian, everything grew silent. The ringing stopped completely, which felt like a relief at the time. I imagined her sitting on the curb with her head in her hands, wondering where she'd gone wrong being assigned to me.

We had an enjoyable evening sitting around the kitchen table talking with the owner and friends of the Victorian. A group had booked the mansion for an investigation, so we tried to stay out of their way out of respect for their evidence, knowing that when someone is walking around, it causes contamination on the audio and video recordings. MJ and I waited until they broke for dinner and made a mad dash to the master bedroom for an EVP session.

We spent about fifteen minutes there, speaking freely to several ghosts in the room, before moving to the third floor Billiards Room. I made the mistake of calling the male ghost forward to talk. He didn't seem very happy, responding with a derogatory comment that was filled with swear words.

As I left that night, I could hear the sounds of several tones in the car with me. None of them were spirits. They were all ghosts. It was enough to make my skin crawl.

"You need to go back to where you came from," I demanded several times. Being appropriately cautious, I'd burned sage before and after leaving the mansion, I said several prayers and even carried religious totems to help keep me protected. None of them worked. I had a car full of ghosts.

Since evicting the Soul Collector for the second time, I was pleased to have my bedroom all to myself. Gone were the constant feelings of being watched and everything else that goes along with a haunting. It wouldn't last for long.

Over the course of the next few days, I watched my sunny bedroom become dark, as though the light were being sucked away into a vacuum. The ghost tones came and went, causing my cats to watch invisible shapes move around the room.

On Wednesday night, as I was taking a bath, one of my cats yelped from outside the door. When I found him cowering on the stairs, I carried him to my room, where he refused to leave my side. My other cat kept coming up to sniff him, as if something was wrong. Seldom do I turn on ghost hunting equipment in my own house, but I needed to know if it was paranormal or not.

"What happened to my cat?" I asked the Ovilus.

"Squeeze" it said. I got chills from head to toe.

I woke the next morning with the feeling of someone lingering very close. The ear ringing was so loud, I couldn't hear anything else. Suddenly, I felt something grab both sides of my head and squeeze. The sensation wasn't painful, but it was alarming. I jumped up and told it to stop.

"Just leave me alone!" I told it, wanting to get another few minutes of sleep. It was bad enough that the cats were frequently waking me up before my alarm, wanting breakfast, but now ghosts? The reprieve only lasted a few minutes before it was repeated.

After I finished my coffee, I knew I needed to do something. I put a message out to Barbara Williams.

Barbara never ceased to amaze me with her abilities. Instead of simply moving the ghosts out of my space, she did something very interesting. If I hadn't witnessed it myself, I probably wouldn't have believed it.

She contacted two other mediums and set up a remote cross-over session. We would all work together to open up a white light and encourage the ghosts to cross through it.

As the time grew near, I could feel the ghosts moving closer to me. I don't always get psychic impressions of what's around me. Usually I just hear the tones and try to figure it out by the register of the pitch, but this time it was very clear to me. There was a woman, a man and a child.

I stood in the middle of my room, feeling foolish as I usually do when talking to invisible people, and closed my eyes.

"It's time," I told them. "You need to move on." I explained about the white light and how it was a place of peace and serenity.

"Why stay here in a world where you don't belong? Why be miserable when you can find the harmony and tranquility you deserve?" After several minutes, the room felt somewhat lighter, but it wasn't as comforting as it should have been. I could still hear one lingering nearby.

I just let it go for the moment. The female had stayed behind.

I saw her very clearly in my mind. She was in her early forties, with long dark hair. She wasn't thin, but she wasn't heavy. She carried the weight of the world in her eyes. If she were alive, we could have probably been great friends.

I've been around malevolent entities before, so I know how that feels, and she wasn't giving me any of the same bad vibes. I felt like she just wasn't ready. She seemed sad. Maybe she had some unsolved issues she needed to attend to. I went back to my Ovilus.

"What do you want to tell me?" I asked.

The Ovilus spoke almost instantly. "Cancer," it said. It then spit out several other words that were seemingly random and didn't make any sense, but then repeated the word "cancer" again two more times. After a few days, I contacted Barbara again and told her I still had one left that I needed help with.

Barbara promised to help me and moments later I heard the tone begin to fade. After several seconds it was gone for good. I reached out to Barbara again, hoping to gain more insight. What she told me was very thought provoking. Being a very talented medium, Barbara was able to talk with the woman. She told her that she died of cancer, but wanted to stick around to watch over her family. She'd found me by happenstance, following me home hoping for help. No one is sure how she ended up at the Victorian, since she is more contemporary, and she didn't seem to know the answer herself. Maybe she followed another intuitive person, hoping for help, and ended up there by accident. It's something we'll never know for certain. What we do know is that she finally crossed after being reassured that she could come back later to watch over her family. It was good to know.

Even though the experience was troubling, it was useful. Maybe I was right in my earlier assessment. I had abilities that were useful to the other side. I just needed to hone them more.

Armed with a fresh boost of confidence, I found myself exploring more haunted locations, hoping to expand on what I learned. What I didn't count on was running into something that didn't want help. That was when I learned that some gifts often come with consequences.

For every ghost that wanted my help, there were several more that didn't want me helping them. They'd try to stop me every chance they got.

Chapter 27

The Toilet Paper Bandit

I felt as though I had opened a portal that hovered right above my head. After my experience with the Soul Collector, I began picking up more and more attachments.

They found me in restaurants, in grocery stores, while driving in my car. I picked them up at my friends' houses, at doctor's offices, and while walking my dog through the woods. It all started with the ear ringing.

I would hear it move through the air, growing louder as it got closer. Despite all my precautions, it usually followed me home once I acknowledged the sound.

"Just turn it off," Barbara Williams told me on several occasions. She tried to walk me through a visualization exercise where I took an elevator up to my special room where all the switches were located. I tried it many times, but couldn't get it to work. No matter what I did, I couldn't turn it off.

At times, it became maddening. Ghosts buzzed around me, swooping around the room like pesky flies. If I tried to ignore them, I was often given a painful pinch or was treated to a loud bang on the wall.

One day, I was out shopping when I heard a tone that I identified as a female ghost. I got a mind picture of a young woman with long dark hair and angry eyes. I attempted to simply ignore her in hopes she'd drift away, but she didn't.

This one was different. She had a definite agenda.

It started one Monday morning. I woke up and made my way to the kitchen, where I planned on making a pot of coffee while surfing the Internet before starting my daily work routine. As soon as I walked into the room, I was stopped short by the overpowering smell of propane gas. It didn't take long to discover the source. One of the gas burners on my stove was turned on.

It was a curious moment for me because I was home alone. In order to turn the burner on, you have to press the button inwards and then turn it. In my eight years in the house, it was something that had never happened to me. My pets lacked opposing thumbs, so I knew they couldn't have turned it on. I hadn't cooked anything in days either. I just shrugged and busied myself opening doors and windows to clear out the potentially dangerous fumes. The thought that it might be paranormal never even graced my mind.

Two days later, something else happened to make me question it. I was walking past the bathroom and noticed that the toilet paper roll was missing. The entire silver cylinder was also gone. I looked around in all the rooms, but couldn't find it. I initially blamed it on the cats. Even though they'd never done this before, it was within reason. I figured I'd find it later under a bed or behind a dresser. What I wasn't expecting was to find it back in place an hour later.

I walked past the bathroom again, on my way to refill my coffee mug, and just happened to glance in the bathroom. I stopped stock-still, just staring at the impossible sight I was seeing. The toilet paper and cylinder were right back in place, as if they were never gone.

I took a deep breath and looked around me. I didn't see anything, but the signature tone I'd been hearing all week was louder than before. Nothing of this magnitude had ever happened to me before. I've had the occasional item disappear, only to reappear somewhere else later, but it was never this obvious before. Usually, it would be something I could blame on myself, like finding my keys on the coffee table instead of in my purse where I swore I left them. There was always a possible explanation. This time, there wasn't one. Toilet paper rolls just don't simply disappear and then reappear.

As I stood there, trying very hard not to allow fear to overcome me, I couldn't help but wonder. What else was she capable of? If she could move toilet paper, could she also move knives? Could she push me down the stairs or harm one of my pets? It was then that I remembered the gas incident from days before. Was she responsible for that as well?

From previous experience, I knew not to allow myself to be afraid. The last thing I wanted to do was feed her.

Keeping myself calm was difficult, given the circumstances. After all, this ghost tried to actually kill me. Being afraid was an instinctive reaction to the situation. I took a deep cleansing breath and tried to ground myself before it could gain a foothold. I took one more deep breath and continued down the hallway to refill my coffee, trying not to think too much.

Over the course of the next few days, I began feeling her growing stronger. Her anger was so powerful, it was almost visible, radiating with spiked thorns every time she was near me. I tried to quiet my mind and ask her what she wanted, but all I got was that sense of overwhelming anger. She was either really mad at me, or I reminded her of someone who'd done her wrong at some point. I tried to reason with her, but she just wouldn't go away.

As it turns out, we had a meet-up event at the Haunted Victorian Mansion that weekend. People teased me, telling me it was turning into my "home away from home," which wasn't far from the truth. I was drawn there for reasons I didn't fully understand. I was comfortable there and the ghosts seemed to like me. They even knew me by name, something we captured several times on EVP.

I think in part, they recognized me as one of the Victorian Helpers – someone who came in to help with events, shovel snow, and keep an eye on the vacant house. They even watched me lean out the third floor window after a hurricane to pull a piece of loose flashing back into place.

At that night's investigation, I was assigned a small group of people who had never investigated before. In some ways, I liked having newbies in my group because they were so willing to learn, but in other ways it was exhausting. They had a difficult time sitting still and continually whispered back and forth to one another, contaminating our EVP sessions time and time again.

"A whisper sounds just like an EVP. If you have something to say, say it out loud so we don't think it's a ghost voice later," I would say, only to repeat myself thirty seconds later when the next person whispered.

When I got to the Red Room, I paused. The room was always quite active. Legends suggeseted that a prostitute was murdered there, but it wasn't something I was able to find documentation on. Regardless of what happened, it was a room I had always felt comfortable with. I decided to appeal to the ghosts there in case any of them could offer me help.

"I get the sense that you like me. I need help though. I have a very negative ghost in my house that might be trying to kill me. Can one of you help me get rid of her?" I asked.

I immediately heard a high pitched tone swoop in and settle near me. Through working Barbara Williams, I knew that the very high pitched tone probably belonged to a spirit. It could have been my spirit guide, my grandmother, or even a soul connected to the house in spirit form. I wasn't sure, but I was happy for the assistance.

I felt a prevailing sense of peace and love come over me. It was almost like getting an invisible hug and a promise that everything would be okay. The moment was so profound, tears came to my eyes.

"Thank you," I whispered into the air.

(Above) Joni on the second floor landing at the Haunted Victorian Mansion

The tone remained with me the entire evening and was still with me when I got into the car. As I made the thirty-minute trek back to my house, she sat beside me on the passenger seat. At one point, I even felt a gentle touch on my hand, as though she was reassuring me that everything would be okay.

Be strong, she encouraged me.

In my mind I saw her as young and blond, dressed in a very plain white dress with an apron. I thought her name was Anna, or Emma, or possibly even Annie. In the end, I called her Emi, after a character in *Ember Rain*, one of my earlier books.

As I pulled up in my driveway, all those old fears returned to me. I didn't want to go inside. Bad things were often inside my house and some of them wanted to kill me.

With a sigh, I pulled myself out of my car and went inside. I walked down the dark hallway to my bedroom, trying to still the fear in my heart.

I quickly dressed for bed and slid under the covers, saying a small prayer before closing my eyes. At first the room was very quiet. I started to relax, thinking that maybe she had left on her own accord, but that wasn't the case.

It wasn't long before I heard her tone move into the room, almost as though she had a trip-wire alarm set up, alerting her when I was in my room. I pressed my eyes together tightly and began counting down from twenty-one, something I've done for years to help me relax enough to fall asleep. Before I got to ten, I could hear Emi's higher pitched tone whoosh into the room. In seconds, the tones began swirling around the room, as though they were chasing one other.

The sounds grew louder, then softer. I opened my eyes, fully expecting to witness a battle, but the room was empty. I somehow fell asleep shortly after. When I woke up the next morning, all I heard was Emi. She had chased the negative woman away.

She stayed with me for several weeks afterwards, almost as if standing guard in case the woman tried to return. In time, she left completely. I was sad at first, but then realized the valuable lesson she taught me. She gave me a clue on how to keep myself protected.

When I began hearing the buzz of a ghost hovering nearby, I could reach out with my mind and ask for help. Soon, I would hear the faint high-pitch tone, growing louder and louder as my protector moved closer.

Within moments, the lower-pitched tone would disappear and I would feel the warmth and love from my guardian. I wasn't sure if it was Emi or someone else who was watching over me. I didn't care.

All I cared about was the fact that I was one more step closer to keeping myself protected. That was all that counted.

(Above) Joni at the Houghton Mansion during an investigation

EVPs available on Soundcloud.com/Jonimayhan

CHAPTER 28

CURTISS HOUSE INN EXPERIENCE

Armed with my new knowledge, I found myself becoming braver than I had been in years. Before my experiences with the Soul Collector, I was often the first one to explore a dark room, but I had lost my nerve. This was all rapidly changing. Knowing that I had a back-up plan went a long way in my development, as well as my bravery.

When Sandy learned that famed psychic medium Lorraine Warren, known from the movie *The Conjuring*, was hosting an event, we quickly signed up.

(Above) Joni and friends Brad Bramble and Breanna McCluskey with Lorraine Warren and her daughter Judy

I had been a big fan of Lorraine's for many years, having read several books about her and her late demonologist husband Ed Warren.

Since the event was being held in Monroe, Connecticut, we would need to find a place to spend the night. Even though it was only a few hours away, we didn't want to drive home in the wee hours of the morning. Besides, staying at a historic inn seemed like an exciting addition to our road trip. Unfortunately, it also presented me with an experience that would impact my travel going forward.

(Above) The Curtis House Inn

The Curtis House Inn was located in Woodbury, Connecticut, just a few miles away from the event.

Built in 1735 by Anthony Stoddard for his son Elikim, the house would open its doors as an inn in 1754. Originally, the house contained two stories, with the second floor sporting a massive ballroom. The ballroom was eventually converted into individual rooms, with a third floor being added in the early 1900's. It has the honor of being the oldest continually opened inn in Connecticut.

Our room was in the carriage house, which is connected to the main house by a charming footbridge. Four rooms had been carved from the structure, with the main floor being used for storage. While the main house is known to be haunted, no one had reported any activity in the carriage house.

(Above) Sandy and Joni's room at the Curtis House Inn

I was tired when we got to the room. The Lorraine Warren event had been pleasant. I was thrilled to get a chance to actually meet her, but we were both exhausted. All we wanted to do was put our heads on our pillows and fall into a deep sleep. Thoughts of ghosts were far from my mind. I actually hadn't given the accommodations much thought. I'd reserved our tickets for the Lorraine Warren event, while Sandy had handled the overnight reservations. A friend had recommended the inn because of its relative proximity to the Warren event.

It didn't dawn on me that we were going to a haunted inn until I walked in the door. It was as if the room was already filled with invisible guests.

As a paranormal investigator, finding a haunted venue is usually very exciting to me, but at that moment it was the last thing I needed. I just wanted to change into my pajamas, read a little from the new book I'd just purchased at the event, and then close my eyes for seven or eight hours until I was properly rested and ready for the next day. Dealing with ghosts wasn't on my agenda.

It was then that I realized Sandy had mentioned we would be staying at a haunted inn. I guess in the back of my mind I'd thought we could wander the grounds and inn to do a few EVP sessions, before retiring to our room. What I hadn't considered was the fact that we'd be hosting a pajama party for the paranormal realm.

The room had two twin beds, so I quickly claimed the one nearest the door, and then retreated into the bathroom to brush my teeth, and change into my sleeping attire. I'd barely closed the door when I realized I wasn't alone. There was a ghost with me.

It was a young female, possibly a maid from the early 1800's, who'd worked and lived at the inn. I saw her in my mind as thin, with long dark hair that she wore in a bun under a white cap. She wore a pale blue dress with a large white apron over the top of it. She didn't mean me any harm, but was curious about me.

I wasn't certain what she wanted. She was probably seeking a human connection with someone who could feel her, after being ignored for the better part of two-hundred years. Unfortunately for her, she caught me at a bad time.

"I know you're here, but I can't communicate with you," I told her. "I'm not a true medium. I can feel you and get an idea of what you look like, but I can't communicate like a real medium can," I told her.

The tone seemed to fade a bit, so I carried on with my nighttime routine.

After getting somewhat settled, I returned to the room to find Sandy already in her pajamas with her digital voice recorder in her hand. She must have gotten a similar visit while I was in the bathroom.

"This room is wall-to-wall ghosts," she told me.

Normally an investigation has more of a formal feel to it. We gather our equipment, including our meters to measure electromagnetic energy, and our beloved Spirit Boxes, and conduct a session. It usually starts with one of us sweeping the room with a Mel Meter, to see if there are any electromagnetic spikes that would show up on our equipment. A false spike could often be caused by faulty electric wiring, or devices like clock radios, that usually emit high levels of energy. We didn't even bother this time. The room was full of ghosts and we knew it. All we needed was a way to record them.

We turned on our recorders and began asking respectful, gentle questions of our invisible guests. As we began, we started sensing the others as well. One entity was male, and was joined by several other females. I didn't like him as much. He felt controlling and a bit hostile. We asked them general questions about where they lived, how old they were, and why they were still lingering at the inn. We even pulled out a Spirit Box to see if we could get a response, but the ghosts just weren't talking. We didn't record a single EVP.

By this time, I was getting really tired. I'd been up since seven that morning and had worked a full day before making the two and a half hour trek south to Connecticut. All I wanted was some nice REM sleep to recover my energy. As I'd soon find out, it wasn't going to happen.

The minute I turned out the light and rolled onto my side, I felt them swoop in. The feeling is very similar to the sensation of a person walking very quietly into a room. Sometimes I just know they're there. I can feel the displacement of air, the sense of their energy behind me. Added to this was the very loud buzzing in my ears. By the sound of it, there were at least a handful of ghosts trying to get my attention.

I quickly created a bubble of protection and prayed it would prevent them from getting too close to me. Unfortunately, that wasn't the case. If anything, it seemed to draw them in closer.

One touched my hair, pulling it back from my face. I nearly jumped out of my skin.

"Stop touching me!" I said, probably jarring Sandy out of early sleep stages in the bed across the room.

I closed my eyes again and tried to fall back asleep, but they weren't finished with me. As soon as I started to drift off, ice cold fingers grasped my ankle.

"Stop it!" I hissed, pulling my knees up into a fetal position, wondering if I would ever get to sleep.

"Are they bothering you?" Sandy asked.

"Yeah, they keep touching me," I told her.

"I can feel them, but they're leaving me alone. They must be too fixated on you," she said.

I tried reciting the Lord's Prayer in my mind, something that usually calms me, but before I could get to the "amen," I was jolted off my pillow in pain. It felt as though someone reached into my eye socket and grabbed a handful of eyeball.

I started to sit up, when the pain moved to my chest. The hand lunged into my chest and grabbed onto my heart. It almost felt as though I were having a heart attack before the feeling eased and then moved to my leg. I was under attack.

I jumped up from bed. The room was dark, with just a gentle glow from the street lights filtering through the window. While I once loved sleeping in total darkness, I just couldn't do it anymore. After my experiences with the Soul Collector, I always slept with a night light.

"Do you mind if I turn on the lamp?" I asked.

"No, go ahead," Sandy said.

I have to give Sandy credit. Being my friend comes with a very large burden. While she had her own ghost situations to deal with, mine were often more disruptive.

I switched on the light and then turned around to look at my bed. It was a cozy little twin bed with layers of covers. To anyone else, it would be the perfect spot to curl up in. To me, it was nothing more than a torture chamber.

"Maybe I can sleep in the car," I mused.

Sandy laughed. "I think they'd find you there just as easily." It was a truth I didn't even need to respond to. If I was in the vicinity, a ghost would be sure to find me.

I considered reaching out to Barbara Williams, but didn't. It was going on midnight and I didn't want to wake her with another one of my paranormal issues. Besides, with her busy schedule she might not even see my message for several days.

I went back to bed, determined to get some sleep. I had already taken my sleep aid, but added another Benadryl to the mix. I read for a few minutes until I felt it kick in and then squeezed my eyes shut. I really needed this sleep. We had a long day ahead of us. Our friends had invited us to investigate at the abandoned Sterling Opera House in nearby Derby.

A few minutes later, I was woken up by another tug on my ankle.

"Enough!" I nearly roared.

Sandy sat bolt upright, jarred from sleep.

"What? What happened?"

"It won't leave me alone," I said, my voice making me sound like a spoiled two-year old.

"Let me see if I can extend my shields to cover you too," she said, quite generously. Sandy's ability to shield was much stronger than mine. She had found a way to harness her energy and push it outwards into an iron-strong bubble. I tried to do the same thing, but my bubble seemed to be made of soap instead of iron.

After about thirty seconds, I felt the ghosts move away from me. I relaxed a little.

"Thanks, that's much better," I said and curled back onto my side.

I managed to fall into a light slumber, but it was frequently interrupted by strange dreams about people I didn't know, trying to urgently pass along messages. When I woke up the next morning, I felt as tired as I had when I walked into the room at midnight.

When we left the room the next day, I stayed close to Sandy and her bubble until we were at the car, preventing anything from hitching a ride with us.

As we took the exit onto the highway, the car was blessedly quiet. We'd managed to escape. It wasn't my first bad hotel experiences, but it also wouldn't be my last. I really needed to figure this all out.

CHAPTER 29

THE LIGHT WORKER

A lot of people would have given up, but I was tenacious. The more the negative entities bothered me, the more determined I became to stop them.

I began researching as much as possible and even gained another mentor, someone who finally taught me how to properly shield myself in a way that was effective for me.

I met Psychic Medium Chris George while I was on his popular internet radio show Second Sight Radio talking about my book *Soul Collector*. He invited me to call him after the show to discuss my situation.

(Above) Psychic Medium Chris George with Joni and his former co-host Victor Furman, who was also key in helping Joni with her spiritual awakening

When I called him, he told me that he was going to start an online psychic development class soon. Sandy and I quickly signed up.

We only ended up taking three classes before they ended, but what I learned was invaluable. While I already knew a lot of the information he taught, he gave me a new method for creating a protective bubble.

He told us to imagine a golden egg surrounding us. He felt that gold was a stronger color than white and it would provide us with better protection.

"Now, plaster the outside of your golden egg with mirrors. That way, if something comes up to you, all they'll see is themselves," he told us.

I found the process to work amazingly well. By taking bits of information from different mentors, I was able to create something that worked well for me. As instructed by Chris, I began creating my golden mirror egg every morning. Because Barbara Williams felt that shields only lasted for several hours, I also instructed my shield to stay in place, protecting me from all energy that wasn't my own for the next 24 hours.

Armed with all of this new information, I took another step forward and began sharing it with others in earnest.

In October of 2013, I began teaching a Paranormal 101 class in the town of Gardner, Massachusetts. It was something that would completely alter my life.

I didn't claim to know everything there was to know about the paranormal world, but I wanted to share my information with others. I knew that information was often difficult to obtain and that mentors were even harder to find. I would teach what I knew to others in hopes that they wouldn't have to go through what I had endured.

Since publishing my book about the Soul Collector, I already knew that there were a lot of people like me. I wasn't the only one that dead people were latching onto. I also wasn't the only one with metaphysical abilities I was uncertain about.

People reached out to me at an alarming rate, sharing their stories. Many of them had lived with this curse for far longer than I had and didn't know where to turn.

I helped them as best as possible, but it was difficult doing this from a distance. What I needed was a way of working with students in person.

The opportunity came to me shortly after I published *Bones in the Basement – Surviving the S.K. Pierce Haunted Victorian Mansion*. A local metaphysical shop called Terrapin Traders in Gardner asked if I would do a book signing there. While I was sitting there, many people came in to talk to me about their paranormal experiences.

"Why don't you teach a class?" the shop owner, Elizabeth Leonard, asked me.

I froze for a second. Besides my work in training employees, I'd never taught a class before. Could I do that?

Could I really stand in front of a group of people and talk about my experiences? It was far easier to hide behind my keyboard and share my stories to people who would never see my face. Actually standing in front of them was a bit mind numbing to even consider.

After all, I didn't know everything. I was still trying to figure out a lot of what I was experiencing. When I voiced this fear to Sandy, she had a logical answer for me.

"Teach them what you do know," she said.

(Above) Several members of my class (L-R) Pamela Howell, Phyllis Fisher, Barbara Kirk Niles, Raymond Richard, shop owner Elizabeth Leonard and Ken Murray

In some way, I hoped that I could also learn by teaching. As I researched information for upcoming classes, it forced me to study more about subjects I wasn't as familiar with. Through this, I transformed into a completely different version of myself. I became spiritual.

Many people believe that being spiritual means being happy, but I came to realize that it went far deeper than that. The happiness came as a byproduct of learning to accept the life lessons that I was dealt.

Everything I had gone through paranormally led me to this place where I could begin to help other people.

Once I began to accept the things that happened to me, I began to see life in a different way. I learned that everything in the universe vibrates. Nothing stays still, even if we can't see it moving. We are all caught up in an ocean of energy.

This made sense to me.

All my life I had been hearing tones. Lower pitches, like what the Soul Collector made, often signified darker entities, while higher tones belonged to spirit guides and loved ones who had passed through the light. Had I been hearing their vibrations?

If lower energies vibrated much slower, it would stand to reason that their sound would be lower too.

While I've always been a positive person by nature, I allowed some past hurts to linger in my heart. This caused a hole in my auric shield, allowing lower vibrational entities to easily latch onto me.

I also began to realize that most things in life happened for a reason. Once I adopted that mentality, I began to see the intricate network of life lessons being served to me. They didn't come written on a chalkboard, they came as moments. How I chose to handle them determined my fate.

My constant battle with the paranormal world became far clearer to me. I was given this gift for a reason. For years, it felt more like a curse than a blessing, but once I latched onto the concept, it turned everything around for me. Not only would I begin fighting back against darkness, I would help make the world a little lighter.

Everything I had learned so far had been about being defensive. It was time to go on the offense and in doing that, I reached out to Barbara Williams for further training.

I had watched Barbara cross over lost souls many times at Parsonsfield Seminary, but I hadn't fully embraced the concept.

I knew how to do it. I had watched Barbara do it many times, but seeing something being done and learning how to do it myself were two distinctly different things.

Barbara set up a special event for us and allowed me to bring some of my students from my Paranormal 101 class.

We met in the schoolhouse building in a room that had been used as an auditorium. From past events, I knew the room was usually filled with ghosts. Many of them were children from the seminary's past. Others had been drawn in by the energy that lingered there.

Barbara instructed us to stand in the middle of the room and link hands, left hand over right, so we created a sacred circle.

"Imagine a column of white light opening up in the center of the circle. It would start several feet above the ground and would continue upwards," she said to our group.

I closed my eyes and tried to hold the vision, but was distracted by the buzzing sounds in my ears. The room was filling up with ghosts.

They zoomed in and out of our circle like moths gravitating towards an open flame. I could hear them so clearly. There were dozens of them.

"It's okay. You're safe here. Come into the circle," Barbara encouraged them. Even more flooded in.

Without warning, I began feeling an electric tingling sensation near my ankles.

What was happening to me?

As I stood there, with my hands linked to the others, the tingling traveled up my body slowly. It filled me up on the inside, making me feel as though my entire body was sizzling with current.

Was a soul trying to cross through me, using me as the column?

(Above) Sandy with Barbara Williams at Parsonsfield Seminary

Before I could even say anything, it zipped all the way up my body and out through the crown of my head.

As it happened, I couldn't move or even breathe. I was utterly and completely paralyzed until it shot through the top of my head. Then, I felt absolute elation.

I opened my eyes, feeling euphoric.

Barbara smiled at me from across the circle.

"One just crossed through you. I call what you're feeling a "spirit-gasm," she said with a short laugh.

I felt the heat rise on my cheeks because she essentially nailed the sensation. It felt like a spiritual organism. I didn't have long to dwell on the experience before another one shot through me, followed by several others. By the time we finished and Barbara closed the light and broke the circle, I was riding the greatest high of my life.

"That was amazing!" I said, breathlessly.

"It was amazing. You just crossed several souls over into the light. Doesn't that feel great?" she asked.

"It feels beyond great." I thought of those souls who had been lingering on our plane for years, if not decades. I had provided them with the peace they had longed for, releasing them from a nightmare they couldn't escape.

My calling became apparent to me. This was what I was meant to do.

"Every time you cross over a lost soul, you make the world a little lighter," Barbara told us after we stopped for a break. Several of the others felt souls cross over, but no one felt it like I had.

It was a bit disconcerting to me. What if they were in the process of crossing through my body and decided to stay instead? Would I become possessed? Barbara was quick to dispel this worry.

"You cannot become possessed unless you allow it to happen. Just move them along like you did before," she told me.

Fortified with this new ability, I would use it to my benefit. Later, when I got home from the event, I crossed over nearly all the souls who were hanging around my house. The only ones I couldn't cross were the ones that didn't want to go. This was troublesome because those were the ones who were there for an entirely different purpose.

They didn't want me to lighten the world and they would try to stop me at every turn from doing what Barbara taught me to do.

(Above) Michael Robishaw with his daughter Sara

CHAPTER 30

MICHAEL ROBISHAW

Sometimes I think we're given exactly what we need when we need it the most. If we're forced to endure a bit of pain before we get it, we are stronger and wiser for the experience. It also forces us out of our comfort zones, which was something I also needed.

Despite my attempts to raise my vibration, the attachments began coming to me so frequently, I no longer tried to figure them out. Some weeks, three or four souls followed me home. I desperately needed help with my attachment issues. While I could now cross over many of them, I was still left with the ones that didn't want to go.

These were the troublemakers.

I began to see them as the gate keepers. They didn't want the world to become lighter. They wanted nothing but pain and suffering to linger on our human plane. They were the energy thieves who pulled energy from me, the ones who banged on the walls to induce a sense of fear and were the ones I feared the most.

No matter how hard I tried, I couldn't move them through the light. They dug in their heels and refused to budge.

While Barbara was amazing, time and distance prevented her from providing me with what I needed, which was constant support.

I got to a point where I didn't want to bother anyone anymore. I've never been someone who has had an easy time asking for help. I liked to figure things out and solve my own problems. Being forced to constantly seek help felt like a weakness to me. I needed to learn how to protect myself. At the very least, I needed someone to help me until I was capable of helping myself. I found this person at a familiar place.

I was invited to the Haunted Victorian Mansion to participate in the filming of a paranormal TV pilot. When I got there, I met several other investigators from out of state. One of these people was a man named Michael Robishaw.

(Above: Michael Robishaw with his cat Spirit

He looked like a modern day cowboy to me. With his Sam Elliot mustache and his deep, resonating voice, he wasn't someone most people easily forgot. Like Barbara Williams, he had a presence to him. He wasn't the kind of person you readily forgot shortly after meeting.

He was a paranormal investigator out of Alexandria, Virginia, and had been exploring the paranormal world for several decades. He ran a team called Alexandria Paranormal, which he deliberately kept small. Joining him that night was his daughter Sara and her husband.

The investigation wasn't memorable. The activity was typical, with bangs occurring in empty rooms and unexplained shadows moving across the walls.

Michael and I ended up on different teams that night, so my encounters with him were brief, but we quickly became friends on Facebook after the investigation ended. I didn't realize that he was more than just an investigator until I had another bad entity follow me home several weeks later.

I wasn't sure where I picked it up, but it swooped around my room with an angry tone. Every time I tried to fall asleep, my body would begin vibrating.

Barbara had confirmed my suspicions about this. When my body vibrated, it meant that the ghosts were pulling energy from me. Stopping them became essential. If I didn't, they might drain me dry.

I took a picture of my bedroom and posted it on Facebook, knowing that I had many medium friends who could read the energy in photos. I hoped that one of them might provide me with a way to make it stop.

I was at the end of my rope by that point. My house was filled to the brim with lost souls and nothing seemed to help. I crossed over as many of them as possible, but a lot of them simply refused to leave. Once I found a possible solution, it didn't take the ghosts long to figure out how to work around it. I needed help.

Michael messaged me shortly afterwards.

"Take the picture down. I'll send my guides in at eleven," he said in his message.

This was a curious moment for me. I had connected with my own spirit guides, but they weren't always successful in removing ghosts from my space. Apparently, Michael's guides were more advanced.

At the specified time, I walked into my bedroom, ready for the show. If I expected to watch his guides zip into the room, I was sadly mistaken. Instead, I heard them.

They sounded like piercing sirens that nearly split my head open. As they zoomed around the room, I could track them by sound, something that hadn't escaped my cats either. Their heads bobbed back and forth as though they were watching an invisible tennis match. Several hours later, everything quieted down. The ghost and the spirit guides were all gone. I was all alone for the first time in months, if not years.

I learned that Michael was more than an investigator. He was also a Shaman.

Before I met Michael, I had only the vaguest clue about Shamanism. All I knew was that a Shaman was typically the "medicine man" of a Native American tribe. He bridged the gap between the living and the dead by being able to communicate with the spirit world.

After learning about his abilities and his connection to his spirit guides, I learned that he was also a spiritual healer, Empath and a medium. He was also able to do something that took my belief system to a brand new level. He was able to astral project.

The process of astral projection is complicated and isn't' something that everyone can master. After doing a series of secret rituals, Michael is able to separate his soul from his body. He can then travel to locations like a living ghost.

I was familiar with the process since both Leesa and Barbara Williams were able to do this too, but Michael's spirit guides always went along with him.

Michael's guides weren't standard issue guides either. They were a band of spiritual warriors, an invisible army who could enter a location and eradicate the darkness inside. He was exactly what I needed.

I told my Paranormal 101 class about my incredible experience. Just like me, everyone was amazed. Could spirit guides really do those things? It was certainly worth checking out.

I taught a class on spirit guides and led the group through a guided meditation. During the meditation, the students were supposed to meet their guides, something that would be helpful in allowing them to establish a relationship with them.

I seldom did the meditations with the class because I wanted to watch them to make sure they weren't having any problems. Later that week, I opened the link to the meditation I used and tried it myself. The results were fairly astounding.

I already knew that I had one guide named Kira. I met her years ago when Kaden walked me through my first guided meditation. What I didn't realize was that I also had another guide, a male I knew as Daniel. I was curious why my guides weren't as talented as Michaels were, so I asked him.

"Your guides are really young and inexperienced. My guides will work with them and train them though," he told me.

My life was getting stranger by the moment.

For most people, the simple act of believing in an afterlife was a stretch. Taking it a step further and buying into the concept of invisible helpers was beyond what most people could grasp, but it all made perfect sense to me. It actually explained a lot.

Many times in my life I had felt as though someone had whispered a message into my ear. Sometimes it was as simple as urging me to slow down while I was driving, other times it was more profound. The messages came to me like thoughts, with the exception that they had a different feel to them. Sometimes, I was suspicious that ghosts were attempting to communicate with me, but other times I had to wonder if it was something else. Was it my spirit guides?

I wasn't sure, but it was something worth looking into. When I felt a ghost drift into my space, I tried to cross them over like Barbara taught me. If that didn't work, I reached out to my spirit guides and asked them for help. Sometimes they were able to move it away, but other times they couldn't seem to budge it. That's when I would reach out to Michael.

"I have a nasty ghost in my house. Can you help?" I would say. Days later, his guides would pop into my house with the same ear-splitting tone I was familiar with and the ghost would be gone.

Was it really this easy? Had I finally found a solution to my problems? Between my spirit guides and Michael, I no longer had to live with unseen entities roaming around my house. If I traveled, I would reach out to Michael to ask him to clear the hotel room for me. For the first time in many years, my life was becoming bearable.

Michael also helped my friends. Sandy used him on more than one occasion and members of my class often used him too. The results were undisputable. When Michael sent his guides in, the ghosts left.

Michael's guides worked closely with the archangels, especially Michael the Archangel. I felt a bit star struck whenever Michael told me that his namesake angel had taken part in several of my home cleansings. After all, I had been calling on him for years while saying his prayer.

In 2015, I asked Michael if I could write a book about his experiences, which I titled Ruin of Souls after the last line in the Prayer to Saint Michael the Archangel. After some serious hemming and hawing, Michael finally agreed. He gave me a list of names of people to contact.

As I reached out to the people on his list, I quickly learned that Michael had been busy over the course of the past few years. Besides helping me and my friends, he had also helped dozens of other people with their paranormal issues. Some of the stories were quite frightening. In several cases, it caused issues in my own life too.

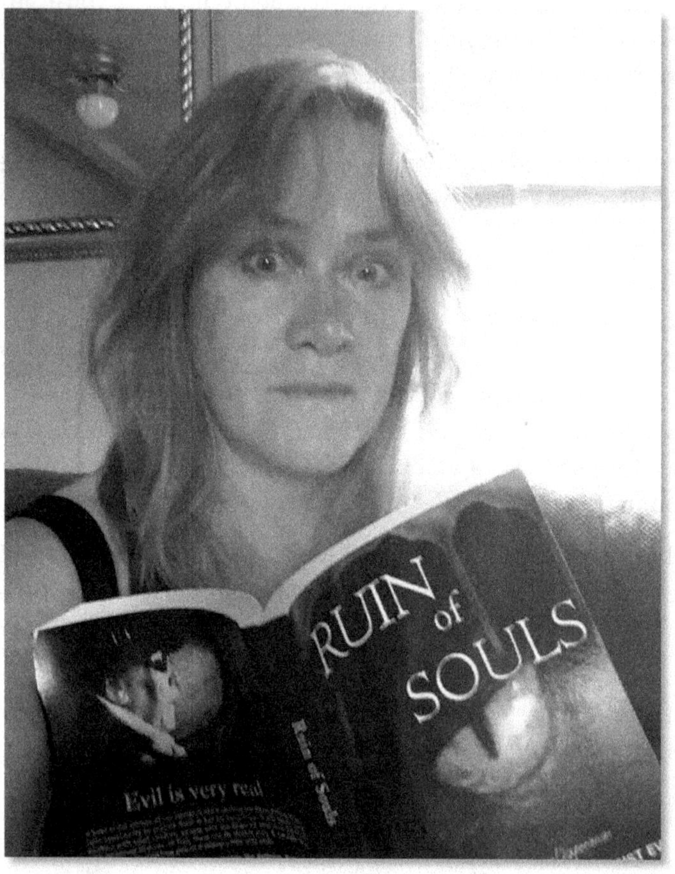

(Above) Joni with her book about Michael

While I was interviewing someone for Michael's book, I felt something drift into the room. It was dark and scary, the tone very similar to the one the Soul Collector possessed. In an instant, I was mentally back in that place in my mind. I remembered the way the Soul Collector hovered inches above me as I tried to fall asleep, and the way he caressed my hair as I lay on my side. I thought about the way he threatened to come after my daughter, holding me hostage with his demands, and the way he followed my son from his room one night. My stomach clenched as the tone moved closer. I could imagine him, licking his putrid lips as he imagined taking me over.

He could have been a serial killer in life. He had no conscience. All he had was the burning need for my soul. In that moment, I knew that I needed to do something to save myself. Thankfully, I had a savior in the wings who was eager to help.

If I'd known Michael Robishaw years ago, the *Soul Collector* would have been a three page book. Since meeting him, he's helped me dozens of times in removing entities from my house. At one point, he recommended that I stop ghost hunting for a while to clear my aura, but it became abundantly clear that it didn't make a difference.

I excused myself from the telephone conversation as quickly as possible, promising to send the woman information that would lead her to more help, and contacted Michael. Shortly afterwards, I heard his spirit guides swoop into the room. It sounded like laser lights zipping around the room. I couldn't see them, but there was no doubt they were there. The entity quickly retreated back to where he came from and the room grew quiet again. Michael had saved me once again.

Michael has helped hundreds of other people in the same way he's helped me. One of those people was the woman I was speaking to. Unfortunately for her, the persistence of the dead will follow her through the days of her life just like it does mine. There will probably never be an escape. There will only be options.

Not all of the entities are as dark as the Soul Collector. Some of them are simply lost souls, looking for help. Those are the easy ones. Thanks to Barbara Williams, I now knew how to cross them over into the light and help them find their way to Heaven.

My connection to Michael would become essential. As time passed by, I became more aware of my purpose. I wasn't given this gift as a means of torture, I was given it for a reason, something the ghosts had been aware of for decades.

I wasn't just a ghost magnet. I was also a light worker, someone who cleared the darkness by making it lighter.

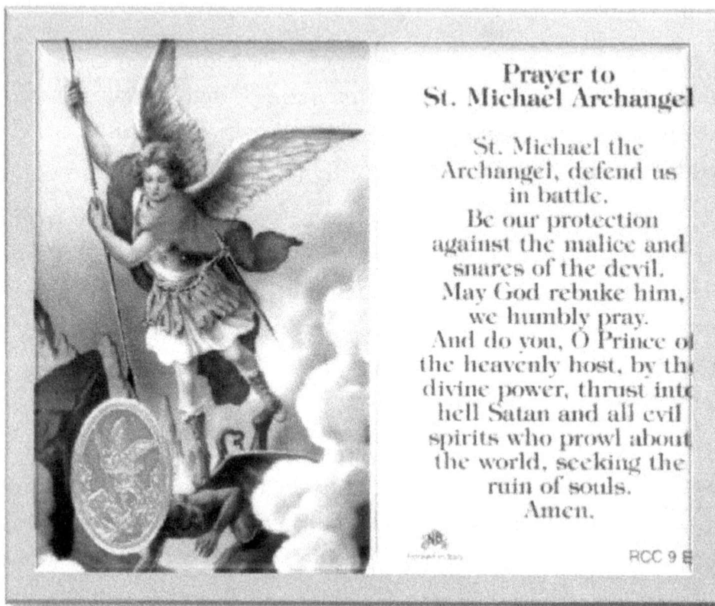

Prayer to St. Michael Archangel

St. Michael the Archangel, defend us in battle.
Be our protection against the malice and snares of the devil.
May God rebuke him, we humbly pray.
And do you, O Prince o
the heavenly host, by th
divine power, thrust int
hell Satan and all evil
spirits who prowl abou
the world, seeking the ruin of souls.
Amen.

RCC 9

CHAPTER 31

AND THE BATTLE BEGINS

After living my life running from the unseen forces that plagued me, it was time to fight back. I chose several of my strongest students and began doing house cleansings.

At first the cleansings were nominal. We would go in and discover that the former homeowners were still in residence, despite the fact that they had been dead for several decades. In these cases, if the activity wasn't threatening, we would educate the homeowner and offer the ghost safe passage to the other side. If they didn't want to go, which was often the case, then we left them in place. In some cases, they acted as guardians of the home, preventing worse situations from happening.

"You are very lucky, actually," I told one home owner after discovering that the shadows she often saw in her hallway were nothing more than the old man who built the house. "He keeps the other ghosts out. It's like having ghost security on duty."

Other times, this wasn't so much the case.

A friend reached out to me to ask for assistance on behalf of another friend.

The woman, who I will call Dot, was in a bad situation. Her house had just burned down, forcing her and her husband Fred to move into another house they planned to renovate and sell. The "flip house" wasn't nearly as nice as the house she and her husband just lost, but they were happy to have a place to stay.

Shortly after moving in, Dot began to have strange things happen to her. When she was alone in the house, she often heard people talking in another room. When she poked her head in to investigate, no one was there. She also frequently heard someone walking up and down the stairs that led to the second floor bedrooms.

At first she thought she was just imagining it, but when she began finding her belongings in strange places, she knew something was wrong.

Dot was terrified. She didn't even watch scary movies because she didn't like the way they made her feel. Living in a haunted house wasn't her idea of fun, especially not after all she and her husband had recently gone through with the fire.

She was afraid to be in the house alone. She made excuses to visit friends and run errands, but she couldn't put off going home forever. Compounding the issue was the fact that her husband was a skeptic. Since he hadn't experienced any of the occurrences, he often chided Dot and told her she was simply imagining the strange happenings.

I hand-picked a small team of students from my Paranormal 101 class and went in, hoping we could help.

I brought along Sandy, Raymond Richard and Ken Murray.

Ray was a true psychic medium, having honed his skills over the past thirty years by doing readings for people and investigating the paranormal. He often helped me out in my classes when the subject matter went beyond my level of expertise.

Ken Murray was my star student. When he began taking my classes, he had very little indication that he possessed any metaphysical abilities, but soon he was leaving everyone else behind in the dust. He was a gifted psychic medium who simply came into his abilities later in life, after opening himself up while taking my classes.

The house was located in a crowded section of Gardner. Small houses were crowded onto small lots with small backyards and even smaller driveways. Older model cars lined the pothole filled streets.

A winter storm had blasted the northeast the night before, which made the roads difficult to navigate. New England back streets are often narrow and winding. Six inches of new snow made them even worse. I tried unsuccessfully to make it up the hill where the house was located twice before giving up and parking at the bottom. By the time I made my way up the slick hill, I was hoping for a warm kitchen where I could knock off the chill.

Ray and Ken were both already inside when I walked up the sidewalk. I could see them through the window, chatting with our mutual friend Marion who had called me about the haunting.

I originally met Marion at the Haunted Victorian Mansion, where she had served as the residence's caretaker for several years, popping in to make sure the vacant house was in good order and fielding questions for the owners. She was a motherly person, the kind who often went out of her way to make sure everyone else was happy and comfortable.

They all rose from the table when I walked in and exchanged brief hugs with me. In many ways, our group of students had become more like family than friends. Our mutual interest in the paranormal created the initial bond, but the time spent together had cemented it into something deeper.

"This is Dot and this is her house," Marion said, gesturing to the woman standing on the other side of the group.

Dot was a heavy-set woman in her early sixties. Worry was etched into her expression, making her look years older. She stood in a corner of the kitchen, worrying her hands together, while her eyes darted back and forth as though she expected to see something appear in midair.

Sandy came through the door seconds later, full of apologies for being the last one there. She too tried to make it up the hill but slid back down again, something that always set my teeth on edge when driving in the winter.

The warmth in the kitchen were frosted over with moisture, causing the outside world to appear distorted. As I peered further into the house, I could see that the kitchen was the only room with opened curtains. The curtains and blinds had been drawn in the other rooms, making the house dark and dreary.

I don't like standing around when there is business to attend to, so I parted through the idle conversations. Some people probably view me as being abrupt at times, something that came from years of working as a manager. When there are tasks to complete, I hate wasting time with chit-chat. I turned to Dot and began explaining what we would be doing.

"We're just going to walk around your house and see what we come up with. We are all mediums and will be able to feel the energy here. When we're finished, we'll come talk to you," I told her.

Marion agreed to sit with her at the kitchen table while we got to work.

We dispersed in different directions, armed with notepads and pens. Ken did a sweep of the house with his EMF detector to see if there were any electrical anomalies that might allude to a haunting, but didn't find anything.

A narrow set of stairs were tucked into the back corner of the kitchen. I stood at the base of them, noticing how they appeared to disappear into shadows at the top. I found myself drawn there, so I followed my nudges.

Ray must have felt this too, because he was right behind me on the stairs. At the top of the stairs, I turned right on the landing and found myself in a small bedroom with a wooden framed bed that was missing its mattress. The walls were painted a stark white. A window on the far right wall looked down over the narrow side yard and into the neighbor's yard. I pulled the blinds all the way up to allow some sunlight into the room.

My ears began ringing with a higher pitched tone, one I always associate with females. As I latched onto it, I opened myself up and allowed the images to flood my mind.

I saw an older woman with wild white hair standing beside the bed near the window. She was dressed in a lemon-yellow house coat that was several shades darker than the walls and glared at me with angry dark eyes.

"What are you doing here? This is my room!" she shouted at me in my mind.

I don't usually do very well with angry people, but I gave her a pass on her hostile behavior. She had probably been trapped in this room for decades, demanding privacy to a world who couldn't hear her. Anybody in her situation would be angry.

(Above) Joni in the room where the angry woman resided. Photo by Raymond Richard

"She's really angry, isn't she?" Ray said from behind me.

I jolted around, not expecting to find him there.

"Yeah, she's not happy. That's for sure."

"Maybe we can calm her down," he suggested.

I walked a bit further into the room and steadied myself against the bedframe. It was time for a counseling session. Talking with the dead was often no different than talking to the living. If we could help her release her anger, we might be able to cross her over into the light.

"I'm really sorry that people have been coming into your room like this without asking for permission first, but you must understand that they can't see you. They might feel funny when they come in here, but they can't hear your words or see your face," I said to her.

"She knows she's dead," Ray told me. "She's just afraid to move into the light."

This was good information to have. Many times, ghosts don't know they have died. They get trapped in a vortex of misunderstanding and spend years not understanding why nobody can no longer hear or see them. It often serves to make their agitation and anger even stronger. If they are left in place for too long, they tend to forget about their former human lives and become whittled down to their strongest emotions.

"You've been here so long and everyone appreciates your dedication, but wouldn't you like to see your family again?" I asked gently, trying to keep my voice pleasant and caring.

"She's calming down. I think she likes what you're saying," Ray said, then added to it. "Your family has been waiting for you for a long time. All you have to do is step through the light and you can be with them again."

"You can trust us. We're here to help you. We want you to be happy again," I said.

"She's thinking about it," Ray said. I loved working with him because he could do something that I often had a difficult time with. He could hear their responses, something I couldn't always do. Since working with my mentors, I was beginning to hear the ghosts more and more, but it wasn't consistent enough to be beneficial.

"We're going to open a white light for you. Call to your family and ask them to help you through it," I said.

"I think she would like a curtain of white light," he said.

I always utilized the column of white light that Barbara Williams taught me, but Ray often gave them a choice. He read their energy and found what would work for them, customizing it in a way that made them feel more comfortable.

"There…can you see the curtain? Just step through it."

"It's okay. We'll watch you to make sure you get through okay. It's time for you to be free and young again. Just let go and step through," I said, feeling tears press against the back of my eyes.

"She went," Ray said with a smile.

I could feel the tears flood my eyes. Releasing a soul who had been trapped on the wrong side of the metaphysical veil was one of the most beautiful things I'd ever participated in. Even though she didn't directly cross through me, giving me the tingle of electricity, I trusted Ray's insight.

The energy in the room lessened as the ringing sound that I initially heard faded away. The room became just another room.

Ray and I moved to another bedroom just as Sandy and Ken came up the stairs. Ray told them about the woman we crossed over in the front bedroom

"That's great. We were just down in the basement and there are two more down there," Ken said with concern in his voice. It made me wonder what we would find. Judging by his tone, it wasn't going to be pleasant.

In the other upstairs bedroom, we found a male soul who had become an invalid in his later days. He too knew he had passed away, but thought he was stuck in the room due to living so many years without the ability to walk. Once we explained his situation to him, he was quick in crossing over.

"Two down, two to go," Sandy said as we moved down the stairs and headed to the basement.

The stairs leading down to the basement were narrow and didn't appear to be used frequently. Cobwebs hung from the rafters and a thick coating of dust covered every horizontal surface.

"Watch your step," Ken said as he got to the bottom. He helped everyone else down the last few stairs before we explored the gloomy space.

The energy in the basement was erratic. It felt like a place for a perfect storm. Lighter energy collided with stronger energy. The two swirled in circles, occasionally bumping against one another. It made my head spin.

While the group checked out the front of the basement, I found myself drawn to the back area. The side of the basement was sectioned off by a long wall, giving the area the appearance of having once been an apartment.

I immediately connected with a sad female. I saw her standing at the back of the area looking forlornly out the window as though she was waiting for someone.

"There's one here," I said, but the rest of the group was focused on the other end of the basement.

"There's a negative male here that we should probably deal with first," Ray said. As I picked my way in their direction, I began hearing the male's tone. I stiffened up immediately. He sounded similar to the Soul Collector. It made me pause in my steps.

After everything I went through, I often balked when I came into contact with negative entities, especially males. The older female upstairs hadn't scared me because I felt her energy and understood her situation. This one was an unknown. All I could feel was his anger.

I began having mental flashbacks of walking into my dark house, not knowing what was waiting for me. I couldn't handle it if another ghost of his caliber followed me. I stayed back and let the other three handle this one, not wanting to get any closer.

(Left) Ken Murray and Ray Richard

They determined that he wasn't necessarily negative, but he was angry. He was a veteran of a war and was angry that his son was taken away from him. Sandy, Ken and Ray talked him down and explained that his son was waiting for him on the other side of the white light and crossed him over fairly quickly.

I heaved a sigh of relief. I didn't need to explain my reluctance about participating. Sandy had lived through my experience and the others had heard my stories. There was never any judgement handed out from any of us. We respected each other's boundaries and took up the slack whenever needed.

The angry energy in the basement faded as his tone disappeared. I felt myself relax a bit.

"Let's take a look at the one back here," I said, guiding them into the area where I found the female.

With the angry male gone, her energy seemed stronger, as though it no longer had boundaries to press up against. I took the lead with her.

"I think she's missing a son who went off to war and never returned," Ray said. Ken felt she was waiting for him to return, which made sense from the mind picture I saw. She was waiting for someone who would never return.

"She's been waiting for him for a long time," Sandy commented and then turned her focus to the female. "We know you've been down here for a long while, but we would like to help you. We can reunite you with your son."

She seemed receptive to our message and it wasn't long before she moved into the light. This time, she crossed over me, allowing me to feel the electric tingle as she swept through my body on her way to Heaven.

There was one more soul lingering in the house, but we decided to leave him as we found him. He wasn't doing any harm and didn't want to leave the house. Ray felt that he might act as a protector to the family, keeping them safe from any further hauntings.

We just stood there for a few minutes, allowing the enormity of what we had accomplished wash through us. These souls had been lingering here for decades without hope. Now, they were in a place where they could let go of all the pain and sorrow and be happy again. It made me feel like a mid-wife for the dead. Death was supposed to be as natural of a process as birth, but some needed help into the next realm. It felt wonderful to be able to provide that for them.

"Let's burn some sage," I suggested and the others nodded.

Even though we had removed the ghosts, the energy in the house was still unstable. By burning sage and filling the empty spaces with love and light, we could help bring the house back to more of a neutral position.

A strong scent of smoke hung in the air. It hit me as I came up the stairs and into the kitchen. I followed the scent to the living room where it seemed to be radiating from the furniture. I leaned over and sniffed a chair in the living room, getting a strong whiff of smoke.

"Was this furniture in the fire?" I asked the homeowner, who was standing in the doorway watching us.

"Yes. We were able to save a few pieces," she said.

"You might want to air it out a bit. Sometimes the energy from a tragic event hangs onto items. When you can smell the smoke, it makes it even stronger because it reminds you of what happened," I told her.

While Ken searched for his sage stick, I explained to Dot what we were going to do.

"When we burn sage, it levels out the energy, removing any negative pockets. Because of the fire and the haunting, there is some lingering energy here that we'd like to neutralize. We're just going to walk around and allow it to fill every nook and cranny of the house," I told her.

As we walked around, I also took some extra time to sage her husband Fred's clothes and tools. His energy was imprinted everywhere inside the house and none of us liked how it felt. Besides being overtly skeptical about Dot's experiences, he had also been edgy and confrontational towards her. I later learned that after we left, his attitude came around immensely.

Before we left, we explained to Dot how important it was to fill the house with light and love. We encouraged her to open the curtains and allow the house to become flooded with sunshine and to play some happy music as often as possible.

"Fill the space with everything that makes you happy," I told her. She seemed relieved. If nothing else, someone else heard her stories and took her seriously.

When I checked back with Marion the following week, she reported that the haunting had ceased completely. Dot's house was no longer haunted and they could finally move on and begin rebuilding their lives after suffering through such a tragedy.

The four of us continued to do more house cleansings in the area, calling on Michael Robishaw when we encountered something we couldn't handle ourselves.

It gave me a sense of confidence and allowed me to put aside the majority of my fears. I now had a safety net to protect me as I put myself in harm's way.

Our actions didn't go unnoticed in the spirit world. For every light worker trying to lighten the world, there is a darker force honing in on them, wanting them to stop.

We would soon meet something dark that none of us were prepared for.

CHAPTER 32

THE DARKNESS

It didn't take long for the darkness to find us.

We were a band of light workers, attempting to make the world brighter, but it rapidly became a contest of good versus evil.

Many of my students were opening themselves up and were discovering hidden gifts they weren't aware of before we started working together. Several discovered they were adept at the art of remote viewing, a process where you tap into information about a location and describe what you see without being there. Others were developing a true knack for interpreting the energy we often felt drift into our classroom.

Our classes were held at Terrapin Traders, a metaphysical shop located in the town of Gardner, Massachusetts, which was just thirty minutes from my home in Barre.

The building was located in the center of town, in a block of old brick buildings that had seen better days. The economy in Gardner was rapidly declining, which was evident in the often run-down conditions of the downtown area. Many of the store fronts were empty, with "for rent" signs taped to the windows. The stores that managed to survive were often niche market stores.

Terrapin Traders was an eclectic mix of spirituality-inspired goods, along with witch supplies and a healthy dose of the Grateful Dead thrown in for good measure. I never knew what I was going to find there, which made browsing the shelves ever interesting.

(Above) Terrapin Traders. Google Images photo

The room where I held my classes was smaller than I would have liked, but we always managed to pack ourselves into the space and soon forgot about the cramped quarters once the class was underway.

Depending on the class topic of the week, anywhere from five to fifteen people would attend. Some of them professed no abilities at all, but were simply intrigued by the metaphysical world. Others were gifted in ways I'd never before experienced.

After so many years of living with my abilities by myself, it was wonderful to have a group of people to share my experiences with.

In some ways, we became a beacon to the spirit world. When we united as a group, our energy soared through the rafters. We often joked that we were probably visible on radar images.

The building also came with its own ghost.

The owner of the shop had known about the ghost for a long time. They called him Eddie.

Eddie was a playful ghost, who was often drawn to the women who visited the store. He would play with their hair and often moved objects. Mediums would feel him when they came into the store, describing him as a former bartender at the bar that had once occupied the space.

People often saw him during my classes. He would walk across the other room, providing them with a quick glimpse of his silhouette as he passed in front of the display case lights. One of his favorite people to torment was Barbara Kirk Niles. He never failed to send her sailing out of her seat after giving her long hair a tug.

We often used him to help us develop our abilities.

"Okay, there's a ghost with us right now," I would say when I felt him drift into the room. "What are you feeling right now?"

Some people would hear the same buzzing tone that I often heard, while others felt a tightening in their guts or a tingling on their arms. Some were able to get clairvoyant images of him and described him as tall and dark haired. It wasn't long before Eddie became a true member of our class.

I would sometimes feel him right behind me, looking at the screen on my computer.

"Is he behind me?" I would ask Ray and Ken.

"Yes. He likes what you're saying. I think he's learning too," Ray told me with a smile.

Week after week, we would meet and discuss a new topic.

I was pleased with what I had accomplished. I brought together a group of people with similar interests and gave them a safe place to talk about their experiences. Through this union, they were able to work with one another and establish a bond that would make them all stronger in the process. My classes became more about the connections and the growth than about the lessons I was teaching. I learned as much from them as they did from me. It was life altering for all of us.

Having metaphysical abilities wasn't something that most people were comfortable talking about. If they tried to tell their friends, family and co-workers, they were often treated with scorn. Our weekly classroom gave them the opportunity to talk freely about what they had experienced and often provided them with solutions to help their progress. Unfortunately, it began drawing in darker energy too.

There is a world of darkness and light that most people can't see. It surrounds us and envelops us, pushing and pulling at us like the tides of an ocean. Sometimes it slithers in unnoticed and other times it rears its ugly head, hoping for a cheap reaction. We didn't always see it arrive, but were forced to deal with the consequences later.

When a man came to the store one evening before my class was due to begin, I recognized him immediately. He was the man with the haunted doll.

I won't divulge his name because I refuse to give him any more publicity. For the sake of the story, I'll call him Dominic.

Dominic had been traveling around the country, showing people a doll that he believed had demonic attachments. He had written a book about his experiences and spent much of his time promoting it. I wasn't sure if the doll was haunted or not, but since he showed up for my class about demonology, I invited him to sit in. If nothing else, I thought the class might find it interesting.

As it turns out, he had the doll with him. He opened the case and sat it on a chair, creating the illusion that the doll was also sitting in on my class.

My students began filing in and were intrigued by the scene in front of them. Many of them also recognized Dominic from social media and began asking him questions about the doll's origins.

(Above) My class listening to Dominic talk about his doll (L-R) Erica Fullum, Crystal Pina, Barbara Kirk Niles, Phyllis Fisher, Raymond Richard, Gina Bengtson, Ken Murray, Pamela Howell

As the class continued, I began feeling the energy drifting off the doll. I could almost visualize it coming off the doll like the tentacles of an octopus, reaching out to each of us. This worried me because people who came in contact with the doll often met with tragic fates. People were pushed down, inflicted with horrible diseases and even died as a result of it.

After my experiences with the Soul Collector, my reaction was predictable. I wanted nothing to do with demons. Just the mere thought of one being in the same room with me was more than I could take.

Halfway through the class, I reached out to Michael Robishaw, asking for his help.

"Yeah," he said, with his slow southern drawl. "I can send my guides in tonight. Let him know what to expect," he said.

"Can you remove the demon too?" I asked, knowing I was probably asking for more than I should have. Something about Dominic made me sad. Through his stories, it was apparent that he felt that keeping the doll was his burden. He'd been offered upwards of $50,000 for the doll, but refused, not wanting it to fall into the wrong hands. Releasing him of the burden seemed like the kindest thing anyone could do for him.

Michael paused. "Yes, but it won't be right away. I'll need to prepare my guides first. Tell him that I'll send them in 48 hours," he said.

When I came back into the room, the energy was stronger than ever. It was clear that the doll knew what was happening. I asked Dominic if he could close the canvas bag. I knew it wouldn't disconnect us from its energy, but I couldn't handle staring into its vacant eyes any longer.

I told Dominic about my phone call to Michael and he seemed relieved. Ken looked up with a startled expression.

"It just told me 'Finally! Someone worthy!" he said. I felt myself go cold inside. In all my encounters with Michael, entities usually run away from him and his guides. Hearing that a dark entity was looking forward to the encounter was less than comforting.

By the time the class ended, four of my students had pounding headaches, but we all rallied around Dominic regardless. We gave him hugs and promised to be there for him until he saw this through. The experience left an indelible mark on all of us. It felt like destiny that he found us.

Soon after I got home, I got a message from Michael.

"It's no match for my guides and the legion of archangels. Darkness will never consume the light, not while the archangels protect us. My guides have been resting and getting ready for the battle. We are going after it Wednesday night. No worries. I am also contacting Jose," he said.

Jose Prada *(shown left)* is a friend of Michael's, someone who is also capable of battling darkness on the Astral Plane. Jose describes himself as a Pagan High Priest and a High Magus, someone who practices true magick. Jose had been helping me learn how to keep myself better protected through a series of phone calls, so I trusted him as much as I trusted Michael. I felt good about what we were doing, right up to the point where I got a message from Dominic. He warned me that the demon said it was going to kill Michael.

A part of me truly panicked. If this thing was powerful enough to hurt people and cause death, then Michael might be in danger. I warned Michael that he might be dealing with a high level demon, perhaps even one of the Seven Princes of Hell, something that Dominic felt strongly about.

Michael's response was reassuring. "I have viewed this doll and the entity attached to it is a low level demon. It's a demon pretending to do the bidding for its leader. It does not have a chance to survive this battle."

I felt a little better, but was still nervous about everything that was unfolding. I thought back to three weeks beforehand when I decided to tackle the subject of demonology for my Paranormal 101 class. Was I led towards this moment? Had it all really started three weeks earlier when I made the decision to talk about demons, something I normally steered clear of?

I tried to relax and pray for everyone. I prayed for Dominic, asking that he find some relief. I prayed for Michael, asking for strength to see this through, and I prayed for all of my class, hoping I didn't lead them into a pit of seething danger. Shortly afterwards, I received a message from Dominic that he was under attack. My heart sank.

Dominic's attack was brutal. After blacking out in the bathroom, he found himself on the floor with his head resting on the tub. Excruciating pain radiated from his chest. It was so powerful, he feared he was having a heart attack. He reached for the phone, wondering if he should call 911, but realized the call would be for nothing. This was a demonic attack. What could emergency personnel do about it? He messaged me instead, asking for prayers.

I messaged Michael again, but he assured me that he wasn't doing anything. "It's bluffing, trying to scare me, hoping I will back down. No chance that is going to happen," he said. He also suggested that Dominic move the doll outside, away from him. "It's using whatever it can. It's scared and has good reason to be I have called in the whole Legion of Archangels, my spirit guides and Jose's spirit guides. That, I hardly ever do."

I called Dominic, worried about his welfare, but he couldn't talk. I hung up and spent the next few minutes worrying.

Moments later, the phone rang. It was Dominic returning my call. He was in so much pain, my heart went out to him. What had I done? I felt horrible for doing something that brought him so much pain. I tried to reassure him with Michael's words. "It's not a high level demon. It's bluffing, trying to gain more power," I told him, but Dominic wasn't convinced.

"It's trying to fool Michael. He hasn't even seen the real demon yet," he told me.

I relayed this information to Michael, who was quick to dismiss the information. "My guides say that it's not. It's more like the opposite. He gives it power by believing it. Until he can separate himself from it, our help will be futile."

At that point, Michael backed off. He called off his guides and archangels and asked Jose to do the same. "We can't help him if he does not have 100% confidence in us or our strengths. With his mind being under control, it can put us all in danger," he told me.

I spent a sleepless night, tossing and turning in my bed. When I did fall asleep, I was assaulted with horrifically bloody dreams where I was being chased by demons. I met Dominic the next day for lunch and found him to be in even worse shape. He could barely walk, the pain was so intense.

The first thing I did was apologize.

"I'm sorry for jumping in and trying to help without asking you first," I told him. "I don't think you're ready for this to end. I think you still have answers you're looking for."

He winced as he leaned back in his chair. "I'm ready for this to end, but I can't end it until those three lost souls are released," he told me. He felt that the demon attached to the doll had also grasped onto three human souls and wanted to help them before he destroyed the doll. I knew my argument was pointless, but I tried anyway.

"Michael can do that. He's that good," I said and then saw my words miss their mark. It became clear to me that everything Dominic had been through had left a mark on him. Many others claimed to be able to help him and hadn't. He didn't know who to trust and who to believe in. Why should he believe someone he just met? I left the restaurant with a heavy heart, feeling I could have helped him through Michael, but also knowing the timing wasn't right.

The following night was filled with more restless demon dreams and the next day found me with an excruciating migraine, something the doll frequently does to people it doesn't like. Other members of my class had headaches and terrifying nightmares as well. Several others experienced a series of bad luck that seemed to come out of nowhere. I tried to talk to Jose on the phone, but had the call cut out five times while we spoke. Later that evening, my four cats and my dog came barreling out of the kitchen, leaving their full bowls of food behind as they stared over their shoulders in fear.

One of my friends reached out to me the next morning. Gina Bengtson was a paranormal investigator and a sensitive. She was also prone to spirit attachment, which made our friendship even more profound. She was worried about what she had experienced at the class the night before and offered to reach out to our mutual friend psychic medium Chris George to get his take on it.

Chris took a look and agreed with Michael's findings. It wasn't a high-level demon and was something that could be removed without much effort. Chris reached out to Dominic, offering to do an exorcism, but Dominic refused.

Things began to become clear to me at that point.

Dominic was enjoying the attention the doll brought to him. He didn't want the attachment removed. I wasn't certain if the demon was impacting his decisions or if he was just riding the wave of fame, but I immediately cut off all contact with him. He brought danger into my classroom, something I found unforgiveable.

I was also angry at myself for allowing it to happen. I should have done more research on Dominic and the doll before inviting him to sit in on one of my classes. Now, we were dealing with something we'd never encountered before as a group.

Demonic encounters aren't something I took lightly.

Michael sent his guides in to clear our energy and soon the attacks on my class abated. Michael had come to my rescue once more.

Unfortunately, it wouldn't be our last battle with a demon. When we decided to take a group trip to Gettysburg, Pennsylvania the following summer, we would soon meet another one.

It would be the one that would nearly take my life.

Chapter 33

The Move

I'm not always transparent about the bad things that happen in my life. I prefer to focus on the positive and keep my life as happy as possible, but that isn't always easy to do.

Sometimes things happen that are out of our control. It's how we contend with them that affect our lives the most. We can either latch onto them, allowing them to sour everything else in our lives, or we can see them as lessons.

In 2013, I allowed my house to go into foreclosure. Due to a calamity of errors, my mortgage company decided to escrow my town taxes, causing my already high mortgage to skyrocket to a price I could no longer afford. Compounding this issue, the housing market had plunged in the eight years since I purchased the house and my house was worth $100,000 less than what I owed on it.

I've always been a big believer in fate and destiny. I also believe that most things happen for a reason. After experiencing one disappointment after another, I began paying attention to the signs that were sent to me and started turning my life around.

This was, hands down, the worst thing that ever happened to me. After all those years of struggling to keep my credit rating high and to pay my bills on time, I was now looking at having to declare bankruptcy to protect myself from the bank due to the foreclosure. I went from hopeful to hopeless in a matter of months. I moved my son and myself into an apartment an hour away, closer to his new college, and did nothing more than survive. Six months later, I was hit with a second major blow. The pet industry chain was moving my national job to the corporate office in Texas. I could either move with it or quit.

Moving simply wasn't an option. I was supporting a son who was only in his first year of college and wasn't even certain I could financially survive in Texas. I ended up taking the severance package and made a leap of faith that everything would work out for me. In less than a year, I went through foreclosure, bankruptcy and unexpected unemployment.

During this period of time, I truly began connecting with my spiritual side. I began communicating with my spirit guides and learning to watch for signs. Several psychic medium friends echoed what I was beginning to suspect. Obstacles were being removed for me so I was able to do what I was born to do: write.

I cranked out 14 books in four years, making just enough to survive on. I'd like to say this was my happily-ever-after, but life had more in store for me. In 2015, as my lease was running out on my apartment, my son hit me with some news. He wanted to move in with his girlfriend and begin his own life. Not only did this mean I wouldn't have his daily companionship, I'd also lose the child support which helped me stay afloat. With a heavy heart, I swallowed my pride and made the decision to move back into my old house, which was still in foreclosure.

I couldn't purchase anything else until the house was out of foreclosure. I called the bank to inquire about their intentions on selling it and was met with indifference. My lawyer told me that houses in my town weren't selling well and that the bank might hold onto it for another five years, for all she knew. "You might as well wait it out in the house instead of paying rent somewhere else," she told me.

Moving back into the house that I abandoned two years previously wasn't an easy feat. Water pipes were busted, heating radiators were cracked and cobwebs draped from every ceiling. Furthermore, I was also moving back into the house where I experienced the Soul Collector.

Unfortunately, I didn't have many other choices. The meager money I make on book sales, classes and events wasn't enough to support an apartment, providing I could even find one that would accept my pets.

I bit the bullet and forked out the money to have the house repaired. Pipes were fixed, an issue with the well was repaired, the house was scoured from top to bottom and walls were painted. Less than a month after I moved back in, I got another heavy blow. The bank was finally jumping into action and were selling my house at auction. After all the work and money, I had less than a month to get out of the house.

I looked for jobs, but found that I wasn't very marketable after so many years of being out of the work force. My Paranormal 101 classes were beginning to dwindle in attendance and book sales were steady, but not enough to support me in New England, which was one of the most expensive places in the United States to reside. What was I going to do?

Digging deep has become a way of life for me. Nothing has ever been handed to me. I took complete ownership of the fact that I made some terrible decisions and was paying for them. If I thought I was at rock bottom in 2012, I was now carving out a cozy space below it. Would I end up homeless? Was this how those things happened, with a slow decline that led to an unavoidable drop off? Would I become one of those sad people who lived in their cars?

I called my mother and told her about my situation and she promised me that no one would let me be homeless. "Why don't you move back to Indiana where the cost of living is much lower?" she asked me. She offered to help me finance a house in the historic town of New Harmony, a place I'd always loved. Could I really do that? Leave everything I knew and loved in New England, including my son and daughter, as well as my friends?

My former step-father stepped in and took over. Doug began tirelessly house hunting for me in New Harmony, but we weren't having much luck. Every house we found had an issue or the deal fell through. Finally, he purchased a modest mobile home that sat on a corner lot and gave it to me.

I've always been the kind of person who bounced back from hardships quickly, always searching for the bright side of situations instead of lingering on the brutal reality. Once I let go of the sense of misery, I was able to see the light at the end of the tunnel. Indiana was my home state. My family lived there, as well as several childhood friends I was still close to. Maybe I could make a fresh start there.

The more I thought about it, the more it made sense. I was born to write and life was clearing a path for me so I could continue.

My last two weeks in my Barre house were somber. I walked around the rooms, remembering all the experiences I had there. In some ways, the house was my paradise, but in other ways it was my private hell.

I never did learn if there was a body buried beneath the floor in the basement, but I did come to understand why my bedroom had always been such a hotspot. Before I left, I brought several members of my class over to check it out.

I didn't tell them anything. I just brought them in through the front door and told them to follow the energy. Every one of them walked directly to my bedroom.

"I don't know how you sleep in here," one of them said. "The energy in here is very heavy."

When Ken walked back there, he identified a possible reason.

"Is there a portal here?" he asked.

It was a good question, one Sandy and I had discussed before. A portal is considered to be a crack in the veil between our world and the spirit world, allowing ghosts easy entrance into our realm. With all the issues I had with attachments, this made perfect sense to me.

I told them about the son who had lived there and how the neighbors saw him dragging a cat across the yard with a lawnmower. Had he somehow opened the portal? If he was the kind of person people said he was, it stood to reason that he might have also dabbled in the paranormal.

"I wonder if he used an Ouija Board here?" Sandy mused.

"I don't know. Maybe," I said.

When people used divination devices such as Ouija Boards, they often drew in darker energy. When they began their sessions, they opened up a doorway to the other side. If they didn't properly close the session, they left that doorway wide open for more ghosts to come through.

"I'm also picking up on an older male that I believe belongs to the house. I think he lived here at one point," Ken said.

"Is he heavy set with a white sleeveless undershirt?" I asked. Since returning to the house, that image had flashed through my mind several times as I felt him linger nearby. I also saw him with grey hair and a mustache. His t-shirt was dirty, as though he wore it for weeks at a time before washing it.

I wasn't sure if I was just fabricating the information, based on what I already knew about the former homeowners or if it was an accurate description of the ghost. I held back the rest of my analysis to see what Ken had to add.

"Yes. His shirt is very dirty and he has short grey hair that is thinning on the top," he said. "He's more than heavy-set though. I see him as almost obese."

The validation was useful for me. It was easy to dismiss the images that popped into my head as imagination. Knowing that someone else picked up the same images gave me more confidence in myself.

We spent a few minutes trying to counsel him and help him cross over into the light, but he refused to go.

"He wants to stay here and oversee the house. I think he still has family that's still living. He checks in on them when he's not here," Ken said.

We attempted to close the portal, but we weren't successful. Instead, we did a cleansing of the house and built a spiritual boundary that would hopefully help the next owners of the house.

My class threw a "going away" party for me at a local coffee shop and the tears flowed like rivers. I felt like I'd finally found my tribe. After all those years of living alone and feeling the pangs of utter loneliness, I was being forced to leave it all behind and start anew.

My only consolation was that I was finally leaving the haunting in Barre behind me. I prayed that my next house wouldn't come with its own portal.

With a heavy heart, I packed up my belongings into a moving truck and headed to Indiana, hoping the road ahead of me held promise.

(Above) Joni's going-away party. Top row (L-R) Ken Murray, Suzie Mendonca Dennehy, Victoria Hanson, Jill Anne, Pamela Howell, Ray Richard, Crystal Pina. Second row (L-R) Sandra Chase, Sandy MacLeod, Joni Mayhan, Katie Bostock, Jackie Kent, Marion Luoma. Front row (L-R) Barbara Kirk Niles, Gina Bengtson, Jo-Anne Burdin

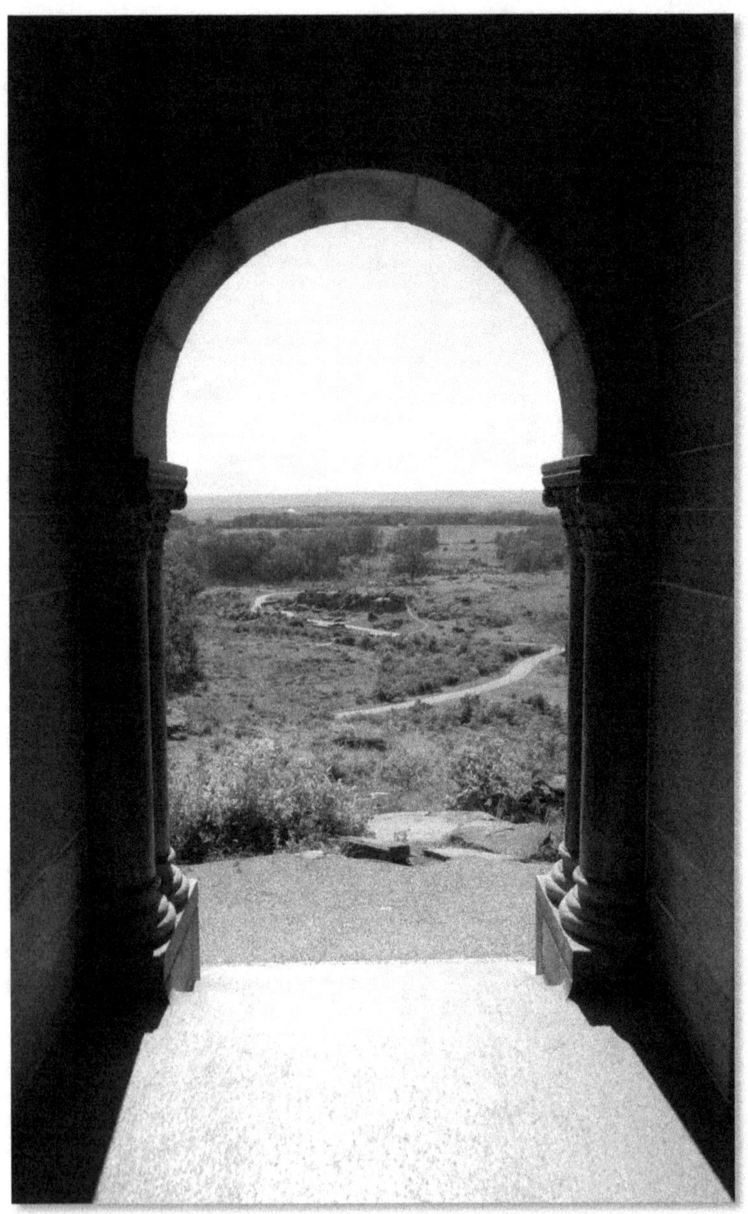

(Above) Photo taken from inside the Little Roundtop monument, looking down at Devil's Den

CHAPTER 34

THE GETTYSBURG TRIP

Instead of caravanning to Pennhurst and Gettysburg with my group, I made the drive alone.

I had only been gone for two weeks, but it felt as though I had been gone much longer. In some ways, it seemed as though I was plopped directly into an alternate universe. The landscape was different, but yet my core existence was the same. I still had my pets, which now included four cats and my dog Ripley, and I still had all my treasured personal belongings. Everything else in my world had been dramatically altered.

I spent my days unpacking and attempting to clean the dirty mobile home that I had been given. While I was happy to have a place to live, I wasn't thrilled with the living conditions. It felt like sliding backwards.

I was at the age where I should have been thinking about an upcoming retirement, but I was starting over again with a broken down trailer. I stayed busy, but thoughts of my friends haunted me. Being away from them had been painful in ways I never expected.

Gone was the easy access to validation. When I felt a ghost nearby, I had to dig deep and rely on my own abilities. In some ways, I think it forced me to grow stronger and trust myself. In that sense, it wasn't a bad thing, but it made life difficult all the same.

As I drove the thirteen hour drive to Pennsylvania, I thought about how swiftly life changes. When I first began making plans to go to Gettysburg, I had no idea I'd be driving there from my new home in Indiana.

I had first suggested going to Gettysburg as a class group in the middle of the previous winter, when we all needed something promising to cling to. The winter winds howled outside Terrapin Traders as we sat huddled around a small floor heater. Thinking about walking through the warm, grassy battlefields seemed like Heaven.

Initially, I thought it would end up as a pipe dream. We would talk about it, but it would never pan out. Those kinds of things seemed to happen frequently in my life. I often adopted a "plan for the worst, hope for the best philosophy." As it turns out, I didn't need the pessimism. This trip was part of my destiny and would happen, regardless of my thoughts. Everything fell neatly into place, like plans seldom do.

As the plans began to formulate, I learned that there was going to be a paranormal convention at an old haunted asylum in Pennsylvania in June. If I could get Michael Robishaw onboard, we could reserve a booth and have a book signing for our book *Ruin of Souls*.

Since Gettysburg was only a few hours away from the asylum, our group could get a chance to visit two haunted locations in the same week.

Once I proposed this to my class, many people were onboard with the plans. Michael confirmed that he was free and was interested. All I needed to do was book the event.

Nothing in my life had ever worked out so simply. I should have been suspicious, but it didn't occur to me that I was following a path that would lead me to my most terrifying experience. I was just happy that the trip was actually going to happen.

The first leg of our trip was to the Pennhurst State School and Hospital.

Located in Spring City, Pennsylvania, the school was originally known as the Eastern Pennsylvania Institution for the Feeble Minded and Epileptic. First opening in 1908, the school and hospital became quickly overcrowded, housing the severely mentally ill side-by-side with patients of lesser handicaps. Due to a lack of sufficient state funding, the hospital soon became "the shame of Pennsylvania." Abuse and mistreatment of the patients became rampant. Patients, which included a large amount of children, sat in their own waste and were often physically abused. The hospital closed in 1987, leaving behind an unimaginable haunting.

(Above: one of the many buildings on the hospital grounds. The Philadelphia Building)

Michael and I were assigned space on the second floor of the old Mayflower Building. It was dusty and dirty with windows that didn't open, which was an issue on a day with ninety degree temperatures.

We set up our table and sent Ken out to a local store to purchase fans and a floor lamp so we weren't sitting in a dark room. Michael's daughter Sara shared a table with Sandy, both selling their hand-made jewelry.

While I loved the concept of being in an old asylum, the reality of sitting there for eight hours was brutal. It was hot, even with the newly purchased fans, and we spent the day sweltering in the heat.

(Above: Sandy MacLeod selling her beautiful jewelry beside Joni's booth with Michael Robishaw)

My friends enjoyed roaming around the grounds. The administrators of the event had opened up an additional building for participants to explore.

Devan Hall was once used as an ambulatory building, housing both male and female patients. Instead of getting the treatment they needed for their mental health needs, the patients were often neglected, with many being bound to metal containers that looked more like cages.

I broke away from the book signing on the second day of the event to explore Devon Hall with Ken. As we wandered around the building, we could feel the souls of the dead following us. At one point, a young female followed us as we made our way through the maze of rooms. She seemed curious about us, but drifted off before we could pull very much information about her.

(Above: Our group at Pennhurst Asylum. Top row (L-R): Barbara Kirk Niles, Mary Lou Moriarty, Ken Murray, Sandy MacLeod. Second Row (L-R): Crystal Pina, Joni Mayhan, Michael Robishaw, Sara Robishaw)

It occurred to me that ghosts in public facilities like Pennhurst probably get used to the constant parade of people passing through. They become like feral cats, never fully trusting the intentions of the people they see.

Getting to put on my author hat was always a thrill for me. After so many years of struggling as a writer, it felt reaffirming to get dressed up and sit at a table and sign my books for my fans. I enjoyed talking with people and listening to their paranormal tales, but after a while I began longing for some down time. Holding a smile in place for eight hours was harder than it seemed, especially for someone who wasn't used to smiling so much.

While I enjoyed getting to spend time with Michael Robishaw, the hot, airless rooms of the hospital made me eager for the second leg of our trip.

We said our goodbyes to Michael and were soon on our way.

***

I booked two cabins at a popular Gettysburg campground to accommodate our group.

(Above: one of the cabins we stayed in that was nicknamed "The Party Cabin")

The campground was nestled in the rolling hills just outside Gettysburg, making it the perfect option. We would be able to enjoy all the benefits of camping, while still getting to sleep in actual beds. An added bonus was that they also had bathrooms and full kitchens where we could prepare all of our meals.

The cabins were nicer than anyone expected and we quickly claimed their sleeping spaces in our assigned cabins. After months of planning, I decided to divide the group up according to sleep preferences. One cabin would be set aside for the group who wanted a quieter environment, while the other group was assigned the second cabin. They were quickly labeled the Zen Cabin and the Party Cabin.

I already knew that we would have a few issues. It's almost impossible to pull together ten people who only saw each other once a week and then expect them to get along perfectly. There were a few battles over sleeping arrangements, cooking duties and overall courteousness, but we managed through it without much bloodshed. Once we got all that settled, we set off to explore the area.

(Above) Looking down from a monument on Little Roundtop to Devils Den and the surrounding valley

Gettysburg was such an amazing place. Besides the hundreds of acres of preserved battlefields, it also offered a quaint downtown area with a plethora of shopping, museums and restaurants.

We spent several days exploring the area, taking in the sights. The battlefields were monumental, holding in the energy from the Civil War battles that ensued there.

As I stood at the top of Little Roundtop, looking down at the valley below where so many soldiers lost their lives, I could feel the energy surging from the ground. The area had a sense of sorrow embedded in it, something you could feel even if you weren't metaphysically gifted.

(Above) One of the cannons alongside the battlefields

The weather was glorious, with nothing but blue skies and pleasant temperatures for the duration of our trip. Evenings were spent at the battlefields until we were forced to leave. We would then retreat back to the cabins where we would stay up until the wee hours of the morning, drinking and laughing. It was a little piece of Heaven wrapped up in one trip.

(Above) Dusk at Gettysburg

Our cabins were rented until Thursday, giving us four full days to experience Gettysburg. On Friday, Sandy and I planned on continuing to Maryland to investigate an old historic mansion that Michael Robishaw had suggested. I was hoping to have enough experiences there to write a book about it, but the plans fell through. The owner of the mansion was called away on an emergency, leaving Sandy and I with two days to spare. It was the first hiccup of the trip, one that seemingly diverted us to another agenda altogether.

"Why don't we just rent a smaller cabin and stay here for a few more days?" Sandy suggested.

"Great idea!" While I was disappointed about the cancellation of the Maryland mansion, I was excited about getting to spend two more days in Gettysburg. Ken and Barbara Kirk Niles decided to stay on with us as well.

As our last night as a group in Gettysburg was coming to an end, we decided to make one more pilgrimage to the battlefields. After spending the week feeling so much sorrowful energy, we wanted to see if we could perhaps cross over a few lost souls.

(Above: Sandy and Ken at one of the monuments shortly before we crossed over several lost souls)

Just the thought made my heart soar. I couldn't imagine being suspended in time, forced to relive all the emotions and tragedy of the battle over and over again. If we could cross a few of them over into the light, we could end their pain and give them the peace and salvation they deserved. It seemed like the right thing to do.

We went out onto the battlefields at dusk and found a location that seemed to call to us. As the sun sank deeply on the horizon, sending a rosy glow across the tall grassy fields, we linked hands and began our process.

"If there is anyone here who would like to join us, we welcome you into our circle. We are going to open a white light above us, one that leads to Heaven. You can now put down your gun and join your family," I said.

"It's okay for you to leave now. You've done your duty. Now it's time to rest," Sandy added.

We felt several souls rush in and pass into the white light. It was one of the easiest crossing-over sessions we'd ever conducted. We wouldn't learn the full impact we made until later that night.

I was tired when we got back, so I headed off to bed shortly afterwards. Fueled by the energy from the evening, Barbara decided to stay up for a while, joining two friends, Mary Lou and Pam in the Zen cabin.

As they were chatting, they began to hear a noise outside. The women paused in their conversation and stared at the dark windows.

"What was that?" Mary Lou asked with wide eyes.

"It sounded like a growl," Pam said.

As the three sat in silence, they began hearing scratches at the windows. It wasn't branches brushing against the windows. It was far more deliberate. The scratching noises were spaced out, sounding exactly like claws on glass.

"It sounds like something is trying to get inside," Barbara said.

"Could it be a tree branch?" Mary Lou asked.

"I don't think so. If it was a tree branch, we would have heard it before tonight," Pam pointed out.

Every time it happened, the women jumped. If something was trying to get their attention, it certainly hit its goal. They moved onto the couch together, watching the dark windows, waiting for the next scratch.

"Oh my God! What is that?" Barbara said, her voice sounding shrill in the quiet room.

"I don't know, but I think we need to wake Sandy up," Mary Lou said. They all stared at one another, thoughts racing through their minds.

Anyone who knows Sandy well knows better than to wake her up unless it's a true emergency. They hemmed and hawed about it for several minutes before they finally made the decision to alert her.

By the time Sandy came into the living room the scratching had stopped.

"It's probably just branches scratching against the windows," she told them. "It's nothing to be worried about."

They weren't convinced she was right, but they didn't have any other options. Everyone else was asleep at the other cabin. Waking up Sandy was one thing, but disrupting a whole cabin seemed unreasonable. They settled back down and finally managed to get some sleep.

By the light of the next morning, the terror of the previous night had lessened. They convinced themselves that it must have been what Sandy had suggested and didn't think much else about it.

We began packing up our vehicles and said our sad goodbyes to the rest of the group in the parking lot. By mid-afternoon, Sandy, Ken, Barbara and I had settled into our smaller cottage and were eager to enjoy our last two days at Gettysburg.

It was a sad time for us. Having friends like those wasn't something that had ever come easy to me. Watching them drive off felt final in some way. I knew we would still get together on occasion, but distance would play a role in our union now. Nothing would ever be the same again.

(Above: several members of our group on the last day of our group stay. (L-R) Joni Mayhan, Crystal Pina, Ken Murray, Barbara Kirk Niles, Mary Lou Moriarty, Sandy MacLeod)

We spent the day visiting the museum and just puttering around the town. We returned to the battlefields and worked on crossing over more lost souls. Several more passed through the white light, making us feel good about the trip as a whole.

Helping the lost souls cross over felt like a rescue mission. I tried to imagine the sense of suffering they had endured for the past century, wandering around a familiar landscape with no hope of finding their way home.

Were they trapped in the Civil War, reliving the event over and over again? Or were they aware of the situation and just couldn't find their way out of it? We couldn't be sure, but it felt so wonderful to alleviate their pain.

By evening, we were settled around the small kitchen table, enjoying a game and a few adult beverages. Something about the evening didn't feel right though. The conversations seemed forced and the laughter was at an all-time low. By 10pm, we were all yawning and ready for bed, something we hadn't done so early all week.

The smaller cabin had two bedrooms and a sofa. We gave Sandy one bedroom to herself, while Barbara and I shared the other queen-sized bed. Ken slept on the couch.

The room Barbara and I shared was barely big enough for the queen-sized bed. The walls were covered with brown wood paneling reminiscent of the 1970's. A television sat on top of a squat dresser at the foot of the bed near the door. It wasn't deluxe accommodations, but it would do.

I changed into my sleep shorts and t-shirt, popped two melatonin tablets and crawled into bed, hoping for a quiet night's sleep. After the four days in the other cabin, where we stayed up half the night partying, I really needed the rest.

I was used to sleeping alone, so the prospects of sharing a bed with someone else made me a little uncomfortable. I planned on hugging my edge of the bed and praying that I didn't make any unladylike snores to keep Barbara awake.

"Do you mind if I keep the TV on?" Barbara asked me as she climbed into the bed beside me.

"No, that's fine. Just keep the volume low." I normally didn't sleep with a TV on, but I'd hardly notice it with my sleep mask on.

I had barely rolled over, when I began hearing a buzzing sound in my ears. Something was there with us.

Even after everything I'd been through with the spirit world, I couldn't help the terror that swept through me, hot and wild. I sat bolt upright and whipped off my sleep mask.

"Something is here and I don't like the feel of it," I said.

Barbara gasped. "Oh my God. I was just going to tell you…I just saw a shadow move across the doorway," she said.

Ghosts were no stranger to either of us. We'd been on dozens of investigations together, but something about this particular ghost set my teeth on edge.

It had a negative vibe to it. I didn't try to reach out with my mind to pull an image. I didn't want to draw it in any closer than it already was. Instead, I called to Ken and Sandy.

"There's something in here," I told them as they appeared in our doorway, looking sleepy.

Sandy had already changed into her nightgown.

"What's going on?" she asked, then narrowed her eyes. "Something is in here. I wonder if it followed us from the battlefield?"

Ken stared across the room, honing in on the far corner beside the bed where I felt the presence.

"Let me go get my cleansing kit," he said and disappeared from the doorway. Several minutes later, he returned with a stick of Palo Santos wood, something we often used in place of sage.

None of us were thinking about the implications of burning the wood inside the cabin. We were too fixated on getting the ghost out. We realized our mistake as the smoke detector above Ken's head began blaring.

"Oh shit!" I swore.

The alarm was maddening, nearly splitting our skulls with its piercing wail. Ken extinguished the wood stick and we all began furiously fanning the air until the detector grew silent again.

Ken shook his head, embarrassed. "I didn't even think about that," he said. "I guess we won't be burning anything inside here. Let's try holy water."

He left the room again and returned with a spray bottle full of holy water, something Michael had given him at the book signing. It seemed relevant that the water came from Michael. It felt more potent.

The three of us watched while Ken sprayed all of the walls inside the cabin. When he finished, we sat on my bed as a group and attempted to connect our energy, similar to what Sandy and I had done with Jeff years ago.

I could feel the energy swell, pushing out from us like a cyclone. It swirled around us, gaining strength as it filled the room. Soon, the buzzing faded. The ghost was gone.

"It's gone now," I said, heaving a sigh of relief.

"I wonder if it followed us from the battlefield?" Sandy asked again.

"Or was hanging around the campground?" I added. I hadn't tried to read the energy. It reminded me too much of the other negative entities I had encountered.

"I don't know, but it's gone now," Sandy said. "I'm going back to bed." She swiveled on her heels and headed out of the room. Ken followed suit, telling us to call them if we felt it return.

As soon as they left, Barbara turned to me with wide eyes. "That was wild," she said. "How weird was it that you felt it at the same time I saw it?" she asked.

"Pretty weird," I agreed. Barbara was the kind of person who needed to talk about the things she experienced, but I didn't want to discuss it anymore. I knew from previous encounters that discussing a ghost could actually pull it back to us. I tried to put it out of my mind.

"Let's try to get some sleep," I told her and rolled back over onto my side.

Sleep eventually found me, but my dreams were filled with demons. They chased me down narrow corridors, always one step behind me. No matter how fast I ran, I couldn't outrun them.

Several times, I awoke to the sensation of energy pushing towards me. It felt as though I was inside a bubble and something was pushing the bubble, trying to reach me.

I would wake up each time it happened and focus my energy outwards, pushing our shields back into place. I could see the shield in my mind's eye, edging back to the outside corner of the cabin. As soon as I fell back asleep, it happened again. By the time morning came, I felt as though I hadn't slept at all. I needed coffee.

I dragged myself down the hallway towards the kitchen, discovering the room lost in shadows. Ken was sitting on the couch, playing with his phone.

"No coffee today," he said glumly.

"What?" I was still half asleep and his words didn't make sense to me. We always had coffee. The first person up always made a pot. It would be sending fragrant tendrils of aroma throughout the cabin by the time I staggered into the kitchen.

"The power's out," he said.

I blinked and tried to focus on the room, his words slowly sinking into my sleep weary brain.

"Really?" I walked to the sliding glass door and poked my head out. I could see a light blaring on the front of another cabin just down the street from us. "Other people have power," I told him.

"Well, we don't."

I groaned. No electricity meant no coffee and no shower. I pulled on clothes and ran a brush through my hair before leaving the cabin to go figure it out.

Due to the early hour, the main office was still closed, so I walked around until I found someone standing outside his campsite.

"Do you have power?" I asked.

He gave me a strange look. "Yeah."

When I explained our situation, he told me to check with the main office. I thanked him and continued on down the street. Many of the campsites were vacant, but all of them had electric meters that were showing signs of having a live electrical source. Our cabin was the only one without power.

I came back in to find Sandy dressed and sitting on the couch with Ken.

"We're the only ones without power," I told them.

"That's so strange," Sandy commented.

None of us wanted to voice it, but we all wondered if it was due to the ghost. Had he somehow cut out our power?

Several minutes later, the power came back on. It was almost as though the ghost was waiting on us to figure it out.

As soon as the power was back, we sprang into action. Coffee was brewed and showers were taken. We didn't want to waste our last day in Gettysburg by sitting on the sofa in the cabin. An hour later, we were ready to leave.

As we walked out, I tipped my head back, trying to listen for the ghost's buzzing sound. I didn't hear anything.

"I think he's gone," I said with relief.

"Maybe what we did pushed him out," Sandy said in agreement.

As we got into my car, I marveled at how far we'd come. If this had happened to us a year or two earlier, we would have been helpless to deal with it. This time was totally different. Our combined energy had been enough to push it out. It made me realize how lost I was going to be without them when I got back to Indiana.

Sadness settled into my soul that day as I realized this was our last day together. By tomorrow this time, I'd be getting into my car alone and driving back to the place I now called home.

Life just didn't seem to be fair sometimes. When was I finally going to get the happy ending I yearned for? Why was I not allowed more than a single moment of contentment?

We spent the majority of the day roaming around the area. We stopped in an antique store to see if we could pick up on any haunted energy, but I just couldn't get my mind off my sorrows.

At Sandy's request, we stopped and had dinner at a local diner before making our way back to the campground. As we sat around on the front porch, it dawned on me that we were missing our last chance to explore the battlefields.

"What do you guys think about going back out to the battlefields and trying to cross over more lost souls?" I asked.

Everyone was a bit tired from driving around all day, but they were agreeable to my idea. It would be a fitting way to spend our last night in Gettysburg.

At dusk, the battlefields became a different place altogether. With most of the tourists gone, it settled into a peaceful and quiet place.

We decided to go to the Peach Orchard which was the site of a major Civil War Battle, resulting in 47 deaths. Sandy has always been a huge Civil War buff and spent some time educating us on the battle. We walked down the street and looked at the monument before spending some time in the orchard itself.

As we stood there, taking in the moment and feeling the energy rising from the ground, we felt several souls drift curiously in our direction.

Ken started us off. "If there is anyone here who would like to cross over into the light, we're here to help you," he said.

I nudged Barbara, urging her to participate. She often held back when we worked together as a group, but I felt that her words were important for the lost souls to hear. She had a tremendously open heart, something I was certain the ghosts could feel. If she told them they would be safe, they would trust her.

"It's okay. You'll be safe. Go find your family. They're waiting for you," she said.

Sandy and I also contributed a few words of encouragement, not stopping until we began to feel them cross over. Each night we had crossed over four or five and tonight was no different.

As the sun disappeared below the horizon, we decided to head back to the car, leaving the battlefields behind us. It was a rewarding trip, one that none of us would ever forget.

Unless you've crossed over souls, you can never fully understand the love and gratitude that comes as a byproduct. As they cross, we can often feel the emotions they experience as they see their long-lost loved ones for the first time in decades, if not centuries. We get a rush of energy that is so filled with happiness, it brings tears to our eyes. It makes everything we go through worth the effort.

As we drove down the tree lined road towards the highway, we held onto the sense of peace. It was our last night in Gettysburg and we rode the high all the way back to the cabin. Unfortunately, the night wasn't over yet.

We had experienced the best the day had to offer, but hadn't even touched the worst. It was waiting for us at the cabin.

CHAPTER 35

THE NECROMANCER

I didn't notice the ghost when we first got back to the cabin. We sat around the kitchen table, playing a game for nearly an hour before I felt it drift in.

I stiffened up and looked around the room, as if expecting to see it hovering over me.

"That thing from last night is back," I said.

"Oh, he's been here for a while," Sandy commented calmly.

I thought it was odd that we hadn't felt him during the day, but he showed up once darkness fell. Was that significant? In most hauntings I'd encountered, the ghosts were there during the day and the night. Why was this one different?

I needed to put my fears aside and pull more information from it. As I tuned into the buzzing tone, images began to pop into my head.

I saw a tall, thin, dark-skinned man with a black hat and topcoat. He wore a white shirt under the jacket that had an odd old-fashioned type collar. Instead of a traditional tie, I saw a string tie that was held together with a silver clip. When he smiled at me, the smile didn't touch his eyes. It felt more like he was baring his teeth at me.

"What do you see when you look at him, Ken?" I asked, hoping to have my mind's eye picture validated.

"He has very dark skin. It's so dark, it's almost black. I see a black hat on his head and a dark jacket. He has a white shirt on with some kind of thin tie and is carrying a silver-tipped cane," he said.

"Wow. That's exactly what I got, but I didn't see the cane. What about his eyes and his teeth?" I asked.

"When he smiles, it's sort of an evil smile. His teeth are very white and his eyes are shot with blood. I get something about voodoo too," Ken said.

"Sandy?" I asked, wondering if she was seeing the same thing. Normally, we wrote down our impressions so we didn't influence one another, but we were getting to a point where we were all seeing the same thing anyway. Sharing information helped us bring the picture into better detail.

"I'm seeing the same thing. I'm getting voodoo too," Sandy said. "He has a very evil look about him. I don't think he came from the campground either."

A word came to my mind, almost as though it were floating in air. I could see it spelled out clearly, refusing to fade.

"I see the word "necromancer," I said. "I don't know why, but it's coming into my mind. Maybe my spirit guides are telling me this."

"Necromancer as in: someone who raises the dead?" Sandy asked.

"Yes, but I think he's also a soul collector," I said, feeling a chill as I released the words I didn't want to speak. "I think he pulls the souls from those who died before they can make their way to the light and then holds onto them."

Soul collectors took the souls from the deceased and forced them to stay close to them. They would then use their energy to become stronger and more powerful. It wasn't something we saw often, but just the mere thought left me chilled to the bone.

A necromancer was something altogether different. I had never heard of a real one, only read about them in fiction books. They were supposed to be able to bring the dead back to life, raising an army of zombies.

"Let's do a cleansing right now and protect our space before he gets a foothold," Ken said.

I loved how Ken often stepped forward, taking charge of situations. He was definitely coming of his own. He wouldn't need our group for much longer. He was strong enough to start his own group and branch out.

Many times, when he explained situations to people, I heard my words come out of his mouth. It meant a lot to me to know that I had given him his start. It felt as though everything I did in teaching the class and mentoring students had a ripple effect that would continue to grow larger and larger, helping more people and more lost souls.

"Let's all go outside and I'll cleanse everyone with the Palo Santos wood," he suggested.

It sounded like a good plan, so we followed him outside. He lit the stick and cleansed each of us with the smoke, making sure it covered us completely. As he finished with each of us, we walked inside.

After the last person was cleansed, Ken walked down to the driveway to extinguish the stick. He was only gone for a minute, but when he came inside, he was whiter than a sheet.

"He's standing outside," he said.

We all jolted around to stare at him, aghast. We began rapidly firing questions at him.

"He's *what*?" I asked.

"You saw him?" Barbara asked.

"Did you see him in your mind's eye or with your normal sight?" I asked.

"I saw him with my eyes," he said, pointing to his face. "He's just standing out there at the edge of the campsite, near the electrical box. At first, I thought it was just another camper, but then he turned and smiled at me. He looked exactly like we described him down to the silver tipped cane," he said.

My mind went numb.

Was this really happening?

Seeing full-bodied apparitions was considered the Holy Grail of ghost hunting, but it was something that seldom happened.

It took a lot of energy for the dead to actually show themselves to the living. If it were easy, we would see them all the time, but it wasn't. Besides the obvious energy required, they also needed to know how to do it. It was a skill that was only known to higher level entities. Random ghosts just didn't do this.

I started towards the door, wanting to see for myself, but Sandy grabbed my arm.

"You shouldn't do that. With all the problems you've had, you shouldn't get close to him," she said.

I pulled against her grip, feeling the emotions inside of me collide. In all the years of paranormal investigating, I had never seen a completely full-bodied apparition. I saw pieces of them, but never the full thing besides the ghost in the pet store. By Ken's description, this one looked as solid as a living person. I wanted to see it.

"He's been targeting you this whole time. Think about it. Last night, he didn't bother anyone else, but he spent the entire night trying to push back our shields to get to you. He wasn't worried about any of the rest of us. He wanted you. You shouldn't go out there," she said, holding me prisoner with her penetrating stare.

Her words rang through me, hitting their mark. What she said was true. If I went out there, he might latch onto me in ways I'd never experienced before, even after everything I had already endured. I was an easy mark for him.

"Let's pull the blinds and create a spiritual boundary," Ken suggested.

"That sounds like a good idea," Sandy agreed.

While Ken walked around and sprayed every door, window and wall in the cabin with holy water, Barbara, Sandy and I pulled the blinds. It seemed almost silly to bother locking the doors against something that could easily walk through walls, but we did it anyway. If nothing else, it set the intention of our desires to keep the apparition outside.

After we finished, we reunited in the living room to say a prayer and build an energy shield. We said the Lord's Prayer and also the Prayer to Saint Michael the Archangel and then filled our bubble with white ethereal light from the heavens.

Even though we were desperate to talk about what had happened, we knew that it wouldn't be a good idea. We didn't want to give him the opportunity to come back inside.

"I think we're good," Sandy said. "We should think about getting to bed. We all have long drives ahead of us."

Sleep was the furthest thing from my mind, but I knew she was right. Gettysburg was a little further west than Spring City, where we went to the paranormal convention, but I was still eleven hours away from home. It was already well past midnight by that point. If I hoped to get home at a reasonable hour, I'd need to leave by 9am at the latest.

We said our goodnights and headed off to our beds, still shaken by the events that had just transpired.

"Can I turn the TV on again?" Barbara asked.

"That's a good idea," I said. I could still hear the faint buzzing of the Necromancer outside the cabin. It wasn't as loud as it had been the previous night, leading me to believe that our shields would hold up against him.

I knew from previous experience that by listening to the tones ghosts made, I often drew them in closer. Over time, I began to think it was part of my problem. When I honed in on them, it somehow gave them permission to come closer to me.

I learned how to "listen around" the buzzing sounds, but I couldn't completely turn it off. If I found another noise in the room that I could listen to, I could put it out of my thoughts. Having the television on would serve that purpose very nicely.

As Barbara turned the TV on, I rolled over onto my side and pulled on my sleep mask, praying that sleep would find me quickly. I knew that ghosts could still get to me in my sleep by impacting my dreams, but they couldn't touch me in any other way. It was my safe place and I yearned for it with all my might.

Barbara climbed into bed with me and snuggled up behind me. Normally, this would annoy me and I'd move the required distance to put a space between our bodies, but I found it oddly comforting. Knowing there was someone else in the bed with me made me feel safer somehow.

I began to drift off to sleep when I was woken up by a loud bang on the window beside me. I sat up and whipped off my sleep mask.

The room was aglow from the light of the television, giving me full view of the space. Nothing seemed amiss and no apparitions skulked in the corners.

"What the hell was that?" Barbara said.

"It was a bang on the window. Apparently someone wants inside," I said.

As soon as the words left my mouth, I felt the energy shield pushing inwards towards me like I had the night before. I sprang from the bed, terror filling every cell in my body.

"It's in the room again!" I shouted out.

Sandy and Ken came running. By their alert appearance, neither of them had fallen asleep yet either.

"Let's build another shield," Sandy suggested.

We sat on my bed and held hands, like we do when we're crossing over souls, and attempted to link our energy. I felt it swirl around us, building strength and radiating out into the room. The more we pushed, the more the Necromancer pushed back against us. After a moment, we dropped our hands and stared at each other.

"Let me try something. I'm going to utilize my Wiccan training and call in a goddess to help us," Sandy said.

We watched her as she worked through the process of summoning the goddess, calling her out by name and asking for her assistance.

The room seemed to grow cold, despite the warm June evening. Something was definitely changing.

I wasn't certain what I thought about many of the Wiccan customs. I respected them, but couldn't fully latch onto them after a lifetime of being Christian. I believed in one God, not two, which was the Wiccan belief. But at that moment, I felt comforted by what Sandy was doing. Something else was now in the room with us and it was pushing the Necromancer out.

I had a small bottle of holy water in my bag, so I fortified our spiritual barrier inside the room with another blast on each wall, window and door. When I was finished, I put my hand on the door frame and imagined all the sprays linking together and creating a solid wall of white light energy.

We sat and stared at each other for a moment, not wanting to celebrate too soon, but the results were apparent. We had pushed the Necromancer back out again and our spiritual boundaries were holding strong.

It was now well after 2am and we were beyond exhausted. Creating spiritual boundaries and contending with the dead are often draining processes. We all needed sleep.

We parted ways once more and headed to our respectful beds, but none of us got much sleep. The night's silence was frequently interrupted by pounding on the windows as he made his way around the outside of the cabin, trying to get inside. Both Barbara and I had horrific nightmares. Barbara woke us both up as she shouted in her sleep several times. By the time dawn crested the horizon, we were more exhausted than we had been before we went to bed.

I got up, lured by the smell of freshly brewed coffee. I filled a mug and brought it out onto the small porch where I found Ken sitting.

"Good morning," I said, sleepily. "Thanks for making coffee. I really needed it this morning," I told him.

"You're welcome. Did you get any sleep?" he asked in a voice that was far too cheery for the circumstances. He was obviously a morning person, something I found inconceivable at the moment.

"A little bit, but he kept pounding on the windows all night."

"I heard them too. He must have spent the night circling the cabin, trying to find a way inside," he said. "He's gone now though. I don't feel him at all."

This seemed to be the pattern with this ghost. He only came to us during the night. I wondered what that meant. It seemed so strange to me.

A thought occurred to me. I was surprised I hadn't thought of it the night before.

"We should get Michael involved in this. We can't leave this thing here to terrorize other people," I said, pulling my phone out of my pocket. I typed out a quick message to him, asking if he could send his guides in to remove the ghost from the area. I didn't provide him with any other details, other than the fact that something had been bothering us. Michael often didn't care about the specifics. It just created a longer message he would have to read. His guides would handle it, no matter what it was.

Sandy and Barbara both joined us. We spent a few minutes discussing the night's events before we started packing up our cars. We hadn't been at the cabin very long, but we still had a lot of work ahead of us.

By 10am, the cabin was empty and the cars were packed. The only thing left were to say our goodbyes and hit the road.

The last time we had parted, we knew we still had our Gettysburg trip ahead of us. Now, there was nothing. We would drive away in separate directions, not knowing when we would see each other again. It felt final in a way, something that burned a hole in my heart.

I followed Barbara's van to the front entrance of the campground, where we threw away the trash and returned the keys. When we met outside the entrance, our faces all reflected the way we were feeling.

We leaned in for a group hug, feeling the energy soar between us like it had the night before. With a final goodbye, we pulled apart. They all piled into Barbara's van, while I got into my car by myself.

As I drove away from the campground, I watched her van grow smaller and smaller in my rear view mirror, feeling the misery grow thorns inside my soul.

I was so caught up in my tears, it would take me several hours to realize that I wasn't alone.

The Necromancer had come with me.

(Above) Joni, Sandy, Ken and Barbara

Chapter 36

Chasing the Miles

I chased the miles, driving as fast as I could manage, my eyes constantly seeking the rear view mirror, terrified at what I might find in my backseat.

In my heart loomed a horror I couldn't wrap my mind around. Had this really happened to me again?

Did another demon latch onto me?

Why was this happening?

Was I marked in some way, creating a beacon they could easily follow?

I could hear the entity's words inside my head. They rattled around like a loose screw in a frantically racing machine.

When it gets dark, I will show myself to you and cause you to have an accident.

I saw his scenario unfold in my mind, playing with such perfect detail that it felt more like a memory than a vision. I would watch dusk settled on the horizon as I crossed the border into Kentucky, still hours away from home. I would feel his presence before I actually saw him, catching movement out of the corner of my eye as a passing car illuminated the interior of my car.

I'd turn with a gasp and he would be there in all his immortal glory, grinning at me with teeth that were crusted with cemetery dirt. His face was as black as the inside of a crypt, making the whites of his eyes seem brighter, almost as though they were illuminated by an internal fire, reminding me of something from a Halloween display. His white shirt was neatly pressed beneath his slim black jacket, but I only saw this detail for a moment. My eyes were too fixated on his horrible sneer. It made me want to crawl inside of myself and find a place to hide where he couldn't find me.

He wanted to tear my flesh from my bones with those horrible teeth, one painful bite after another, and then spit me out, claiming my soul as his own until he had pulled every ounce of light from it.

"God, help me," I whispered.

I wanted a cigarette, even though I hadn't smoked for more than two years. The need was so strong, I nearly pulled over at the next exit to purchase a pack, before I realized that cigarettes weren't going to help me with this.

What I needed was someone to sweep in and save me. I needed a miracle because this thing was in my backseat, patiently waiting for darkness to fall.

That was all I could think about.

Darkness and what it would bring.

I needed gas, so I took an exit that promised a gas station in West Virginia. The road winded off to the left until it came to a stop light. A sign for the gas station pointed to the right.

I pulled up to the pump and got out of my car, my legs feeling as though they were made of rubber bands. When I put my credit card into the slot, it came up with an error message, telling me to see the attendant. This was the last thing I needed. I had to get home before dark. If I didn't, I was afraid I wouldn't make it home at all.

I ran in to see the clerk, waving my credit card in front of me. I told her about the message and she looked at me questioningly.

"Really? I've never seen it do that before. Let me come take a look," she said.

She was a fresh-faced girl of eighteen or nineteen, with long strawberry blond hair and an earnest smile. I couldn't remember how long it had been since I was that way. Life and all its experiences had hardened me over time. Earnest smiles didn't come easily to me anymore.

She swiped my card, only to get the same message.

"This is really weird," she said, frowning at the machine.

I didn't think it was weird at all. High level entities could perform amazing feats when they set their minds to it. Delaying me at the gas station was only one of his tricks.

"Let's go inside and I'll plug in the numbers manually. Don't worry! We'll get you your gas!" she said, probably reading the frustrated expression on my face.

As I followed her back into the store, the Necromancer was close on my heels. I could hear his tone buzzing loudly in my ear, like he'd been doing for the past several hours.

I hadn't realized the Necromancer was in the car with me until I'd been on the road for several hours. Once I realized what had happened, I called Sandy immediately.

"He followed me. He's in the car with me now!" I nearly shouted into her ear.

There was some commotion inside the car as she relayed the information.

"That's strange that you can hear him now. When we were at the campground, none of us felt him during the day. I wonder what changed?" she asked.

I thought about it, then the realization hit me.

"He needs to gain more energy, so he's allowing me to pick up on him. That way I'll feed him with fear," I said breathlessly. He must have tapped my inner thoughts and discovered what scared me the most. Now, he was threatening to use it against me in hopes that I fed him energy.

"We'll do what we can from our end. Have you contacted Michael?" she asked. Michael had become our savior in more ways than one. Reaching out to him was usually my first reaction to bad ghosts.

"Yes. I contacted him when we were still at the cabin. I'll send him a message when I stop for gas next to make sure he's coming," I told her.

"Be careful," Sandy said before hanging up. She'd been through all this with me before. Going through it again seemed almost surreal.

(Above: I tried to take a picture while I was at the gas station, hoping to capture what was going on, but all I found was my own scared face)

Something about this particular ghost bothered me. He had a different texture. It felt slimy and uncomfortable, the way you feel when a lecherous sexual predator stares at you. I hadn't been this creeped out since the Soul Collector first latched onto me. It made me wonder if this was more than just a ghost.

Hours later, as I watched the fresh-faced woman type in my credit card information, I realized that I was putting her in danger just by being in front of her. I had become a walking time bomb. I could feel him in my head, whispering words he knew would bring me terror.

"She looks interesting. Maybe I'll come back to visit her after I'm done with you," he said inside my head.

If I hadn't been through so many years of mediumistic experiences and the corresponding validation to prove they were real, I might have wondered if I was crazy. Crazy people heard voices in their heads, didn't they? Fortunately -- or maybe unfortunately -- for me, they only happened when ghosts were nearby. I knew I wasn't crazy, but that was the least of my problems.

She finished my transaction, so I ran back to the bathroom to relieve myself. The Necromancer was still tagging along with me, as if he was afraid I was going to try to escape through a back door.

Normally when a ghost follows me into the bathroom, I yell at it to give me some privacy, but I didn't bother in this case. It would only serve to encourage him.

I got back into my car and messaged Michael, telling him that the ghost from the campground had followed me and that I needed immediate assistance.

I waited a few minutes, hoping to get a response, but none came. Michael was sometimes away from his phone for hours at a time. If I didn't hear from him in an hour, I'd call him directly.

I had spent the first several hours of my drive home crying, missing my friends and worrying about what the future would bring without them. I had the music turned up loud as I listened to the songs that we played while we explored Gettysburg. It wasn't until I turned down the music that I heard the tone in my backseat.

Despite everything I'd gone through in the past, it never once occurred to me that the ghost might follow me home. I thought he was grounded to the land in Gettysburg.

My first reaction wasn't necessarily fear. It was agitation.

"Why? Why would you follow me?" I asked, my eyes darting to the rear view mirror to the backseat where his tone was radiating from.

"Because I want you dead. Dead like me," came the response.

It startled me because I seldom hear voices so clearly. Usually if I hear something, or think I hear something, the message feels similar to my own thoughts. I often dismiss it as my imagination. This time, there was no doubt. It was as clear as if I heard it spoken.

He then began feeding me movies in my mind.

I saw dusk settling on the horizon in the distance as I drove. Headlights appeared in my rear view mirror as cars followed me down the highway.

I looked in the rear view mirror and saw him sitting there, as real as life. He grinned at me, showing me a mouthful of white teeth that were bared to the gum line. His eyes were manic, full of rage and hatred.

I screamed, my foot finding the brake petal as I steered the car to the breakdown lane.

As I pulled the car to a sudden stop, I glanced back up at the mirror. He was now leaning forward, ready to pounce on me. I didn't know what he would do once he got me, but I didn't want to find out.

I threw the door open and raced down the breakdown lane, my mind filled with utter panic. Headlights flashed on my back, sending my shadow racing ahead of me. I ran for all I was worth.

I don't know where I was running to. I just wanted to get away from the ghost in my backseat.

Then, like magic, he appeared in front of me with his arms raised.

"Boo!" he said, laughing in my face.

I attempted to turn around, but he appeared behind me.

My mind simply shut down as I raced onto the highway. The last thing I saw were the bright lights of headlights bearing down at me before the movie ended.

I snapped myself out of it, but he played it for me again and again until it was all I could see.

My phone rang, making me jump. It was Jose.

"Are you okay?" he asked, his voice filled with concern. "I was picking up on your energy and felt as though you were in trouble."

Jose often worked with Michael and had been mentoring me over the past few months via phone calls, trying to help me get a better grasp on my abilities.

"I'm not okay. Something followed me from Gettysburg," I told him.

He paused for a moment. "Take your next exit and find a quiet spot so we can talk," he told me and ended the call.

The next exit came in five miles, so I took it and found a gas station with a parking lot. I pulled in and called Jose back.

The line was filled with static. It was so bad, I couldn't hear him and he couldn't hear me.

The call ended.

Jose called me back again, but it was the same situation.

I was fairly certain the ghost in my backseat was manipulating my phone, attempting to prevent us from talking, but I didn't want to take any chances. I started my car and drove several miles until I found another gas station. I called Jose back.

The connection was much better this time. I was ready to blame it on poor reception, but Jose was quick to squash that theory.

"He doesn't want us to talk. I just sent my archangel in to restrain him," he said.

"Thank you," I said, feeling the first sensation of relief since I first noticed the ghost. I suddenly didn't feel as alone anymore.

"Did you contact Michael about it?" he asked.

"Yes, but I haven't heard from him." I eyed the rear view mirror again, helpless to look away.

"I'll give him a call when we get off here. This one isn't good. It's a shadow demon," he said, sending a chill through my body.

I'd never heard of a shadow demon before, but the term alone made sense to me. It never appeared during the daylight. It only came out at night.

"I see him as a high voodoo priest. He was called to Gettysburg back before the battle to punish the racist land owner who had slaves. The land owners eventually died off and just left him there. He's been collecting souls ever since," he said.

"So, we picked him up at the battlefields?" I asked.

"Yes. Were you crossing over souls?" he asked, not waiting for my response. "I think you angered him because you removed some of his collection."

I almost hated to ask, but I needed the validation.

"What does he look like?"

Jose paused for a moment. "Let me hone in on him," he said, allowing almost a minute to pass before he spoke again. "He's dark-skinned, possibly of Haitian descent. He's wearing a black jacket with a white shirt and black hat. He has a cane."

I gasped. There was no way Jose could have known that. We hadn't told anyone about our experience. The information hadn't left our group.

If I'd ever doubted Jose's abilities, it became crystal clear that he was the real deal. His next words nearly sent me over the edge.

"When it gets dark, he plans to physically manifest in your backseat, hoping to make you crash," he said.

My eyes welled up with tears.

Why was this happening to me?

Was I somehow marked as an easy target? Did my encounter with the Soul Collector so many years ago mark me as demon bait?

What was I going to do?

"Get back on the road and continue driving. I'll talk to Michael and explain how urgent the situation is. My archangel will stay there and hold him back until Michael's guides can get there. Hang tight," he said and then ended the call.

I got back on the highway and drove.

As the miles passed beneath the tires on my car, my mind reeled. Sandy called asking how I was doing and I told her about Jose's call.

"We'll be praying for you. We're almost home," she said, making me even sadder with her well-intended words. If I was with them, I'd be almost home too. As it stood, I still had four hours left to go and darkness would be falling in two hours.

I like to think of myself as a brave person. For the sake of research, I've put myself into some dangerous positions and then have shared them with the world. Some of my medium friends felt that made me a target as well.

"You're sharing information they don't want made public. You've become a danger to them," I was told.

It wasn't something I would ever stop doing. Despite the fear and the constant attachments, I felt as though this was part of my destiny. I was supposed to share this information so I could help others. I wouldn't stop, no matter what happened.

I was nearing my breaking point though. My hands wouldn't stop shaking and I couldn't stop glancing up at the rearview mirror. Would this be the end for me? Would my children believe that I died in a horrible car crash, not ever knowing the truth?

I felt like I had so much more to give, so many more books to write and people to help. I wanted to live to see my children get married and be there for the birth of my first grandchildren. I wasn't ready to die.

I began to pray.

The sun sank lower on the horizon, an hour away from sunset when I felt Michael's guides come into my car.

"Oh thank God," I whispered.

They battled for an eternity, the sounds zipping around my car like lasers. Finally, it grew silent.

The demon was gone.

I felt tears press into my eyes as I drove the final two hours home.

I was safe again, for now.

I knew that this wouldn't be the end for me. The experiences would continue. More ghosts would follow me. If history held true, they would become darker and scarier as time passed, a progression of dead souls sent to halt my progress. Thankfully, I was now better prepared to handle them. I now had a team of warriors helping me. I was no longer handling this all alone.

As I pulled in my driveway two hours later, I felt a sense of peace wash over me. I had survived.

Now, it was time for me to begin the next phase of my life.

I was safe.

EPILOGUE

I quickly settled into my new life in New Harmony, Indiana. I reconnected with several childhood friends and began to allow the stress and worry fade away like distant memories.

If I had been reluctant to leave my friends in New England behind, I didn't need to worry. They began visiting me in my new home. Within three months of my arrival, both Sandy MacLeod and Barbara Kirk Niles made the journey to see me.

Being away from the constant reminder of the paranormal world was actually good for me. I no longer spent the majority of my days talking about ghosts. I now talked about new restaurants, day trips to scenic caves and getting together with my old friends for drinks and games.

As my focus drifted, the ghosts didn't flock to me in such abundance. I still felt a few drift in from time to time, but armed with the information Barbara Williams gave me, I was able to cross most of them over. The ones I couldn't handle were swiftly eradicated by Michael Robishaw.

Slowly, I began to heal. I walked for miles every day with my dog Ripley and finally shed the 25 pounds I'd been carrying around for nearly a decade. I began to smile more, laugh frequently and open my heart to new experiences.

I know I will never be fully released from the dead, but I've learned how to deal with them more effectively.

Through all this, the biggest lesson I learned was that despite everything we go through, friends will pull us through.

And I'm thankful for every one of them. Even the ones I no longer talk to.

People come into our lives for a purpose. Whether it's for a lifetime, a moment or a lesson, they're all part of our overall life plan.

I will continue to explore the paranormal world and expand on my knowledge. One thing you can count on is that I'll never stop, no matter what is thrown at me.

Fear no longer controls me.

To learn more about the work that Shaman Michael Robishaw does, please continue reading for a sample of *Ruin of Souls*.

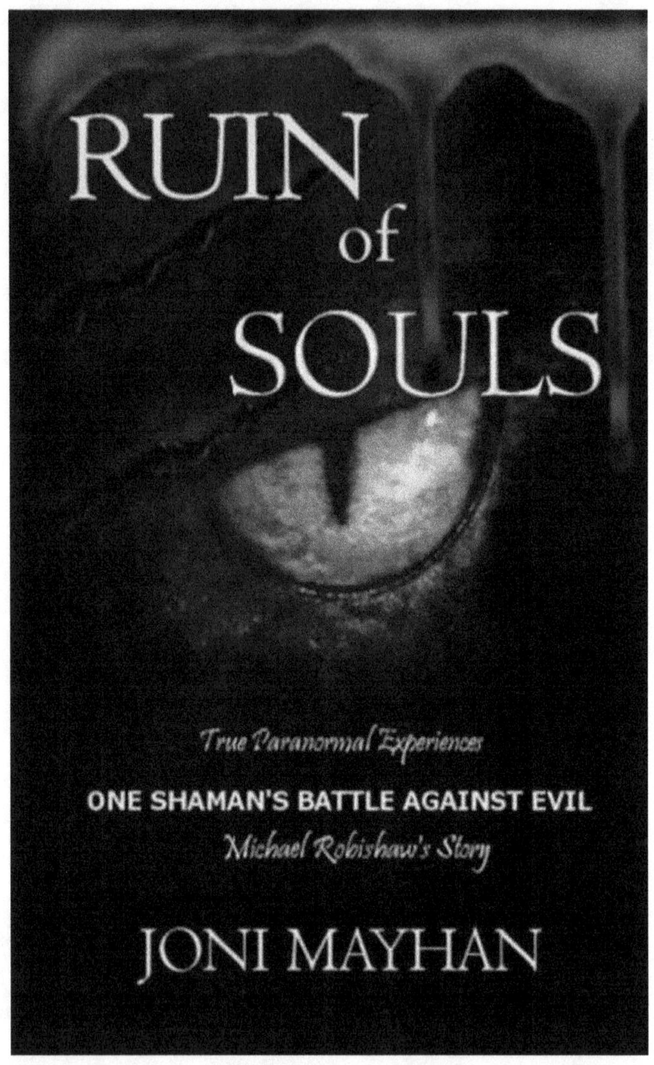
RUIN
of
SOULS
True Paranormal Experiences
ONE SHAMAN'S BATTLE AGAINST EVIL
Michael Robishaw's Story
JONI MAYHAN

RUIN OF SOULS

BY

JONI MAYHAN

PREFACE

I first met Michael Robishaw in the autumn of 2010 at a paranormal investigation. A mutual friend was filming a pilot for a television show he hoped would get picked up by a national network. Unfortunately, the show never materialized, but the evening wasn't a complete loss. It was the place when two souls met and founded a friendship that would bring an amazing story to life.

I didn't know it yet, but Michael had a secret.

He possessed an ability that was beyond comprehension. It was so powerful, so other-worldly, most people would have dismissed it as fiction, but it was very real. He played around with it from time to time, testing it to see if it was genuine, but he didn't tell anyone about it, especially not people he met on the sidewalk in front of a haunted house.

The investigation was held at the Haunted Victorian Mansion, a Victorian era mansion located in Gardner, Massachusetts. Over the course of the next four years, the Victorian would draw me into her web. I eventually went on to write my 2014 book *Bones in the Basement – Surviving the Haunted Victorian Mansio*n about the owner's experiences. At the time, I was just an extra investigator, invited to tag along to watch the filming of a television show.

Michael and his paranormal team drove in from Alexandria, Virginia to participate in the filming. His team Alexandria Paranormal was well respected in the paranormal community, making him a valuable asset for the pilot. When we broke into groups, I was teamed up with Michael's son-in-law at the time, a man who said very little during the course of the night. Michael and his daughter Sara were dispersed into other teams, along with the group who was responsible for the filming.

The activity in the mansion didn't disappoint. My group saw a mirror move on the floor in front of us and experienced knocking on the door of the master bedroom, a place that saw its fair share of death over the course of the past 135 years. I didn't really get a chance to talk to Michael until we decided to take a break.

He stood on the sidewalk, smoking a cigarette. Being a former smoker, I missed the smell of a freshly lit cigarette, so I happily joined him and we began chatting. I don't remember what we talked about during that first meeting, but I'm sure it lingered around the subject at hand. We didn't pick up the end of the conversation until some months later, when he was safely back home in Virginia and I was ten miles away from the Victorian, enduring another paranormal hitchhiker.

As a sensitive, I was prone to bringing ghosts home from investigations. I endured it as best as I could, begging the few mediums I knew to help me de-ghost my house from time to time to keep it from becoming a ghost hotel. At some point, Michael must have seen one of my many postings on social media, whining about my lot in life. He messaged me, telling me he would send me a Saint Michael's medallion and a few prayers that might help me.

I received the promised package several days later and hung the medallion on my equipment bag, where it remains to this day. I said the prayers and moved on, not seeing a significant difference in my situation. All the same, I was happy to have someone on my side rooting for me.

Years later, my situation became far more serious. The entities that came home with me grew darker and more dangerous. Even when I moved from one town to another, the activity didn't lessen. I could feel them swirling above my bed at night, making my ears ring with a maddening tone that wouldn't dissipate, no matter what I tried. I reached out on social media, asking if anyone could help me. I had enough. I couldn't handle it any longer. To my surprise, Michael responded to my plea in a private message.

"I'll send my guides in later to help you," he said simply.

I was truly at the beginning of my spiritual journey. I knew that I too had spirit guides, but I didn't know it was possible to send them places and ask them to do things for you.

I responded back favorably. At that point, Santa Claus could have walked through my door to save me and I wouldn't have turned him down.

"Don't be surprised if you see flashes of light or strange sounds. I'll send them in at 11pm. You may want to stay out of your bedroom until I'm finished," he added.

Okay then…

I wasn't sure what to make of this, but I hadn't slept in several nights. The activity was at an all-time high. If I wasn't hearing bangs on my walls, I was seeing misty shapes attempting to materialize beside my bed. My four lazy house cats were actively watching invisible things moving around the room, validating my suspicions.

I did what he asked and moved the pets out of my bedroom. They weren't any happier about the situation than I was. I needed to get some sleep so I wouldn't be completely foggy-headed for work the following day, but we all relocated to my study and waited.

As the clock ticked towards the given hour, I began to hear a strange tone. It was high-pitched and loud, sounding like laser lights zipping around the room. I couldn't handle the suspense any longer, so I tiptoed to my bedroom and put my ear to the door. The sound was far louder inside.

After a minute of eavesdropping, I finally cracked open the door and peered inside. A part of me was fully expecting to see ghosts and angels battling above my bed, but the room was empty. I was greeted by the sight of my unmade bed, with the covers thrown half-way off. I closed the door behind me and tiptoed to my bed, feeling the unfounded need to excuse myself like I would in a movie theater.

I slipped under the covers and leaned against the headboard, wanting a front row seat for the show. If I was expecting to see something, I was disappointed. There weren't any flashes of light or any bangs; however, the deafening sound of lasers swooped around the room, chasing the sounds I always heard when a ghost was near.

A full-on battle was raging in my bedroom, but all I could get was the audio portion of the presentation. I watched for nearly an hour before I succumbed to exhaustion and found myself slumping down into my pillow.

If I dreamed, I don't remember. All I know is that I woke up the next morning to the blissful sound of nothing. I had grown accustomed to the static sound that ghosts make when they are hovering over my bed, but there was pure silence.

I got ready and headed to my home office, where I worked for a pet supply company, managing several of their in-house training programs. By noon, it was still quiet. I messaged Michael, not expecting a response until later.

"How did it go?" I asked, and then went back to work.

I was surprised to find a return message waiting for me.

"You had a couple of them, but they weren't too bad. Just energy leaches who were draining your energy," he responded with the same lack of enthusiasm a plumber might use to tell you that you had a clogged drain.

Over the course of the next several years, Michael helped me dozens of times. Even though he was always humble, telling me that he was simply fulfilling his calling, he changed my life in so many ways.

He took away the fear that lingered in the back of my mind every time I left the house. Now, if I encounter something deadly, I have a back-up plan. I will no longer have to suffer in silence. While I still continued to search for methods to better protect myself, he became my safety net, preventing me from falling into a pit I could never climb out of alone.

As I would soon find out, Michael had a secret.

He has helped hundreds of other people just like me with their paranormal inflictions.

These are the most horrific cases.

(Above) Michael Robishaw

CHAPTER 1

Something pinned Tracy Gudeman to the bed.

She couldn't move, not even an inch, as invisible fingers ruffled through her hair, taunting her. All around her, the sounds of the night kept a maddeningly normal cadence. The crickets chirped outside her bedroom window and the clock in the living room ticked steadily. She could hear a car pass by on the street outside, the sound momentarily silencing the crickets.

What was happening?

After a few agonizing moments, the pressure eased and Tracy was able to move again. She pushed herself up to her elbows, listening intently to the sounds of the house.

Was it gone?

Everything remained exactly the same. It was as though nothing had happened. She heard her daughter roll over in bed, which should have eased her mind, but it didn't. She still got up to check.

She tucked a strand of long dark hair behind her ear and reached for her glasses on the nightstand. Petite in stature, she was no match for an intruder, but she wasn't sure that would matter if her suspicions were correct.

As she pushed open the door to her daughter's room, she was greeted by the sweet smell of the toddler's bedroom. It smelled of baby powder, Playdough, clean laundry, mixed with an underlying tang of urine. Gracie was two and had moved into a big bed, leaving the crib in the corner vacant and ready for her new baby sister, who would be arriving in a few months. Potty training a two year old was often hit or miss, something she was dealing with on a daily basis. She checked her daughter's sleep diaper, the one that prevented overnight accidents, and then planted a soft kiss on her daughter's forehead, feeling a tug of emotions sweep through her.

Being a mother was one of the most rewarding things she'd ever done, but it was also one of the most exhausting. When she thought of having children, she didn't realize she'd be doing most of the child rearing herself. With her husband in the military and her family so far away, she was almost always left to her own devices.

She glanced around each room to make sure nobody had broken into the house before making her way back to her bedroom. Everything looked the same as it did when she went to bed earlier. With a sigh, she climbed back into bed and pulled the covers up to her chin despite the warmth of the night, hoping she'd be able to finally get some sleep. She closed her eyes, wishing she could pretend it had just been a dream. Under normal circumstances, she would have brushed it off as a nightmare or just her imagination, but too many other things had happened to allow for that.

Tracy was thirty-seven when she moved into the house in Rutherglen, Virginia. Shortly after moving into the house, strange things began happening to her and her family. At first, she blamed it on the hassles of moving and the sadness of missing her family, but it wasn't long before she realized it went beyond normal anxiety.

Tracy always knew there was something different about her. Ever since she was a small child, she could pick up on other people's emotions, sometimes feeling the same sensations they felt. It often left her feeling drained and confused, but it wasn't something she could talk about. People would think she was crazy.

Needing to supplement her family's income, Tracy took a babysitting job for a family in town. The first day Tracy babysat for three year-old Chloe, she knew something was wrong. The little girl refused to sleep or play in her bedroom, telling Tracy there was a shadow man in her room. Chloe drew chilling pictures of the man, showing an entity with a dark face and scary eyes.

"What's the matter, honey?" Tracy asked, leading the girl into her bedroom.

The toddler pointed to her closet, holding tightly to Tracy's hand.

Tracy sat on the child's bed and something strange happened to her. Her chest tightened up and she couldn't breathe. Her heart began racing with anxiety and she couldn't move or speak. Pictures began popping in her head of a man. He was dressed in the uniform of a Confederate soldier. Tall with dark hair, he stared at Tracy in her mind's eye, glaring at her menacingly. She managed to break the spell and launched herself out of the room. She and Chloe spent the rest of the day playing in another room.

What happened in that room?

The thought wouldn't leave her. Were the girl's stories true? Was there something hiding in the closet in that room?

When the little girl's mother came home, Tracy filled her in about the day's events. The woman was shocked. Tracy's description was identical to what Chloe had already told her. Something triggered in Tracy's mind as she made a connection. There was a small cemetery near the family's house.

Could the two be linked?

She took a walk to the cemetery before heading home, feeling the bite of the January wind against her face. The landscape was bleached of color, leaving the landscape trapped in varying shades of brown. Above her, the sky churned with turbulent grey clouds. If the sun was up there, it was hiding in the darkness.

She felt a sense of uneasiness as she approached the cemetery. She couldn't put her finger on it, but something felt wrong. It was almost as if eyes were watching her from somewhere in the distance. She turned and looked around, but saw nothing more than the quiet street behind her.

The cemetery appeared to be a family plot, the kind that people once put on their land. There were only a handful of graves and the plot was overgrown and forgotten. She found herself drawn to a specific grave. It was as though she was being pulled there by an invisible string. When she stopped in front of it, she gasped.

It was the grave of a Confederate soldier.

Could this be the same soldier who lurked in Chloe's bedroom? She looked around, getting the distinct impression that someone was watching her. The feeling was so strong, she spun around in a slow circle, studying the landscape around her. Nobody was there, at least nobody she could see. Another shiver climbed her spine, but she shrugged it off and started back towards her car.

The experience wasn't over yet, though. As soon as she got home, more strange things began happening. Items started disappearing in her house and then reappearing in strange locations. She initially blamed it on her daughter, but as the events continued, she had to reconsider. Sometimes the items were left in places where her daughter couldn't possibly reach. When she started hearing footsteps and having horrific nightmares, she began to wonder if it was something paranormal.

The nightmares came on quickly. She saw images of a dark man, similar to the one Chloe described. The man presented himself to her in shadows. She couldn't make out any details of his face, but could feel the sense of anger that radiated from him. In her dreams, he approached her bed, looming over her with evil malice. The nightly advances swiftly turned to attacks of terror as invisible hands climbed up her body.

As the days progressed, she began losing track of time, finding herself zoning out for long moments. One afternoon, she found herself sitting in front of the mirror with no knowledge of walking there. When she checked her watch, she saw that nearly an hour had passed since she was last aware of her surroundings.

Things soon got worse. Tracy became despondent, never wanting to leave the house. Even her husband began noticing a difference in her. Being a career Marine, John wasn't prone to flights of fancy, especially those broaching on paranormal topics, but he couldn't explain what was happening to his wife.

He dug out an old family Bible and showed it to her, curious to see her reaction. She immediately retreated from him, a strangled growl coming from deep within her chest. Something was wrong, but he wasn't sure what to do about it.

He knew that Tracy's life hadn't been easy. After being sexually abused by her own step-brother as a child, she had a difficult time trusting people. Before they met, she attempted to take her own life over a failed relationship. Allowing other people into her private thoughts wasn't something that came to her easily, so he didn't push her initially. He just kept an eye on the situation and kept the worry to himself.

They needed help. That much was clear. As the days passed and the issues became more urgent, he knew they needed to find someone to help them. He was losing her day by day. Sometimes he'd find her just sitting there, staring into space, while the rest of the world moved around her. He would touch her arm and she would look at him as though she'd never seen him before. This wasn't like Tracy.

"Let's see if we can find someone to help us," he suggested, but she balked at the idea. Bringing other people in made it more real somehow. It turned it into something that *might have happened* into something people would whisper behind her back about. She really wanted to fit into her new community. What would the neighbors think if they saw a troop of paranormal investigators tromping into her house, armed with cameras and paranormal equipment?

John refused to let it go. They couldn't continue to pretend it wasn't happening. Every time they looked the other way, things got worse. Besides the attacks on Tracy, they also had a child to consider. If this entity was attacking Tracy, it might also come after their daughter and they couldn't let that happen. After much discussion, they reached out to a local paranormal group, who promised to come to their house to help.

The group arrived several days later, accompanied by a minister. Tracy told them the story about the mirror and the missing time periods, as well as the experience of being pinned to the bed. The minister pulled out his bible and said a prayer for her. When he asked her to recite it back to him, she couldn't do it. She could feel the words tangling up inside her mouth, but she couldn't release them. She began getting hot flashes, feeling as though her skin was being seared off her body. She felt the strongest need to flee the room, as a sense of anger filled her soul.

The minister pulled a chair over in front of her. He was an older man with balding hair and kind eyes.

"Sit down here," he told her.

She held his gaze for a long moment, wondering how something like this could be happening to her. She was born and raised in a small town. Ghosts weren't something her family ever discussed, but here she was, just the same.

Reluctantly, she sat on the chair, tucking her feet beneath her.

As the minister pulled another book out of his bag, the energy in the room seemed to change. The air felt thick and unbreathable, as though it was weighted down with sand. She took a deep breath and tried to steady her nerves.

Hopefully, this would all be over soon.

The minister flipped the book to a specific page and began reading passages from it. She would later learn that he was doing a deliverance, which was the layman's version of an exorcism. As he continued praying, he called on the entity that was inside her, demanding that it gave its name.

"Tell us your name!" he said in a stern voice.

Tracy stiffened in her chair.

"Tell us your name!" he said louder.

Tracy's face began to change, the skin molding over features that were no longer hers. The energy in the room grew intense, transforming into something forceful and strong, like an invisible cyclone. She was swept into it, feeling her thoughts fade away to nothing.

A picture flew from the wall and crashed to the floor, followed by the howl of wind against the windows. The room became filled with sounds, as though every entity in the house was smashing against the walls.

Tracy suddenly stiffened in her chair.

"If they go, I go with them," she said in a deep, grating voice that wasn't her own.

Everyone in the room paused, casting fearful glances at one another over the top of her head.

John felt his stomach clinch into knots.

What was going on?

The minister pulled a bottle of holy oil from his bag and attempted to anoint her, but she struggled away from him, sending her chair flying halfway across the room. They tried to hold her down, but it took all five of them to manage it, despite the fact that she only weighed a hundred pounds.

John could feel the adrenaline pumping through his body. Something wasn't right and he knew it. The longer they held her, the more visibly upset she became. He worried that the stress was more than her body could take.

He released his hold on her and sat back on his heels.

"We need to stop," he told the others.

They exchanged worried glances, all of them thinking similar thoughts.

If not this, then what? What would it take to make this all go away?

As the others released her, the energy in the room softened, like a storm that lost its power. They pulled themselves off the floor and subconsciously retreated away from her, feeling a sense of relief that would later turn to guilt.

The minister stood up, wiping the sweat off his brow. It was clear that this was much more than he was prepared to handle. The group hurriedly gathered their gear, shoving it into their silver cases with an urgency that was undeniable. John watched them rush out the door, feeling a sense of overwhelming helplessness overcome him.

"What now?" he called out to the minister who was halfway to his car.

The man turned to meet his eyes, the expression on his face a mixture of fear and relief.

"I don't know," he said simply.

John felt the first pangs of panic come over him. As a Marine, this wasn't an emotion he was comfortable with. "Will you come back to finish this?" he asked.

"Yes, we'll be in touch," the minister said, pushing through the door.

He stood at the door, watching them pile into their vehicles as though they were retreating from a murder scene. He had a feeling this was the last time he'd see them, something that proved to be true.

As the days progressed, Tracy's emotional well-being became more and more disruptive. Not only was she still losing track of time, finding herself with tremendous gaps in her memory, she was also watching her personality change. Through a mutual friend, they learned about a man named Michael Robishaw who lived nearby in Alexandria, Virginia. Maybe he could help.

Michael in action at a 2013 investigation

CHAPTER 2

As far as his friends were concerned, Michael Robishaw was a dedicated paranormal investigator. Having spent most of his life in the communications field, people often came to him for advice about their phones or electronics as frequently as they came to him about their ghost issues. While he was patient with the requests, he wasn't the kind of guy who suffered fools. He knew when to cut his losses when he needed to. This made him not only well-liked, but also well-respected.

When I first met him on the sidewalk of the Haunted Victorian Mansion, he was very much dedicated to his small team of investigators. He founded Alexandria Paranormal Investigations in 2005, keeping the group small to eliminate the drama that seemed to persistently plague the paranormal field.

The group assisted the communities in Virginia, Maryland, Washington DC, West Virginia, North Carolina, Delaware and Pennsylvania, never failing to turn down a request for help. They didn't charge for their services, paying all expenses for the investigations out of their own pockets.

As was often the case, people frequently came to him as a last resort, feeling overwhelmed by the paranormal activity that plagued them. Even though the paranormal world was becoming more mainstream, through the constant barrage of paranormal television shows and movies, people were still shy about admitting something was happening to them. They worried that other people would laugh at them and call them crazy, so they dealt with the haunting until it became too much to bear.

What most people didn't know about Michael was that he was far more than just a mere paranormal investigator. He kept his mediumistic side hidden from view. Like the people he often helped, he was fearful of the backlash he would receive if people were aware of what he could do. He often worked in the background, silently helping friends and family when they encountered something dangerous, never professing to possess any special abilities. It took him years to get comfortable with his gifts. Even though he was accomplished with his capabilities, he wasn't certain how others would react to them.

People with mediumistic abilities are typically born with them. If they have a strong mentor, like a parent or relative, to shape their abilities, they grow strong and capable of handling their gifts. Often though, this isn't the case. Like many others, Michael was forced to traverse the ocean of the dead alone, often wondering if his experiences were real or imagined.

I drove to Virginia in the spring of 2015 to interview him. Despite the fact that we frequently chatted on social media, I knew very little about the man himself. He keeps everything close to the belt, something that often comes with the territory of being metaphysically gifted.

Like many mediums I've met over time, Michael's introduction to the paranormal world came when he was a child.

Since his father was a Marine, the family often moved around frequently, bringing him to locations he might have never experienced otherwise. It also made it extremely difficult to make and keep friends. He learned how to evaluate people quickly, separating friend from foe by the end of the introduction. Much of this was due to an internal ability known as empathy, but Michael wouldn't understand this until he was much older. All he knew at the age of nine was that moving was often difficult, especially for someone with metaphysical gifts.

One tour brought his family to the island of Hawaii. His father was stationed at Kaneohe Bay for several years, which meant that the entire family got to enjoy the bounty of the island. While Hawaii was beautiful, Michael's adventurous spirit often led him to places most kids avoided.

One weekend, his mother suggested they check out a flea market held in an old airplane hangar near the base. While his mother poked around the various tables, Michael wandered off with several of his friends to explore the hangar.

The hangar was obviously old, the far end filled with rusted hunks of forgotten metal and dusty remnants of the past. As they roamed farther away from the flea market, the buzz of voices grew fainter and their sense of intrigue grew stronger. The shadows at the edges of the hangar were thick and heavy, filled with murky shapes they couldn't quite make out. It looked like a perfect place for a game of hide and seek.

As they spread out and began their game, they nearly bumped into a Marine sergeant who watched over the area. At first, they paused, waiting for him to scold them for wandering so far away from their parents, but he didn't. He seemed to enjoy the boys' enthusiasm. He gave them a quick tour of the hangar, answering their questions, while pointing out the bullet holes in the ceiling from World War II Japanese fighter planes.

As he turned to leave them to their explorations, he turned with a smile.

"Just stay out of the basement area," he said. "There are some things going on down there that you don't need to experience."

Being typical nine-year-old boys, they waited for him to leave and bolted for the stairs. Being told to stay away from an area only made it more enthralling.

The other boys raced ahead, but Michael took his time, letting all the details sink in. He could feel the sense of history in the building and could imagine American soldiers from the past walking down those same stairs. He put his hand on the rail that thousands of others had used over the decades, trying to imagine their lives. He could almost feel the energy radiating off the metal.

"Hey guys! Wait up!" he called, when he realized the boys were nowhere in sight. As he looked up, he saw something that made him stop short.

A shadow moved up the stairs towards him. At first, he thought it was the sergeant coming back to check on them, but as the man grew closer, he realized it was someone else. It was a Japanese soldier.

His breath caught in his chest.

The man was dressed in a traditional khaki uniform, perfect in every detail, down to the small gold star on the center of his field hat. Michael was rooted to the spot as the soldier continued up the stairs and walked right through him.

Was that a ghost?

He didn't take time to contemplate his experience. He raced back up the stairs with his heart pounding heavily. He told his mom and dad about what he saw, but they shook their heads and laughed, telling him that he had a good imagination. It was a lesson he would carry with him for years. Talking about ghosts wasn't always a welcomed conversation.

The experiences continued to pile up, one after another.

After leaving Hawaii, his family moved to Virginia. The conditioning he received while growing up as a military brat left a mark on him as a teenager. He was prone to acting out, often skipping classes and experimenting with drugs and alcohol. After his parent's divorce, his father moved to Connecticut. Thinking that a change of pace would be good for him, his mother sent

Michael to live with his father. Once he crossed the Connecticut state line, his life took an interesting turn.

Something about the state of Connecticut unnerved him. He could feel a strange sort of energy swirling around him. The sensation was similar to the way he felt in Hawaii when the Japanese soldier approached him. He wasn't sure what to make of it. Was the entire state haunted?

Was this a sign of things to come?

It wasn't long before he started having odd experiences. It started with horrific nightmares he couldn't wake up from. In his dreams, faceless beings chased him down dark corridors. He would often wake up feeling as though something was sitting on him, trying to choke the life out of him. Even after he woke and was conscious of everything going on in the room, the activity didn't cease. If nothing else, it seemed to escalate.

He wasn't sure what to make of it. Did he have a ghost in his room? The only experience he had to draw from was the one in Hawaii, but this one seemed different. While the Japanese solider didn't appear to be aware of him, this one was intent on making his life a living hell.

Every time he walked into his bedroom, he could feel it hiding in the corner. Soon, it began showing itself, slinking across the walls in shadow form. Drawers would open and close right in front of him and the door to the old iron stove in his room would bang. He needed his rest, but the entity in his room wouldn't let him sleep.

He didn't know what to do. He told his father about the events that were transpiring in his bedroom every night, but being a life-long military man, it wasn't a part of his nature to believe in such things. He told Michael to, "Lay off the weed," and it would go away.

Michael knew what was happening to him was real. He could feel the energy of the entity, pinpointing its location as clearly as if he could actually see it. There was no way this was his imagination.

Other strange things began happening, as well. His dreams became more vivid and lucid. Sometimes, he felt as though he was actually visiting the places he dreamt of because the textures were so perfect. As he focused on them, he learned he could actually change the course of a dream, often traveling to places where he'd never been before. One of these travels nearly got him into trouble.

A girl at his high school caught his interest, and he thought about her frequently. One night while he was sleeping, he found himself outside her house, beneath her window. Thinking it was just a dream; he opened the window and slipped inside. The girl woke up with a start, which caused him to jolt awake in his own bed miles away.

She tracked him down at school the next day.

"I had something really weird happen to me last night," she said, tucking her long brown hair behind her ear, scrutinizing him as though she knew more than she was admitting to.

"Yeah, what was that?" he asked.

"I think I had a ghost in my room," she said, and then went on to tell him about seeing her curtain move.

He felt his stomach knot up.

Did she see him?

How the hell could he explain that?

"That's really weird," he said and just left it at that. He didn't want to scare her, but it was a perplexing turn of events. Could he really go wherever he wanted to go, just by thinking about it?

The thought was mesmerizing. He began reading every book he could get his hands on and learned that what he had experienced was something called astral projection. He had somehow separated his soul from his body and had traveled to the girl's house.

It wasn't something he'd ever heard of before. No one he knew could do such things and he was hesitant to discuss it with other people, knowing their reactions would be similar to the way his parents dealt with the Japanese soldier.

Not long after, he began having strange dreams where he was talking with several etheric people who claimed to be his spirit guides. One of the guides was a petite older woman who was of European descent. She seemed like an old soul, with her last human life having taken place in the seventeenth century.

Another guide was a massive Cherokee warrior. He was intimidating, reminding Michael of a Roman gladiator. They didn't sugar coat anything with him. They told him they were there to help him on his spiritual journey and asked him to pay closer attention. This was definitely something he didn't share with his friends or family.

What would they think if he started talking about spirit guides and astral projection? He was at the age where most of his friends were preoccupied with music, girls and cars. If he told people he was visited at night by angelic beings, they'd tell him to lay off the weed, like his father had done.

He slowly grew into his abilities, experimenting with them as much as possible, but other interests began pulling him away from the paranormal. Music was always a big interest of his, and he spent a lot of time practicing both the guitar and the harmonica. He joined a local band and began playing at small events, when he wasn't on the football field, playing for his high school team. As much as he wished they'd go away, the ghosts wouldn't leave him alone.

As the weeks turned to months, they became more invasive. The more he ignored them, the more disruptive they became. They began impacting his sleep. As soon as he would nod off, a drawer would slam or an invisible fist would pound against the wall, leaving him bleary eyed and exhausted the following day.

He needed help, but he wasn't sure where to go. His father was obviously not going to be helpful and he was afraid to approach his friends about it.

What about the church?

The voice came to him as though it was spoken directly into his hear. It almost sounded like the older woman who claimed to be one of his spirit guides.

(Left) Michael at 13 – middle)

He stared off into space, wondering if that was the right option.

"Really? The church?" he asked, but didn't receive a response. He shook his head, feeling like he was losing his mind. If someone saw him talking to himself like this, they'd surely think he was crazy. Regardless, he went to his church the next day. He needed answers.

Since Michael attended a Catholic school, he knew what to expect when he approached the church. Opinions about the supernatural world varied among the priests as widely as they did in the outside world. They would either help him or ignore him. He just needed to find the right person who shared his beliefs.

As he made his rounds, he was met with a few raised eyebrows, which were always followed by the advice to pray. He was almost ready to give up when he came across a nun in the hallway of his school. She was always patient and kind with the students, so he felt comfortable sharing his story with her.

"You should talk to Father Patrick," she told him. "He's from Ireland and is spending a year with us on sabbatical. They deal with more things of that nature in his country, so he might be able to help you." She told him where he could find Father Patrick and wished him well.

Michael was nervous as he approached the room where the Irish priest was teaching. As he neared the door, he could hear a thundering voice reverberating from inside the room. It was the kind of voice that spun wild, adventurous stories, the kind of voice you wanted to listen to.

Michael stood outside the door until the catechism class ended and the students filed out, filling the otherwise empty hallway with the happy chatter of their voices. He found the young priest at the front of the classroom, tidying up his notes.

As Michael scrambled to search for the right words to say, the priest stuck out his hand, a warm smile on his ruddy face.

"Welcome, my son. I'm Father Patrick O'Malley. I don't believe I've had the pleasure of meeting you yet," he said with a thick brogue that filled his words with music. Standing just under five and a half feet, Father Patrick was nearly the same height as many of his students, making him feel like one of them. The man radiated with exuberant joy, making him someone you wanted to get to know better.

"I've been experiencing some things I can't understand," Michael said, working up his courage as he spoke. He'd been through this speech several times before with the other priests and hoped it wouldn't be met with the same results.

Father Patrick surprised him.

"Let's sit down for a spell," he said, ushering Michael to a seat near his desk. As soon as Michael was settled, he joined him in a nearby chair, giving him his full attention, something the other priests seldom did. He wasn't distracted by his pile of papers or his list of things to do. He was there, one hundred percent, and was willing to give Michael the guidance he needed.

"Tell me about it from the beginning to the end," he said with a wry smile. "And don't go leaving anything out. I want to hear it all."

Comforted by his warmth of positive energy, Michael told the young priest about his experiences. When he finished a half hour later, Father Patrick patted him on the hand.

"They know you have abilities. That's why they're trying to communicate with you," he told the boy. "We deal with this on a frequent basis in my country. The power of prayer will carry you far."

The conversation was life altering for Michael. The priest spent hours talking with him, sharing his experiences and knowledge. He taught Michael that prayer and self-fortitude were the building blocks for the foundation he would build on. Not only would they help him deal with his paranormal issues, but they could also help the entities themselves.

"There are many lost souls lingering in our realm. They need help and you can help them," the priest told him.

He then went on to teach Michael several prayers that he could use.

Michael took Father Patrick's words to heart. He knew it wouldn't be an easy matter. Unlike most other weary lost souls who wanted help, this entity was fixated on causing harm. It wanted nothing more than to wrack havoc on Michael's life.

Armed with a crucifix and the new prayers, Michael returned to his father's house and began battling the entity.

Every night, he repeated the prayers and asked his spirit guides to help him. After the first night, he noticed a dramatic difference. The entity appeared to be weaker than before. He increased his efforts and continued to wear it down, prayer by prayer, until it was nothing but a memory. The entire process took him several years until it was finally gone.

While he wasn't eager to repeat the experience, he appreciated the lessons it taught him. He was capable of handling more than he originally thought. It also helped him learn more about his spirit guides.

Working with his guides was almost like building a team. Even though they were experienced guides, they weren't trained in spiritual combat. He had to work with them over a period of time and train them on the virtues of keeping him protected. In the process, they grew stronger, making him stronger, as well.

Michael was thirteen years old when he investigated the paranormal for the first time. Even though he experienced a horrific haunting in his own house, he still yearned for validation.

A big part of him wasn't convinced that his experiences were real. He needed real proof. All it would take was a haunted house and the right opportunity.

The opportunity came to him after he discovered an old abandoned house at the end of his street. The kids at school had been talking about it for years. One of them even claimed to see a ghost in one of the rooms. If he could capture a photo of the ghost, or even record its voice on his tape recorder, then he would have the proof he needed.

He headed down the street, armed with his paranormal gear. He had a Polaroid camera and a tape recorder that he frequently used to record music off the radio. If something paranormal happened to him at the house, he wasn't going to miss it.

One of his friends was interested in going, so they made arrangements to meet in front of the old house at dusk.

His plan was simple. They would sneak in and walk around while recording on the tape recorder. If they saw anything, Michael would snap a photo of it, giving them the proof they needed.

The friend was ten minutes late and was a bundle of nerves by the time he got there.

"Are you sure we should do this? What if…something happens?" he said, eyeing the house with a nervous glance.

"We'll be fine. We'll just walk in, take a look around and then leave," Michael told him. As soon as the words left his mouth, he felt a strange sensation.

The house was calling to him. He could feel it beckoning him. He needed to get inside now.

"Something in there wants me to come inside," he told his friend.

It was enough to tip the boy over the edge.

"I can't do it, man," the boy said. He didn't give Michael a chance to argue. He simply turned on his heels and ran back home. Michael shook his head. How were they ever going to learn anything if they didn't try?

The house was in a traditional neighborhood setting, but was so far off the street that nobody would see him. Weeds and bushes had grown up all around it and most of the windows were broken.

He slipped inside quickly. The last of the daylight warmed the rooms, the sunset painting the white walls a pale orange. He stepped over some trash and broken beer bottles and made his way deeper into the house, looping the camera strap around his neck to make it easily accessible. He held the recorder in his hand, not wanting to waste his valuable tapes until he was ready. If anything happened, he was ready this time.

As he approached the center of the house, he heard footsteps on the floor above him. He paused, his heart beating heavily.

What was that?

He listened for a full minute, but didn't hear it again.

Maybe it was just an animal that climbed in through a window.

He tightened his grip on his recorder and moved forward again. The floor was littered with trash, making it evident that it was a popular hangout for kids in the area. As he moved towards the back of the house, he heard the footsteps again.

This time, they were directly overhead. He stopped mid-step, his heart racing even faster.

There was no way it was an animal. It sounded like carefully placed footsteps. He retraced his steps back to the staircase.

"Who's up there?" he shouted.

More than anything, he wanted to run up there and confront the person or thing that was making the footsteps, but he didn't want to chance the stairs. They were nearly caved in. The last thing he needed was to fall through them and end up in the basement.

"Let me know who you are right now!" he yelled again, making his voice twice as loud. If it was animals, they would run away when they heard his voice.

He was met with silence.

Something stirred deep inside him. He could feel another presence. It wasn't something he could explain, it was just a knowing. It was similar to the way it felt when someone slipped silently into a room behind you. It was the stir of the air, the displacement of space. It made him want to turn around and look to see if anyone was there or not.

When he did, the room was empty.

He felt the first spike of fear fill his veins with adrenaline.

What were ghosts were capable of doing? Could they actually hurt people?

He paused, balancing the camera in his sweating palms. Should he leave while he had the chance?

"Get a grip, man," he whispered to himself. He was here to see if he could find a ghost. He wasn't going to go running out like his friend did. He put the camera back to his eye and snapped another photo. As he shook the photo, watching the image form on the square photo paper, the footsteps sounded again.

There was no way it was animals.

You need to get out now.

He took the message as a cue and made his way back out to the front yard.

He didn't realize it at the time, but it would be the first of many paranormal investigations, something that would one day dictate his life.

When Tracy called him, some forty years later, he remembered what it was like to be afraid. He immediately made plans to make the two hour drive to her home, hoping he could help.

Ruin of Souls is available where you purchased this book

About the Author

Joni Mayhan is a paranormal investigator and author who teaches a popular Paranormal 101 class. After living in New England for nearly all of her adult life, she recently relocated to her home state of Indiana, where she is working on her next paranormal book.

To learn more about her, check out her website Jonimayhan.com

A Note to My Readers

I wanted to take a moment and thank you for being a part of my journey. Everything you've read here really happened. I've always dug my heels in about telling my stories exactly like they happened. It hasn't always worked in my favor either. I've been turned down several times by paranormal television shows because they didn't feel the stories were scary enough. Trust me, living through them wasn't exactly a fun experience.

I will continue to share my experiences in the hopes that it helps someone else. After publishing Soul Collector, I was absolutely inundated with emails from people who have experienced similar hauntings or feel they have metaphysical gifts like mine. I've also had several people thank me for talking them out of delving into paranormal investigating. It looks like fun, but reality can be a completely different story, especially if you are a sensitive.

If you enjoyed this book, please consider leaving a reader's review at the location where you purchased this book. As an self-published author, I don't have access to the marketing teams that traditionally published authors enjoy. Reviews help me more than you can believe. If there's something you feel I can do better, please contact me. I'm always open for suggestions and honest feedback.

If you'd like to learn more about me, please visit my website: Jonimayhan.com. You can find a link to all of my EVPs, as well as my email address to contact me.

Thanks again!

CPSIA information can be obtained
at www.ICGtesting.com
Printed in the USA
LVHW052226080723
751901LV00032B/511

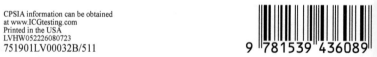